Counterterrorism and the Comparative Law of Investigative Detention

Counterterrorism and the Comparative Law of Investigative Detention

DAN E. STIGALL

Foreword by Amos N. Guiora

CAMBRIA
PRESS
Amherst, New York

Requests for permission should be directed to:
permissions@cambriapress.com, or mailed to:
Cambria Press
20 Northpointe Parkway, Suite 188
Amherst, NY 14228

Library of Congress Cataloging-in-Publication Data on file.

Hardcover
Counterterrorism and the comparative law of investigative detention / Dan E. Stigall.
p. cm.
Includes bibliographical references and index.
ISBN 978-1-60497-618-2 (alk. paper)
1. Detention of persons—United States. 2. Detention of persons—Great Britain. 3. Detention of persons—France. 4. Terrorism Investigation—United States. 5. Terrorism Investigation—Great Britain. 6. Terrorism Investigation—France. I. Title.

K5437.S75 2009
344.05'32517—dc22

2009009971

To Jack, who taught me to work hard;
to Norma, who taught me to read well;
and to John, who taught me to fight both hard and well

Table of Contents

List of Tables

Foreword

Dan Stigall has undertaken a project of great importance. He has carried it off with aplomb and gusto. By engaging the question of detention in a robust fashion, he deserves both our praise and ear. He has also done something else which is of particular importance to me. Dan has engaged the subject of detention from a comparative perspective, thereby earning double accolades—one for addressing detention in the post-9/11 world and the other for doing so from a perspective that extends beyond the American coastline.

With those warm words behind us, a word of personal introduction is in order. When Dan graciously asked if I were willing to pen these few words, I asked to read the manuscript prior to agreeing. A quick read warmed my heart because it quickly became apparent to me that Dan had undertaken a project I would have been happy to undertake. Precisely because the detention issue is, in many ways, at the confluence between the legitimate rights of the individual and the equally legitimate rights of the state, we must discuss it openly and candidly.

The discussion ultimately centers on the question of limits—what limitation of freedom can we impose on the individual? How long will he or she be held and subject to what independent judicial review is a question critical to the debate. Similarly, whether the detainee will be allowed to consult with an attorney is a question of extraordinary importance. American jurists have long discussed these questions; American courts have struggled to create and maintain "bright line rules" in the criminal law paradigm. While any U.S. law student can recite case law addressing detention and interrogation questions, that same student will have a difficult time articulating that courts have addressed these issues uniformly and consistently.

Needless to say, the uncertainty and ambiguity—what is politely referred to as a "case-by-case" approach—is magnified when the detainee is not a common criminal, but rather an individual suspected of involvement in terrorism. Whatever one's political perspective, many—if not most—commentators suggest that civil democratic regimes must conduct operational counterterrorism subject to the rule of law. Where the rubber hits the road is in how the detainee is treated not in the fully articulated paradigm where the rules are largely known, but in the developing counterterrorism paradigm.

Developing the tools—legal and policy—to simultaneously protect the nation-state while protecting the detainee from the excessive use of power by that very nation-state is an extraordinary challenge. Policy makers are, frankly, searching for answers and guidance. The past seven years are the manifestation of how not to seek answers, for they are a reflection of unwarranted and inexcusable hubris and arrogance. Moving forward, President Obama must reach out to a wide array of experts; he and his administration must also listen and understand and respect the limits of their own understanding and comprehension of the issues.

And that is precisely where Dan Stigall comes in—while not "long in the tooth," Dan has exhibited an unusual sensitivity in how he has approached this issue. He has also exhibited unusual maturity in examining the issue from a comparative approach. The choice of comparing to the United Kingdom and France is interesting; while others may quibble as to the efficacy and wisdom of choosing those two countries (an inevitable response to a comparative study), I suggest that is not the main issue. What is critical—and this is the important contribution—is the essence of the study. By examining how other democratic regimes address the very issues we have struggled with over the past seven years, Dan truly grabs the "tiger by the tail." A comparative analysis is never easy nor is it warmly received in all quarters. While Justice Scalia's criticism of comparative approaches is well-known, it is, I suggest, very wrong and highly shortsighted.

Dan Stigall's analysis highlights the danger of dismissing a comparative approach, for he has most effectively used the British and French experience in discussing detention. While no regime has *the* answer (an illusion, at best), democratic nations can well learn from each other's successes and failures. Precisely for that reason, policy makers, jurists, and the concerned public owe Dan a collective thanks; in addressing the extraordinarily complicated issue of detention from a comparative perspective, he has truly bitten off a very large bite of a problematic apple. That he has done so is to our benefit; that he has done so successfully is to his credit.

While we shall continue to struggle with the limits of detention and what legal paradigm is the "correct" one, we are the richer for Dan's book. It can serve as an effective "guide" as we continue to traverse the never-ending field of terrorism and counterterrorism.

Amos N. Guiora
Professor of Law
S. J. Quinney College of Law
University of Utah

Preface

I watched the Twin Towers fall from my room in The Judge Advocate General's Legal Center and School ("the JAG School") on the campus of the University of Virginia. I was a first lieutenant and had just graduated from the 155th JAG Officer Basic Course a few days earlier. I was soon to ship out for my first assignment in Germany and turned on my television that morning expecting to find some anodyne entertainment—only to see an image of thick, black smoke rising from one of the towers and to hear a news anchor's reticent, halting commentary. What follows is something of a blur. I remember being in uniform, staring at the television, and feeling a sense of violation along with a certain feeling of confusion. I also remember the sound of footsteps in the building—both busy and purposive. The televisions throughout the JAG School were tuned to news programs, phones were busily ringing, and—as we all helplessly watched the horror unfold—the world was changing in ways more profound than I could have anticipated.

This experience, at the outset of my legal career, was certainly a formative one and served, in part, as the motivation for this book. Watching my country being attacked from my room within the complex central to the U.S. Army's legal community, I contemplated the relationship between law and terrorism. What legal tools could have prevented this tragedy? What laws could have been used to stop this? What laws could be put in place to avert such attacks in the future? What happens next? I was obviously not the only one pondering such issues. Officials at the highest echelons of government would soon take action—much of which is discussed in the pages that follow. Ever since, the legal world has been busily discussing the relationship between law and terrorism. It is my hope that this book contributes—however modestly—to this important discussion.

This book focuses narrowly on the concept of investigative detention of terrorism suspects and outlines the investigative detention powers of the United States, the United Kingdom, and France. This is important in order to attain an understanding of the powers available to law enforcement in those countries (for joint international operations that involve domestic law enforcement entities), as well as to see if any of the laws in force in those European jurisdictions could possibly find applicability—or at least provide inspiration—here at home. Throughout its analysis, the book maintains two assumptions: (1) that we need to aggressively ferret out, detain, and interrogate terrorists in order to prevent another catastrophic attack; and (2) that we must do so in a way consistent with our Constitution and international human rights law. While I recognize some inherent tension between those two ideas, my hope is that the book demonstrates that they are not mutually exclusive.

Likewise, the book demonstrates that the investigative detention regimes in the United Kingdom and France are far more potent than anything in the United States—but it also reveals areas of "plasticity" in U.S. law that would allow for a more robust investigative detention regime. I, therefore, conclude by offering a series of legislative proposals that would make the most of those areas of malleability and foster greater domestic counterterrorism capabilities without abandoning our constitutional values or violating international law.

My proposals are not intended to displace other arguments, such as those who call for a special terrorist court, possible preventive detention mechanisms, military tribunals, and so forth. My proposals are somewhat distinct from those arguments (though obviously related). I, instead, seek to demonstrate how other countries have used their ordinary criminal processes for counterterrorism purposes and how U.S. criminal law can be better attuned to the problem of terrorism. I further seek to demonstrate that issues of terrorist detention do not necessarily require the utter abandonment of our criminal model.

Acknowledgments

Every comparativist is, to some degree, an autodidact. As jurists trained in one system, intellectual curiosity or professional necessity (or both) at some point compels us, for myriad reasons, to cast our gaze upon a foreign system of laws. On numerous occasions throughout my career as a military lawyer—which has placed me at various times in Europe and the Middle East—I have been called upon to quickly attain some understanding of another country's legal system and, based on that understanding, render advice or take action. At such moments, I have been most grateful to the jurists before me who took the time to sit down, set pen to paper, and assiduously detail the legal system in question—splaying out its underlying theories, explaining the structure, and illuminating the legal landscape. It is only through such efforts that the rest of us may rise to become comparativists in our own right. Likewise, in writing this book, I have heavily relied on the works of others who have performed the public service of explicating the legal systems relevant to this study. To each of them, I owe a debt of sincere gratitude.

Obviously, a work of this length makes use of numerous statutes and legal texts, but I felt it worth the effort to highlight a few secondary sources of which I made significant use. With regard to the law of the United Kingdom, I have chiefly relied on John Sprack's *A Practical Approach to Criminal Procedure* (2006) as well as *Blackstone's Guide to the Anti-Terrorism Legislation* (2002) by Clive Walker and *Blackstone's Guide to the Terrorism Act 2006* (2006) by Alun Jones, Rupert Bowers, and Hugo D. Lodge. Similarly, my discussion of French law relied heavily on Jacqueline Hodgson's excellent work, entitled *French Criminal Justice* (2005), as well as Catherine Elliott's *French Criminal Law* (2001). Lastly, my discussion of comparative counterterrorism legislation was deeply informed by Yonah Alexander's fascinating work, entitled *Counterterrorism Strategies: Successes and Failures of Six Nations* (2006). I commend each of these works—along with all of the others cited in the succeeding pages—to any serious student of comparative law or counterterrorism.

In addition, there are numerous people without whom this book would not have come into existence. The first among them is Professor Peter Raven-Hansen, currently the Glen Earl Weston Research Professor of Law at George Washington University. Professor Raven-Hansen, while acting as the advisor for the thesis that would later evolve into this book, reviewed numerous drafts of this work and generously lent to this project his unrivaled expertise in the area of counterterrorism law. This book simply would not have been possible without him. Any contribution this work makes to the field is directly due to his assistance and encouragement. Any error is purely my own.

I must also thank Monsieur Roger Errera, *Conseiller d'Etat honoraire*, for his reviews of the discussion of French law and for generously allowing me—a jurist of far less stature—to bother him with numerous questions about French criminal law. Similarly, I wish to thank Professor Geoff Gilbert, Professor of Law, University of Essex, for taking the time to read my chapter on the law of the United Kingdom. My interaction with both of these gentlemen has constituted a profound learning experience all on its own.

Finally, and perhaps most importantly, I must also profoundly thank my beautiful wife, Elizabeth, and my wonderful daughter, Madeleine, for enduring those long hours without me as I researched and wrote this work. I owe you both many nights and weekends that we can never get back. But I will try.

ANY OPINION EXPRESSED IN THIS BOOK IS PURELY MY OWN.
I REPRESENT NEITHER THE U.S. DEPARTMENT OF DEFENSE
NOR THE DEPARTMENT OF JUSTICE.

Counterterrorism
and the Comparative Law *of* Investigative Detention

CHAPTER 1

INTRODUCTION

When you see a rattlesnake poised to strike, you do not wait until he has struck before you crush him.[1]

The years since the devastating attacks of September 11, 2001, have seen dramatic developments in the recognized challenges to U.S. national security and in the ways the United States reacts to terrorist threats. Those reactions have demonstrated both the flexibility and limitations of U.S. criminal law in its ability to adapt to terrorism. A focus on the perceived limitations of U.S. criminal law in this regard has led to calls from key players within the U.S. national security apparatus for an improved regime of investigative detention, such as those currently in place in the United Kingdom and France. But what do the laws of those countries permit that U.S. law does not? What aspects of U.S. criminal law—if any—set it on unequal footing with its European counterparts? What desirable aspects of those systems in the United Kingdom and France are needed and capable of implementation in the United States?

In an effort to answer these questions, this book explores the investigative detention capabilities of the United States, the United Kingdom, and France. One obvious purpose in endeavoring to compare counterterrorism legislation in these various countries is to provide useful information for those conducting joint international counterterrorism operations. A proper understanding of which laws best facilitate the capture of counterterrorism targets—and the manner in which they function—is critical in the planning of such operations so that the various partners in such an enterprise understand the relative strengths and weaknesses of the laws in each jurisdiction.

An equally important purpose of such a comparison, however, is served by looking to the legal systems of each country to determine whether the capabilities of each detention regime are exportable to other legal systems or—at the very least—if those capabilities can somehow inform domestic counterterrorism policy. In undertaking to explicate the investigative detention laws of each country relevant to this study, this book reveals that, in spite of some recent adaptations, overall, U.S. law is far less permissive than U.K. and French law in the ability to detain and interrogate terrorist suspects. Legislative modifications in the United States are, nonetheless, possible, which could serve to increase U.S. detention powers and "narrow the gap" that exists between the United States and our European allies—all in a way that is consistent with international human rights law, the U.S. criminal model, and the U.S. constitutional tradition.

BACKGROUND

On January 9, 2003, a U.S. naval officer, Vice Admiral Lowell E. Jacoby, completed a declaration that would be submitted as part of the record in the matter of *Jose Padilla v. George W. Bush, et al.*[2] The United States, still reeling from the attacks of September 11, 2001, was engaged in an aggressive new counterterrorism strategy. Federal agents had captured and detained Jose Padilla—a U.S. citizen—because it was suspected that he was engaged in terrorist activity. The suspect had been, thereafter, labeled an enemy combatant, handed over to the Department of Defense, and was being held incommunicado by the military without access to an attorney or anyone else except those interrogating him.

As one might expect, Padilla filed for a writ of habeas corpus in an attempt to challenge his detention. The U.S. government, therefore, needed someone to explain this strikingly extreme situation to a federal court—to explain why it was necessary to hold someone in detention for a prolonged period without granting that person access to an attorney or outside assistance. For that, they turned to Vice Admiral Jacoby, who was the director of the Defense Intelligence Agency (DIA).[3]

In his declaration, Vice Admiral Jacoby noted that interrogation—"the art of questioning and examining a source to obtain the maximum amount of usable, reliable information in the least amount of time to meet intelligence requirements"—is a fundamental tool used in the gathering of intelligence.[4] Prolonged incommunicado detention, the vice admiral argued, was critical to "minimize external influences on the interrogation process" and, thus, maximize the quality and quantity of intelligence produced.[5] He concluded by declaring the following:

> In summary, the War on Terrorism cannot be won without timely, reliable, and abundant intelligence. That intelligence cannot be obtained without robust interrogation efforts. Impairment of the interrogation tool—especially with respect to enemy combatants associated with al Qaida—would undermine our Nation's intelligence gathering efforts, thus jeopardizing the national security of the United States.[6]

Four years after that memorandum was completed, in a 2007 op-ed in the *Wall Street Journal*, Michael B. Mukasey, the former district judge who signed the material witness warrant authorizing Padilla's arrest and who would soon after become U.S. attorney general, publicly called out for a statute that would give U.S. law enforcement investigative detention powers similar to their European counterparts, stating that

> [the U.S. material witness statute] was used frequently after 9/11, when the government tried to investigate numerous leads and people to determine whether follow-on attacks were planned—but found itself without a statute that authorized investigative detention on reasonable suspicion, of the sort available to authorities in Britain and France, among other countries.[7]

The issue confronting both Mukasey and the vice admiral was a central quandary of modern counterterrorism in both military and domestic law enforcement operations: how to assert control over a terrorist suspect in order to get the information needed to understand the enemy, discover the truth, and stop the next attack. A central aspect of that dilemma is the fact that the need for intelligence and/or usable evidence requires governments to not simply kill terrorists—but to capture them so that information may be gleaned (for the intelligence officer) and evidence collected (for the prosecutor). Otherwise stated, rather than simply crushing the rattlesnake when it is poised to strike, governments must instead find a way to ensnare it in order to obtain needed intelligence, convict terrorist suspects, and prevent future terrorist attacks.

This is true whether one is seeking to thwart terrorists at home or on the battlefield abroad. As Jacoby noted, interrogation is important for military reasons, such as developing information needed to counter the "asymmetrical" threat posed by terrorists.[8] It is pellucidly clear, however, that such information is equally essential to civilian criminal institutions in their effort to ferret out terrorist operations domestically and prosecute offenders. In either case, it is axiomatic that, in order to accomplish such interrogation, one must first detain a person so that he or she can be interrogated. There can be no doubt that if interrogation forms a critical part of the counterterrorism effort, detention is its necessary antecedent.

This challenge is certainly one that is shared by other countries. The threat posed by terrorist activity is a matter of utmost concern to modern governments across the globe.[9] The sickening brutality demonstrated by international terrorists in New York, Madrid, London, and elsewhere has mobilized action by those governments on both the domestic and international fronts. Governments must act to counter foreign terrorist threats while simultaneously seeking to address domestic terrorist activities occurring within their borders, among their own populations, and perhaps by their own citizens. Thus, while the vast machinery of the military is unleashed to do battle abroad, governments must also formulate strategies for addressing the problem of terrorists at home through domestic counterterrorism legislation. As demonstrated throughout this book, a central feature of such counterterrorism legislation has been a regime of law allowing for investigative detention.

Investigative Detention

In his excellent article on the subject, Professor Doug Cassel has noted that there are two purposes underlying the post-9/11 detention of terrorist suspects: criminal law enforcement and/or preventive detention.[10] The two types of detention are conceptually distinct in that the former (detention for criminal law enforcement purposes) envisions an eventual criminal prosecution while the ultimate aim of the latter (preventive or "security detention") is—in its purest form—the mere prevention of action through detention of the individual.[11] As one commentator has noted in distinguishing the two concepts, "Pure preventive detention is defined…as a deprivation of liberty that is based on a prediction of harmful conduct and that is not time-limited by culpability or other considerations (such as a pending trial)."[12] As will become apparent throughout the discussion in this book, there is a significant degree of interplay and synergy between these two concepts, owing to the fact that each entails essentially the same action (locking up a suspect) but for ostensibly different purposes. On that note, even the differences between these purposes can become blurred when mechanisms for preventive detention are used for investigative purposes and vice versa. Nonetheless, the distinction between the two concepts remains and their treatment in both domestic and international law has been notably different.[13] The focus of this book is primarily on the detention of terrorist suspects for criminal law enforcement purposes—specifically the type of detention identified by Mukasey as a critical tool found in the counterterrorism legislation in numerous countries—investigative detention.[14]

The term *investigative detention* is subject to various meanings in legal literature. For instance, in the United States, it is sometimes used to refer to a brief stop of a suspect who falls short of a full arrest. In some cases, the phrase is conflated with preventive detention or detention without trial.[15] *Investigative detention*, as the term is used in this book, however, specifically refers to the detention of a suspect for the purpose of obtaining evidence for use at a subsequent criminal prosecution. This necessarily implies (a) a certain lack of evidence at the outset of detention, (b) an investigation of some sort during the period of detention designed to obtain useable evidence, and (c) the eventual release of the suspect or subjection of the suspect to a criminal proceeding where his or her guilt or innocence can be determined.

The concept of investigative detention has been the subject of a certain degree of neglect in both scholarly and policy-making circles. As Cassel has noted, "[I]n many cases, the obstacles to prosecution may lead States to look for other, more practical ways to remove suspected terrorists from the streets."[16] The strictures of domestic criminal law can sometimes drive governments to seek extrajudicial means of dealing with terrorists, such as military detention and preventive detention.[17] But to focus attention to such other means of detention to the neglect of investigative detention is to ignore an important aspect of effective counterterrorism. As one UN report has noted, "A forward-looking, preventive criminal justice strategy against terrorist violence requires a comprehensive system of substantive offences, investigative powers and techniques, evidentiary rules, and inter-State cooperation mechanisms."[18] Investigative detention has been expressly identified by some experts as an element of such a system.[19] It is a means of empowering law enforcement to seize an individual and hold that person for the purposes of interrogation, obtaining evidence, and ensuring the integrity of an ongoing investigation.[20]

In spite of its importance, however, while a surfeit of literature has recently appeared that addresses military and preventive detention in connection with terrorist suspects,[21] the subject of investigative detention has remained largely in the shadows. While an absolute neglect of preventive or military detention would be imprudent (given their conceptual overlap) this book seeks to cast greater light on investigative detention within the domestic criminal process—illuminating its characteristics, capabilities, and limitations.

The Comparison

For its comparative analysis, this book looks to the European comparators identified by Mukasey (the United Kingdom and France) to see how those countries operate and what their law provides, and to ascertain the essential elements of their investigative detention regimes. These countries share a great deal in common with the United States in that both France and the United Kingdom are liberal democracies that have had experience with both domestic and international terrorism. The manner in which France and the United Kingdom have chosen to deal with terrorism and the detention of terrorist suspects, however, marks a point of distinction. Kenneth Roth has noted that "[a]mong liberal democracies, the United Kingdom and France are arguably the most aggressive in granting the state latitude in detaining terrorist suspects."[22] France, in particular, has been singled out as possessing an especially effective counterterrorism regime—based in large part on its potent investigative detention apparatus.[23]

In spite of what common attributes the three countries share, the legal systems of each country present areas of contrast, posing challenges to comparativists seeking compatible tactics and exportable elements from each legal system. This also, however, presents a fantastic opportunity for useful exploration, as the juridical heterogeneity among these three divergent legal systems has given rise to different legal approaches to investigative detention—each designed to conform to the country's specific legal requirements. The comparative analysis, therefore, is not a mere academic exercise, but a quest for ideas that have succeeded abroad that could be effectively implemented at home. "Comparative law is an *ecole de vérité* which extends and enriches the supply of solutions and offers the scholar of critical capacity the opportunity of finding the 'better solution' for his time and place."[24]

Accordingly, each chapter begins by detailing the experience of the relevant country with terrorism and its legislative response to the threat. It then analyzes the general nature of the criminal justice system of that country, how that country's criminal law defines terrorism, and the country's law of detention, including what provisions exist for investigative detention in standard criminal matters. Thereafter, the chapter analyzes counterterrorism legislation in force and how that legislation augments the ordinary criminal law regime in cases of terrorism. Through an analysis of each country's domestic criminal procedure, this book determines where the U.S. regime of counterterrorism legislation stands in relation to its European counterparts, what lessons—cautionary or otherwise—can be learned from across the Atlantic, and how our domestic policy can be informed by their experience.

CHAPTER 2

INVESTIGATIVE DETENTION AND INTERNATIONAL HUMAN RIGHTS LAW

In order to attain this book's goal of comparing the investigative detention regimes of the United States, the United Kingdom, and France, this chapter outlines the criminal procedures of those countries in detail, exploring the powers and restrictions of each country's domestic criminal justice apparatus. At the outset, however, there is another dimension that must be considered in the analysis of all three legal systems—a regime of law on the international plane that can influence, or in some instances control, domestic criminal law. That regime of law is commonly referred to as international human rights law.

Commentators note that international human rights law is, in some respects, a new body of law that has been rapidly evolving since the end of World War II.[25] It has been defined as "the law that deals with the protection of individuals and groups against violations of internationally guaranteed rights, and with the promotion of these rights,"[26] and consists of those international rules, procedures, and institutions developed to protect and promote international human rights obligations.[27] The core of this field of law is composed of the United Nations Charter and related instruments. Three instruments, however, are largely considered to be among the most important: the Universal Declaration of Human Rights of 1948, the International Covenant on Civil and Political Rights (ICCPR), and the International Covenant on Economic, Social, and Cultural Rights (ICESCR).[28] Other regional instruments, such as the European Convention on Human Rights (ECHR), also play an important role. Cassel detailed a list of several international human rights instruments that touch upon a state's power to detain individuals.[29] The most salient instruments for purposes of this analysis, however, are the ICCPR and the ECHR.

The International Covenant on Civil and Political Rights

The ICCPR was adopted in New York on December 16, 1966. It entered into force for the United States on September 8, 1992. The Senate resolution giving its advice and consent to ratification was adopted on April 2, 1992, subject to five reservations, five understandings, and four declarations.[30] The ICCPR articulates many of the same human rights articulated in the Universal Declaration of Human Rights, but focuses (as its name implies) on those rights that are considered "civil and political."[31] These rights are "essentially those civil and political rights reflected in the Western, liberal, democratic tradition,"[32] and are "primarily limitations upon the power of the State to impose its will upon the people under its jurisdiction."[33]

Specific rights enumerated in the ICCPR include freedom of thought, conscience, and religion; freedom of opinion and expression; freedom of association; the right of peaceful assembly; the right to vote; equal protection of the law; the right to liberty and security of the person; the right to a fair trial (including the presumption of innocence); the right of privacy; freedom of movement, residence, and immigration; freedom from slavery and forced labor; protection from torture, or cruel, inhumane, or degrading treatment or punishment; and the right to life.[34]

The provision of the ICCPR that most directly touches on the subject of investigative detention is article 9, the first paragraph of which states that

> everyone has the right to liberty and security of the person. No one shall be subjected to arbitrary arrest or detention. No one shall be deprived of his liberty except on such grounds and in accordance with such procedure as are established by law.[35]

That same article goes on to spell out specific requirements that must be met when detaining an individual.

Another provision is article 14 of the ICCPR, which lays out the principal obligations regarding due process in criminal trials. Pursuant to article 14, state parties must ensure that criminal defendants receive a fair and public hearing before a "competent, independent and impartial tribunal established by law."[36] In addition, article 14 requires numerous substantive rights, such as the presumption of innocence, due process rights, and the right to appeal a conviction to a "higher tribunal according to law."[37] States must also ensure that all persons are tried without undue delay.[38]

Enforcement Mechanisms

A key part of the ICCPR is the establishment of the UN Human Rights Committee, an institution created to ensure that member states comply with their obligations pursuant to the ICCPR. The Human Rights Committee has two principal mechanisms at its disposal to encourage compliance with the ICCPR by member states: (1) the review of periodic reports that member states must submit on measures they have taken to implement the rights delineated in the ICCPR, and (2) an interstate complaint mechanism that allows member states to assert that another member state is not fulfilling its obligations under the ICCPR.[39] In addition, pursuant to an optional protocol, states may agree to allow the Human

Rights Committee to consider complaints (called *communications*) filed by individuals through what is known as the individual communication process.[40]

All states under consideration in this analysis are party to the ICCPR,[41] though, of the three, only France is a party to the optional protocol.[42] Neither the United States nor the United Kingdom has ratified it. Individual complaints, therefore, can be brought against France, but not against the United States or the United Kingdom.[43]

The nature of the HRC and its jurisprudence is not the easiest to ascertain. It is considered neither a judicial nor even a quasi-judicial entity, yet it issues general comments intended to clarify its understanding of the ICCPR and "final views" intended to conclude the individual communication process.[44] The Human Rights Committee's decisions, nonetheless, have no binding force—even among parties to the Optional Protocol. Member states are, therefore, not always legally obligated to comply with the committee's findings.[45] The question of the direct binding force of the committee's decisions is not, however, the end of the inquiry. Though not binding, the committee's decisions are considered a highly persuasive authority for ICCPR interpretation. This is because the Human Rights Committee is considered the authoritative interpreter of the rights articulated in the ICCPR.[46] As such, its decisions and views are given great credence internationally and have a norm-creating property that can serve to create customary international law.[47]

> What can be stated with a high degree of certainty is that the HRC is the sole body which is authorized to make authoritative interpretations of the ICCPR, thus when the Committee pronounces upon the content or meaning of a right contained in the Covenant, it does so with undeniable authority.[48]

Unlike France, when ratifying the ICCPR, the United Kingdom accepted the competence of the HRC to hear interstate complaints.[49] Likewise, the United States "accept[ed] the competence of the Human Rights Committee to receive and consider communications under article 41 [state-to-state complaints] in which a State Party claims that another State Party is not fulfilling its obligations under the Covenant."[50] The United States, thus, is subject to the interstate complaint mechanism, which allows the committee to receive and consider communications from one state party claiming that another state party is not fulfilling its obligations under the ICCPR. It should be noted, however, that no state party has ever filed an interstate complaint against another state. Should a state party ever file such a complaint against the United States, the committee would have a role in evaluating the alleged violation.[51]

The European Convention on Human Rights

A separate instrument that pertains exclusively to European states is the European Convention for the Protection of Human Rights and Fundamental Freedoms (ECHR), which was signed in 1950 and entered into force in 1953.[52] This convention was, in part, a response to the human rights atrocities committed during the Second World War and represented an attempt to integrate European powers in a way that would prevent the repetition of such large-scale violence and global conflict.

> The ECHR is of particular importance within the context of international human rights for several reasons: it was the first comprehensive treaty in the world in this field; it established the first international complaints procedure and the first international court for the determination of human rights matters; it remains the most judicially developed of all the human rights systems; and it has generated a more extensive jurisprudence than any other part of the international system.[53]

Both France and the United Kingdom are parties to the ECHR, though the United States—being located in North America—is not.

There is no hierarchy of rights under the ECHR, though commentators distinguish between those rights in the convention that are "unqualified" and "qualified."[54] Those which are unqualified are the right to life; the prohibition on torture, inhuman, or degrading treatment; the prohibition on slavery and forced labor; the right to liberty and security; the right to a fair trial; the prohibition on punishment without law; the right to marry; the right to an effective remedy; the prohibition on discrimination; the right to education and the right to free elections; and the prohibition on the death penalty.[55]

The primary article impacting investigation detention under the ECHR is article 5—the fountainhead for the right to liberty and security of the person.[56] This article provides that everyone has the right to liberty and security of person. It goes on to state that no one shall be deprived of his liberty except in certain enumerated cases, such as lawful detention after conviction by a competent court; the lawful arrest or detention of a person for noncompliance with the lawful order of a court; and

> the lawful arrest or detention of a person effected for the purpose of bringing him before the competent legal authority on reasonable suspicion of having committed an offence or when it is reasonable considered necessary to prevent his committing an offence or fleeing after having done so.[57]

This article has generated a fair amount of jurisprudence, which has had significant effects on the investigative detention regimes of European countries.

Commentators note that the purpose of article 5 is to limit detention to those circumstances where it is strictly necessary in the public interest and to provide guarantees against arbitrariness.[58] Article 5(1)(c) of the ECHR allows the "lawful arrest or detention of a person effected for the purpose of bringing him before the competent legal authority on reasonable suspicion of having committed an offense."[59] The European Court of Human Rights (ECtHR), in interpreting this provision, has held that the test of "reasonable suspicion" is an objective one that "presupposes the existence of facts or information which would satisfy an objective observer that the person concerned may have committed the offense."[60]

Further, article 5(3) of the ECHR requires that those arrested and charged with any offense be brought "promptly" before a court.[61] In interpreting this provision, the ECtHR has held that the initial arrest and the continuing detention must be justified, so long as it lasts, by adequate grounds. Further, the duration of the detention must not exceed a reasonable time.[62] In the specific case of terrorism, the ECtHR has demonstrated a degree of flexibility in defining reasonableness, noting the following:

> Because of the attendant risk of loss of life and human suffering, the police are obliged to act with utmost urgency in following up all information, including information from secret sources. Further, the police may frequently have to arrest a suspected terrorist on the basis of information which is reliable but which cannot, without putting in jeopardy the source of the information, be revealed to the suspect or produced in court to support a charge.[63]

Another key provision is article 6, which lays out substantive requirements in the criminal process, such as the presumption of innocence, the right to be promptly informed of the charges, and the right to legal assistance. Article 15(1) of the ECHR, however, provides that "in times of war or other public emergency threatening the life of the nation, any High Contracting Party may take measure derogating from its obligations under this Convention to the extent strictly required by the situation."[64] As the following discussion demonstrates, European countries have made use of this ability to derogate for purposes of counterterrorism.

Enforcement Mechanisms

The ECHR provides for two different procedures to ensure member state compliance with its provisions: an individual petition procedure and an interstate procedure.[65] Pursuant to these two procedures, member states may be held accountable by the ECtHR for violations of recognized rights.[66] Unlike the ICCPR, the ECHR's interstate complaint mechanism has been used in the past—albeit infrequently.[67] Further, in contrast to the ICCPR, all member states are subject to the ECHR's individual petition procedure, and final decisions by the ECtHR are largely considered to be binding.[68]

HUMAN RIGHTS AND INVESTIGATIVE DETENTION

Cassel noted that, for member states of the Council of Europe, the ECtHR's interpretation of article 5 and its jurisprudence have served to limit European investigative detention powers—at least in theory.[69] Those limitations—and the resultant legislative responses—are discussed more fully in the chapters addressing the United Kingdom and France. It is worth noting here, however, that the nature of the ECHR and its robust human rights regime has resulted in a far more detailed body of law on the subject for European countries than exists vis-à-vis their North American counterpart.[70]

The key instrument bearing on detention to which the United States is a party, the ICCPR, implicitly permits the practice of investigative detention. The language of General Comment 8, which elaborates on the rights contained in article 9 of the ICCPR, never expressly mentions investigative detention but does state that preventive detention—its more potent corollary—is permissible so long as it is controlled by the provisions of article 9. This means that preventive detention is permissible so long as it is not arbitrary, it is based on grounds and procedures established by law, information of the reasons for detention are given to the suspect, courts are in control of the detention, and compensation is available in the case of a breach.[71] From this express allowance of preventive detention, one may deduce a fortiori (a maiore ad minus) that investigative detention is permissible so long as the same safeguards are granted.

Further, the HRC's General Comment 8 states that

> in criminal cases any person arrested or detained has to be brought "promptly" before a judge or other officer authorized by law to exercise judicial power. More precise time-limits are fixed by law in most State parties and, in the view of the committee, delays must not exceed a few days.[72]

Thus, a delay of a few days for investigative purposes before bringing a suspect before a judge would not violate the provisions of the ICCPR.[73] This allowance of "a few days" of detention before presentment before a judge is another implicit acknowledgment of the practice of investigative detention—albeit with some time constraints.

There are, in addition, other strong indicia of the acceptance of investigative detention under the provisions of the ICCPR. The United Nations Office on Drugs and Crime, Terrorism Prevention Branch, has subtly indicated that investigative detention may be required in order to safeguard the rights contained in the ICCPR:

> A forward-looking, preventive criminal justice strategy against terrorist violence requires a comprehensive system of substantive offences, investigative powers and techniques, evidentiary rules, and inter-State cooperation mechanisms. Such an integrated system is necessary to implement the right to life guaranteed by the ICCPR.[74]

That same report also noted that "there is no precise or universally authoritative answer to how many hours or days the rule of law permits a person to be detained in a terrorism case before being charged or released" and that "[n]ational legislation varies widely, and many systems allow extended investigative detention under judicial supervision once a preliminary determination has been made by a neutral magistrate that grounds for investigation or trial exist."[75] Thus, a regime of investigative detention is compatible with the ICCPR so long as such detentions are not arbitrary, remain controlled by the judiciary, and otherwise comport with the requirements of article 9.

Lastly, it is worth noting that one of the key requirements of article 9 is that the detention must not be arbitrary. According to the UN Working Group on Arbitrary Detention, the deprivation of liberty is arbitrary when a case falls into one of three categories.[76] The first category is when there is no legal basis to justify the deprivation of liberty. The second category is when the deprivation of liberty violates certain articles of the Universal Declaration of Human Rights or the ICCPR, namely, when it is used to infringe upon a person's freedom of thought, conscience, and religion; freedom of opinion and expression; or the right of peaceful assembly and association.[77] The third category is when the international norms relating to the right to fair trial are so ignored or abused that the governmental action confers on the deprivation of freedom, of whatever kind, an arbitrary character.[78] A regime of law allowing for the investigative detention of individuals suspected of terrorist activity, so long as it is normalized in a legal framework and comports with the requirements previously discussed, is not violative of the ICCPR.

CONCLUSION

As this discussion has demonstrated, the practice of investigative detention is not violative of international human rights law per se. Nonetheless, there are definite restrictions and limitations on the detention of an individual and many opportunities for a nation to run afoul of limits set by international instruments. The influence of international human rights law on each nation under consideration in this book differs depending on the governments involved, their approach to terrorism, and each treaty's varying degree of applicability. The effects of these international instruments are considered in the discussion along with the requirements of each country's domestic legal structure.

CHAPTER 3

THE UNITED STATES

In 1979 the U.S. Supreme Court held that "detention for custodial interrogation—regardless of its label—intrudes so severely on the interests protected by the Fourth Amendment as necessarily to trigger the traditional safeguards against illegal arrest."[79] Based on such an assertion, the likelihood of investigative detention in the context of U.S. criminal law would seem somewhat dismal. But is this statement true—or is it something of a shibboleth?

This chapter analyzes the law of detention in the United States and reveals that, while U.S. law does tend to restrict the abilities of law enforcement agents to detain suspects for investigative purposes, there still exists in contemporary U.S. law a rather impressive array of detention powers—especially where national security concerns are present. While a host of judicial decisions decry the possibility of investigative detention in the United States, numerous other statutes and judicial decisions, in certain circumstances, allow limited approximations of it. Furthermore, numerous areas of exception exist that allow for the possibility of a formalized, limited investigative detention regime—even in the context of ordinary criminal law.

Overview of the U.S. Criminal Justice System

The contemporary system of American criminal justice is the product of the English legal tradition, but centuries of evolution now separate it—like an ocean—from its European ancestor.[80] It does, however, share the same basic adversarial traits that prevail in England, such as a procedural model in which the defendant, with the advantage of legal counsel, faces off against the government in a series of adversarial proceedings.[81] This model of criminal procedure prevails throughout the country.[82]

It is worth noting that, under the American system of government, each of the fifty states retains the power to promulgate and enforce its own criminal laws within their respective territories.[83] Even though a significant portion of the law of criminal procedure—at every level—is derived from the U.S. Supreme Court's interpretation of the U.S. Constitution and its amendments,[84] some lack of procedural and substantive uniformity remains among those disparate jurisdictions.[85] These various state courts will not, however, be the focus of this study, as current U.S. law gives the U.S. Department of Justice the authority to investigate all offenses related to terrorism.[86] Thus, for purposes of clarity, as well as for practical reasons, as it is the U.S. federal criminal justice system that will predominantly handle any criminal terrorism matter, this chapter shall focus on federal criminal procedure—though similarities in the laws of every political subdivision of the United States will often make what is said here equally true at the state and local levels.[87]

American Pretrial Investigation

Mary Clifford has noted that the American system of policing was modeled after the London Metropolitan Police.[88] In accordance with its legal structure, the police in the United States are decentralized, with separate police entities at the local, state, and federal levels of government.[89] The basic investigatory model is also similar to that of its English progenitor—a binary system in which police investigate crime and then bring the evidence to a prosecutor who then decides if prosecution is appropriate.

The standard criminal case generally begins with the police making an investigation prior to the arrest of the suspect.[90] This investigation begins once the police are notified of a potential crime. Police then will begin investigating the activity made known to them in order to determine whether a crime was committed. Police will seek to determine who committed the crime, collect evidence of that person's guilt, then locate the suspect and—quite importantly for purposes of this book—take him or her into custody.[91]

In that process, the initial decision to charge a suspect is usually made by a police officer when arresting the suspect.[92] Lafave, Israel, and King described the normal postarrest process:

> The arrestee is then transported to a police station or other facility where various aspects of arrest processing occur—e.g., the arrest is recorded (i.e. "booked"), and the arrestee is photographed and fingerprinted. At this point also, the police will review the arresting officer's initial decision to charge and set the proposed charge. Assuming the police do not decide against charging (and therefore release the arrestee), the arrestee will have to be taken before a magistrate within a relatively short period (typically 24 or 28 hours.) Ordinarily, during this period, as to felony charges, a member of the prosecutor's staff will "screen" the charge recommended by the police.

Thereafter, the case is in the hands of the prosecutors (known as assistant U.S. attorneys in the federal system) who make the decision of whether to prosecute the arrestee and make the final decisions regarding the charges to be brought.[93] As one popular American television series phrases it, "In the criminal justice system, the people are represented by two separate, yet equally important groups: the police who investigate crime and the district attorneys who prosecute the offenders."[94] Barring the use of some exceptional mechanism, it is within the context of this procedural model that terrorist suspects will be investigated.

The U.S. Experience and the U.S. Response

At the time of this writing, the terrorist attacks of September 11, 2001, are the events most immediately associated with the U.S. experience with terrorism. Yet, the United States has been dealing with terrorism—in one form or another—since its inception. Commentators note that counterterrorism legislation in the United States may have appeared quite early in the nation's history with the trial of a Jamestown Colony leader in 1607 for an unknown crime that threatened the colony's existence.[95] Another example of such early legislation in the United States is the Alien and Sedition Acts of 1798, which authorized the president to remove any alien who was deemed dangerous to the peace and security of the United States.[96]

In the nineteenth century, the United States experienced terrorist acts conducted by anarchists associated with trade union movements.[97] The most famous example of this sort is the Haymarket Square incident in 1886 in which an anarchist in Chicago threw a bomb into a crowd of police.[98] More recent examples of terrorism in the United States include other "homegrown" groups such as the Ku Klux Klan (KKK), which came into existence roughly 140 years ago and conducted terror campaigns against minority communities[99]—principally against African Americans, Jews, Catholics, and certain liberal groups.[100] The methods employed by the KKK were classically terroristic in nature, as they were deadly, theatrical, and designed to intimidate those who opposed their white supremacist world view.[101]

The practice of domestic terrorism, however, was by no means confined to the KKK. In the 1960s, leftist radical groups with violent tendencies emerged, such as the Black Panthers, the Weather Underground, and the New World Liberation Front,[102] all of which managed to successfully carry out some form of attack on U.S. soil. The Weather Underground, for instance, claimed responsibility for the bombing of the Gulf Oil Building in Pittsburgh in June of 1974.[103] The Black Panthers, likewise, were involved in plots to bomb a number of targets in New York City, including department stores, police stations, and public buildings.[104]

Domestic terrorism, therefore, has been a feature of American society for some time. Foreign organizations have also historically carried out acts of terrorism on U.S. soil. Examples of such terrorism include a Croatian group called Otpor, which hijacked a commercial airplane traveling from New York to Paris in 1976 in an attempt to garner attention for its separatist agenda, which included obtaining independence from Yugoslavia. That same group later took over a West German consulate in Chicago in an effort to obtain the release of a Croatian leader in Cologne.[105] By employing such tactics, a relatively obscure foreign political agenda was thrust into the eye of the American public.

Although certain militant groups remained active through the 1980s, there were relatively few terrorist attacks on U.S. soil during that period.[106] Abroad, however, numerous dramatic attacks against U.S. interests were perpetrated by foreign actors. For instance, in 1988 Pan Am Flight 103 was bombed while over Lockerbie, Scotland, destroying the plane in midair and killing 270 passengers—of which 189 were American citizens.[107] Other notable attacks abroad included the hijacking of the cruise ship *Achille Lauro* and the bombing of a West Berlin disco that was frequented by U.S. soldiers.[108] More direct attacks against U.S. interests included a suicide bomber who detonated a truck full of explosives in front of the U.S. embassy in Beirut, Lebanon, killing sixty-three people.[109] Only a few months after that attack, on October 23, 1983, the most devastating attack of the decade occurred when a U.S. barracks in Beirut was bombed by Islamic extremists—causing 241 deaths.[110] Thus, although the 1980s were relatively free of domestic terrorism, the level of international terrorism directed against American interest abroad was still significant.

In the 1990s, however, the number of domestic terrorist attacks in the U.S. would increase. Professor Yonah Alexander explained,

> Between 1990 and 1999, some sixty terrorist attacks perpetrated by both domestic and foreign groups occurred in the United States, killing 182 people and injuring more than 1,932. In 1990 the perpetration of only four events was the lowest number in any year since 1970. The most dramatic event was the assassination of Rabbi Meir Kahane, the Israeli leader of the Jewish Defense

> League (JDL), by an Egyptian immigrant to the United States. Other events included: an abortive plot by militant "skinheads" to pump cyanide gas into a synagogue; the explosion of a bomb outside a Cuban museum in Miami; and the arrest in Florida of individuals affiliated with the PIRA while attempting to purchase a heat-seeking anti-aircraft Stinger missile and other sophisticated weapons.[111]

Among the most stunning attacks of that era was one that occurred in 1993, when a car bomb was detonated below Tower One of the World Trade Center in New York City. That attack, masterminded by an individual named Ramzi Yousef, was perpetrated by terrorists linked to foreign terrorist organizations from the Middle East, including Al-Qaeda.[112] While this particular bombing only killed six people, it wounded 1,042 and caused widespread damage.[113] It was a dramatic and deadly attack against a symbolic target—a classic terrorist operation.

What foreign terrorist organizations had not yet done in the way of fatalities would soon be accomplished by domestic terrorists. Only two years after the World Trade Center was bombed, an American citizen named Timothy McVeigh, with the assistance of another American citizen named Terry Nichols, detonated a truck full of explosives beneath the Alfred P. Murray federal building in Oklahoma City.[114] This attack destroyed the federal building, severely damaged or destroyed an additional twenty-five structures in Oklahoma City, and—most tragically—claimed 168 lives (including 19 children) and wounded 674 people.[115] The fact that this attack was perpetrated by two American citizens highlights the danger of domestic terrorism and the fact that such violence can be the result of purely domestic actors—individuals living and operating on U.S. soil and subject to all the rights and privileges afforded to U.S. citizens.

These dramatic attacks had an impact on the way Americans viewed the threat of terrorism,[116] and legislation to address the problem soon emerged. In 1996 Congress passed the Anti-Terrorism and Effective Death Penalty Act (ATEDPA) the first modern attempt by an American government to comprehensively address the problem of terrorism.[117] Among its many provisions, ATEDPA put into effect new rules empowering the secretary of state to designate certain groups as "terrorist organizations" if those groups were found to engage in activities that threaten the peace and security of the United States or its citizens. The act also prohibited the financing of such organizations by individuals and barred even humanitarian assistance to such groups.[118] In addition, ATEDPA authorized the agency then known as the Immigration and Naturalization Service (INS) to refuse asylum or citizenship requests from any member of a terrorist organization and created a special federal court that could utilize secret evidence in making its findings.[119]

ATEDPA augmented governmental powers to fight terrorism, but it did not prevent what was to follow in a few short years. The worst was still to come. On September 11, 2001, four U.S. airliners were hijacked by terrorists associated with Al-Qaeda and Osama bin Laden.[120] Two planes filled with passengers were flown directly into the both towers of the World Trade Center (the "Twin Towers") in New York City, one plane filled with passengers was flown into the Pentagon, and a third—which may have been headed toward the White House—crashed in a field in Pennsylvania after the passengers on board overcame the hijackers.[121] The burning jet fuel exacerbated the damage of the attack, ravaging the structures they impacted, creating enormous explosions, and melting metal—which, in New York, caused the skyscrapers to collapse. In all, three thousand people were killed.[122] As Gerard Chaliand and Arnaud Blin noted,

> The 9/11 attacks were the biggest achievement yet by a terrorist group: in media terms (the attacks were broadcast live around the world); symbolically (the attacks struck at the core of America's financial center and military establishment); and statistically, with a large number of victims (the term "megaterrorism" was used.) There is no doubt that psychologically, America and much of the rest of the world, especially in the West, were in a state of shock.[123]

Within one week of the attacks, new counterterrorism legislation was developing, which would give the U.S. government even greater power to combat terrorism.[124] With very little debate and a pressing sense of urgency, Congress passed the Uniting and Strengthening America by Providing Appropriate Tools Required to Intercept and Obstruct Terrorism Act (the USA PATRIOT Act).[125] This legislation amended numerous laws regarding a wide range of criminal matters, but is most noted for the broad surveillance powers it grants the federal government. Its main elements allow for broader, more flexible warrants; for enhanced ability to subpoena electronic and financial information; and for the punishment of those who aid or harbor terrorists.[126] Notably, however, and as this chapter explores in greater detail, it did not provide for a regime of investigative detention and left U.S. law in that regard largely unchanged.

U.S. Law of Detention

In order to understand how terrorist suspects may be detained, it is necessary to understand the basic detention mechanisms available under U.S. criminal law. The U.S. criminal justice system contains a complex body of law governing detention. Different standards and mechanisms apply depending on the status and circumstances of the individual to be detained. Moreover, there are distinct bodies of law developing in the U.S. that treat the possibility of pre-charge detention quite differently—including a strictly criminal detention regime, which is generally hostile to the notion of investigative detention, and a quasi–criminal detention regime, which is somewhat more permissive. Reconciling these divergent voices on the law detention can prove a daunting task and requires close attention to the specific statutes being used to effect detention, as well as the circumstances of the detainee.

The Fourth Amendment and Detention of Criminal Suspects

The Fourth Amendment of the United States Constitution states that

> [t]he right of the people to be secure in their houses, papers, and effects, against unreasonable searches and seizures, shall not be violated, and no Warrants shall issue, but upon probable cause…, and particularly describing the place to be searched, and the persons or things to be seized.[127]

In the context of detention, U.S. jurisprudence has interpreted this rule as requiring probable cause to arrest an individual. Probable cause has been defined "in terms of facts and circumstances 'sufficient to warrant a prudent man in believing that the [suspect] had committed or was committing an offense.'"[128] The effect of these provisions is to limit police action in the criminal context and to impose upon them requirements that serve to inhibit their ability to detain a suspect for investigative purposes. As the analysis in this chapter demonstrates, however, the protections of the Fourth Amendment are not inflexible, and there are exceptions to its restrictions where greater matters of public safety or national security are implicated.

The Power to "Stop and Frisk" Suspects

In spite of the language of the Fourth Amendment, police in the United States do have a limited power to stop and search individuals without probable cause that the individual has committed a specific offense. This is known as a "Terry stop" under U.S. law due to the Supreme Court case entitled *Terry v. Ohio*, which established the rule that police, without a warrant or probable cause, may briefly detain an individual suspected of criminal activity, question him or her, and perform a limited search for weapons. It allows, therefore, not only the brief detention of the individual, but also a limited search.

> [T]here [is] a narrowly drawn authority to permit a reasonable search for weapons for the protection of the police officer where he has reason to believe that he is dealing with an armed and dangerous individual, regardless of whether he has probable cause to arrest the individual for a crime. The officer need not be absolutely certain that the individual is armed; the issue is whether a reasonable prudent man in the circumstances would be warranted in the belief that his safety or that of others was in danger.[129]

This judicial exception to the protections of the Fourth Amendment, thus, was based on the practical needs of law enforcement and the recognition that a strict prohibition on such searches and seizures was neither practical nor tenable. Accordingly, police in the United States may stop an individual based on reasonable suspicion of criminal activity and perform a limited search for protective reasons. Before a police officer initiates an investigative stop, however, the officer must, based on the totality of the circumstances, "have a particularized and objective basis for suspecting the particular person stopped of criminal activity."[130] Thereafter, the officer may perform a cursory search, which allows the officer to frisk an individual, and pull out objects found on the suspect if it is believed that it is necessary to protect the officer from bodily harm.[131] The degree of suspicion required to effect the stop is referred to as "reasonable suspicion"—a criterion that is somewhat less demanding than the higher standard of "probable cause."[132]

The Supreme Court has adopted a two-part inquiry for evaluating the reasonableness of an investigative stop involving something less than probable cause: (1) The officer's action must be justified at its inception, and (2) the seizure and search must be reasonably related in scope to the circumstances that justified it in the first place.[133] With regard to that second element, the stop must be temporary, it must last no longer than is necessary to effect the purpose of the stop, and the search must employ the least intrusive means available to verify or dispel the officer's suspicion.[134] Accordingly, so long as the police have an articulable and reasonable suspicion that the suspect is engaged in criminal activity and that the subsequent seizure and search are reasonable, the Terry stop is permissible.[135] As later articulations of this rule have confirmed, this standard is not a very demanding one and affords U.S. law enforcement a great deal of flexibility.

> The officer, of course, must be able to articulate something more than an inchoate and unparticularized suspicion or "hunch." The Fourth Amendment requires some minimal level of objective justification for making the stop. That level of suspicion is considerably less than proof of wrongdoing by a preponderance of the evidence. We have held that probable cause means a fair probability that contraband or evidence of a crime will be found, and the level of suspicion required for a Terry stop is obviously less demanding than that for probable cause.[136]

According to this rationale, investigatory stops of suspects have been found valid where the indications of wrong-doing were quite vague, such as where the only basis for a stop was the perception that a suspect was acting nervously, along with the fact that the suspect was in a high-crime area and fled from police.[137] Therefore, although the officer must be able to articulate more than an "inchoate and unparticularized suspicion or 'hunch' of criminal activity," U.S. jurisprudence demonstrates that he or she will not have to articulate a great deal above that. As the Supreme Court has noted,

> Even in *Terry*, the conduct justifying the stop was ambiguous and susceptible of an innocent explanation. The officer observed two individuals pacing back and forth in front of a store, peering into the window and periodically conferring. All of this conduct was by itself lawful, but it also suggested that the individuals were casing the store for a planned robbery. Terry recognized that the officers could detain the individuals to resolve the ambiguity.[138]

It is important to emphasize, however, that such an investigative stop is not a full arrest. Although a warrantless stop for protective reasons may include a brief and limited investigation of sorts, U.S. law does not generally permit police to detain a suspect for a prolonged period of time based on such minimal criteria. Such detention, justified by reasonable suspicion, must be reasonable in its scope or it risks transcending the limits of a Terry stop and becoming a full-blown arrest—which requires more than mere reasonable suspicion. There is no bright-line rule to determine when such a stop crosses the line and becomes an arrest, although the Supreme Court has held that a ninety-minute detention was unreasonable and constituted an arrest.[139] The inquiry a court will use to determine whether an investigative stop has crossed the line will focus on the diligence of the police in conducting their investigation. Once, however, a suspect has been moved to the police station or moved to a separate location, such as a small room in an airport, U.S. jurisprudence generally holds that the police have effected an arrest and left the realm of the brief, limited, investigatory stop allowed by *Terry*.[140]

Arresting Suspects

As noted, the protections of the Fourth Amendment of the Constitution apply during the early stages of a criminal investigation in the United States.[141] The "stop and frisk" power previously described stands as an exception to the general rule that seizures of persons must be based on probable cause.[142] Likewise, it is a settled rule of U.S. jurisprudence that a warrantless arrest in a public place is permissible as long as the arresting officer had probable cause.[143] U.S. criminal law, in that respect, follows the common-law rule that a police officer may arrest a suspect without a warrant for either a misdemeanor or a felony offense.[144] In *United States v. Watson*, the Supreme Court held that so long as a police officer has probable cause to believe that a person has committed a felony, then the officer may arrest the suspect in a public place without a warrant.[145] Further, in *Atwater v. City of Lago Vista*,[146] the Court ruled that, where there is probable cause, the Fourth Amendment does not forbid peace officers from arresting a suspect without a warrant for misdemeanors not amounting to or involving breach of the peace.[147] If the suspect is in his or her home at the time of arrest, however, then an arrest warrant is still required.[148]

U.S. law enforcement agents may, therefore, arrest a suspect without a warrant so long as there is probable cause to believe there has been a crime and the suspect is not in his or her home. Certain procedural protections after a warrantless arrest apply nonetheless, such as the suspect's entitlement to a prompt postarrest assessment by a magistrate to determine whether there actually is probable cause to believe that the suspect committed the offense.[149] Prolonged delays between arrest and a magistrate's review are only permissible in situations where police are acting diligently and the delay is unavoidable.[150] Further, as previously noted, U.S. police may not generally detain a suspect at a police station for the sole purpose of interrogation.[151]

Border Searches

Another marked exception of the requirements of the Fourth Amendment exists in what are typically described as "border searches." The Supreme Court has noted that

> searches made at the border, pursuant to the long-standing right of the sovereign to protect itself by stopping and examining persons and property crossing into this country, are reasonable simply by virtue of the fact that they occur at the border.[152]

According to this rule of law, no probable cause or suspicion of any sort is needed to detain and search individuals attempting to enter the United States.[153]

> These routine border searches may be made at the border when entry is by land from Canada or Mexico, at a place where a shop finally docks after coming from foreign waters, or a place where aircraft land at the end of an international flight, and there is also authority that they may be conducted inland at a functional equivalent of the border or if there has been virtual constant surveillance since the time of the border crossing, thus ensuring that whatever is found in the search can be said to be an object that crossed the border.[154]

There are, nonetheless, more intrusive types of searches that would still require actual suspicion of some sort of criminal activity in order to effect, such as a strip search. The sort of suspicion required for such a search "lies somewhere in the nebulous region between mere suspicion and probable cause."[155] For instance, a greater level of suspicion—clear indication of smuggling—is required to search an individual's body cavities, although no search warrant is needed.[156] Likewise, where border agents reasonably suspect a traveler is smuggling contraband in his or her alimentary canal, and where such a detention is reasonably related in scope to the circumstances, border agents may detain an individual at the border without a warrant until the individual defecates in order to determine whether the individual is attempting to smuggle previously swallowed contraband.[157] Such an intrusive detention and search would obviously require probable cause (at the least) under ordinary circumstances. But at the border—due to the sovereign's right to protect itself—the protections of the Fourth Amendment must give way.[158]

The "Critical Zone" Theory

The rationale underlying border searches has been extended by some courts to airports in accordance with what has been called the "critical zone" theory.[159] According to this theory, a search in a "critical zone," such as an airport gate area or security checkpoint, does not require probable cause or even reasonable suspicion, but instead requires only "mere suspicion of possible illegal activity."[160] The basis for this increased ability to stop and search individuals is one derived from a utilitarian calculus. Courts weigh the competing interests of law enforcement in the context of a certain threat—such as the problem of air piracy—against the rights of individuals. In the context of airports, for instance, courts have "concluded that airport searches designed to protect the heavy volume of interstate and foreign travel by air could be conducted under a less stringent standard than ordinary probable cause because of the unique circumstances of time and place."[161]

The key critical zone theory case is *United States v. Moreno*.[162] In that case, the Fifth Circuit confronted the issue of a search of a suspicious passenger in an airport. The defendant, Moreno, was in an airport, behaving oddly, was unusually nervous, and seemed unusually wary of airport security.[163] It also appeared to law enforcement as if the defendant was covering up something in his clothing.[164] Police officers, therefore, followed him into the bathroom, stopped him, and conducted a search, which revealed that Moreno was carrying quantities of heroine.[165]

At trial, Moreno filed a motion to suppress the evidence obtained from the search, including the incriminating heroin. Moreno argued that, even if there were sufficient circumstances to justify a stop and frisk, the detention and subsequent search went far beyond the constitutionally permissible intrusion contemplated by *Terry v. Ohio*.[166] In rejecting this argument and finding the search lawful, the Fifth Circuit noted the following:

> Although the personal safety of the police officer is a valid governmental interest at stake in deciding the proper scope of a warrantless airport security search, that is not the only governmental interest involved. Of equal importance to airport secu-

> rity searches is the central purpose of thwarting air piracy which often involves the safety of passengers and crew on tremendous aircraft after the plane is airborne with a heavy cargo. At this point in time the security officer is usually safe in the airport. However, the "others" involved, the passengers and the crew, are in the air.[167]

The court noted that airports are special in that they are the

> one channel through which all hijackers must pass before being in a position to commit their crime. It is also the one point where airport security officials can marshal their resources to thwart such acts before the lives of an airplane's passengers and crew are endangered.[168]

But the special nature of the airport was not the only consideration. The nature of the threat of "air piracy" and the unique nature of the crime factored largely in the analysis. In fact, the court noted that the hijacker was "at the core" of the analysis in the *Moreno* decision and that

> [a]lthough the crime of air piracy exceeds all others in terms of the potential for great and immediate harm to others, its undesirable consequences are not limited to that fact. Among other things, it has been used as an avenue of escape for criminals, a means of extorting huge sums of money and as a device for carrying out numerous acts of political violence and terrorism.[169]

In addition, the court noted that hijackers are unusually difficult to detect:

> Apart from the unusual dangers inherent in the crime itself, aerial hijacking has created equally unusual detection problems. Unlike most other crimes, hijacking is one in which secrecy is not a principal concern. Once the hijacker decides to act, he doesn't care if there are numerous witnesses. Indeed, according to the pattern developed thus far, he prefers as many as possible because each one is a potential hostage to shield him from apprehension until he can be flown to a political sanctuary or place of concealment. Obviously, in order to jeopardize the lives and safety of the smallest number of people, the hijacker must be discovered when he is

> least dangerous to others and when he least expects confrontation with the police. In practical terms, this means while he is still on the ground and before he has taken any overt action.[170]

Thus, as early as 1973, a federal court allowed for an exception to the normal rule of *Terry* based on the location of the offense and the nature of the threat posed. Location and threat combined to allow a search and seizure based on a decreased level of suspicion. It is worth noting that practically all of the factors justifying the exception to the Fourth Amendment in critical zones, due to air piracy and so forth, are applicable with equal force to contemporary terrorists.

"Special Needs" Exceptions to the Fourth Amendment

Since the decision in *Moreno*, the idea has ramified in U.S. jurisprudence that there are cases where the government has "special needs" that justify greater intrusion than that which would ordinarily be allowed under the Fourth Amendment. The term *special needs* first appeared in a concurring opinion by Justice Blackmun in *New Jersey v. T. L. O.*[171] In that case, Justice Blackmun noted that there are limited exceptions to the probable-cause requirement, in which reasonableness is determined by "a careful balancing of governmental and private interests," but concluded that such a test should only be applied in exceptional circumstances in which "special needs, beyond the normal need for law enforcement" make the warrant and probable-cause requirement impracticable.[172] The Supreme Court has since recognized a series of circumstances in which the Fourth Amendment becomes pliant, such as suspicionless stops of motorists at a fixed Border Patrol checkpoint designed to intercept illegal aliens[173] and similar stops at a sobriety checkpoint aimed at removing drunk drivers from the road.[174]

In *Chandler v. Miller*,[175] the Supreme Court discussed the analysis that courts must use to determine whether a particular governmental search falls within the "closely guarded category of constitutionally permissible suspicionless [Fourth Amendment intrusions]."[176] The Court explained that when "'special needs'—concerns other than crime detection or ordinary evidence gathering—are alleged in justification of a Fourth Amendment intrusion, courts must undertake a context-specific inquiry, examining closely the competing private and public interests advanced by the parties."[177] In applying the special needs doctrine, courts must weigh "the government conduct—in light of the special need and against the privacy interest advanced" through the examination of three factors: the nature of the privacy interest involved; the character and degree of the governmental intrusion; and the nature and immediacy of the government's needs, and the efficacy of its policy in addressing those needs.[178] If these three factors so warrant, the requirement of any sort of individualized suspicion can be dispensed with.[179]

In recent cases analyzing detention schemes under the special needs doctrine, the Supreme Court has emphasized that, in determining whether individualized suspicion is required for a stop and seizure, a court must consider the nature of the interests threatened and their connection to the particular law enforcement practices at issue. In that regard, the Court has noted that "[w]e are particularly reluctant to recognize exceptions to the general rule of individualized suspicion where governmental authorities primarily pursue their general crime control ends."[180] For that reason, in *City of Indianapolis v. Edmond*, the Court struck down a road block scheme that served the primary purpose of detecting ordinary wrongdoing.[181] Even so, the Court noted examples of cases that would be permissible under the Fourth Amendment:

> Of course, there are circumstances that may justify a law enforcement checkpoint where the primary purpose would otherwise, but for some emergency, relate to ordinary crime control. For example, as the Court of Appeals noted, the Fourth Amendment would almost certainly permit an appropriately tailored roadblock set up to thwart an imminent terrorist attack or to catch a dangerous criminal who is likely to flee by way of a particular route. The exigencies created by these scenarios are far removed from the circumstances under which authorities might simply stop cars as a matter of course to see if there just happens to be a felon leaving the jurisdiction.[182]

Similar lines of dicta, indicating that constitutional protections might yield in situations where the specter of terrorism is implicated, have appeared in recent Supreme Court cases addressing the Fourth Amendment and its limitations. For example, in *Illinois v. Caballes*, the Court considered the question of whether the Fourth Amendment required reasonable, articulable suspicion to justify using a drug-detection dog to sniff a vehicle during a legitimate traffic stop.[183] In that case, the Court avoided use of the special needs doctrine and simply found that the use of a well-trained narcotics-detection dog during a lawful traffic stop generally did not implicate legitimate privacy interests where the dog sniff was performed on the exterior of the suspect's car while he was lawfully seized for a traffic violation. In dissent, both Justices Ginsberg and Souter found that the search violated the rule set forth in *Terry*—but in a separate dissent, Justice Souter noted the following:

> I should take care myself to reserve judgment about a possible case significantly unlike this one. All of us are concerned not to prejudge a claim of authority to detect explosives and dangerous chemical or biological weapons that might be carried by a terrorist who prompts no individualized suspicion. Suffice it to say here that what is a reasonable search depends in part on demonstrated risk. Unreasonable sniff searches for marijuana are not necessarily unreasonable sniff searches for destructive or deadly material if suicide bombs are a societal risk.[184]

Thus, although the Fourth Amendment normally provides a barrier against police seizures, the Supreme Court has allowed exceptions to the requirement of the Fourth Amendment at borders, in other critical zones, or where there are "special needs, beyond the normal need for law enforcement," which make the warrant and probable-cause requirements impracticable.[185] Those cases have generally allowed law enforcement great latitude where some threat to the sovereign is implicated. Further, there is some indication in recent jurisprudence of greater toleration of exceptions to Fourth Amendment protections—a greater malleability in the protections required—in situations related to terrorism.[186]

The ordinary protections against searches and seizures in U.S. law must be understood in light of these exceptions and the particular way in which U.S. law has allowed for constitutional protections to apply differently where national security is threatened.

"Stop and Identify" Statutes

Another interesting caveat in U.S. law is the way that the Supreme Court has interpreted the Fourth Amendment vis-à-vis statutes requiring citizens to give information to law enforcement. As discussed, the holding in *Terry* allows for a suspect to be stopped for reasonable suspicion of criminal activity. State legislatures in the United States have, however, further built upon this ability of law enforcement and passed legislation that also requires suspects to identify themselves. In 2004 the U.S. Supreme Court considered the application of *Terry v. Ohio* to a Nevada statute that required any suspect detained by police to identify himself or herself.[187] The statute in question provided that any peace officer may detain any person whom the officer encounters under circumstances that reasonably indicate the person has committed, is committing, or is about to commit a crime. The officer could detain the person pursuant to this section only to ascertain his or her identity and the suspicious circumstances surrounding his or her "presence abroad." The statute further provided that "[a]ny person so detained shall identify himself, but may not be compelled to answer any other inquiry of any peace officer."[188] Failure of a suspect to identify himself or herself could result in criminal prosecution.[189]

That statute resulted in the arrest and prosecution of Larry D. Hiibel, an individual who refused to identify himself when police asked him to do so during an investigative stop.[190] The local sheriff's department had received a phone call reporting an assault allegedly committed by a person driving a red and silver truck.[191] When police officers arrived in the area, they found Hiibel standing next to just such a vehicle.[192] A police officer approached Hiibel and asked him to produce some form of identification. This request was repeated eleven times. Ultimately, after continued refusals to comply with this request, Hiibel was arrested and charged with "willfully resist[ing], delay[ing] or obstruct[ing] a public officer in discharging or attempting to discharge any legal duty of his office" in violation of Nevada's criminal statute.[193]

In considering the validity of such police action, the Court noted that such "stop and identify statutes" have long existed in Anglo-American criminal law, currently exist in numerous states, and "often combine elements of traditional vagrancy laws with provisions intended to regulate police behavior in the course of investigatory stops."[194] Such statutes permit an officer to ask or require a suspect to disclose his or her identity—and many criminalize the failure or refusal to do so.[195]

> The principles of *Terry* permit a State to require a suspect to disclose his name in the course of a Terry stop. The reasonableness of a seizure under the Fourth Amendment is determined by balancing its intrusion on an individual's Fourth Amendment interests. The Nevada statute satisfies that standard. The request for identity has an immediate relation to the purpose, rationale, and practical demands of a Terry stop. The threat of criminal sanction helps ensure that the request for identity does not become a legal nullity. On the other hand, the Nevada statute does not alter the nature of the stop itself: it does not change its duration, or its location. A state law requiring a suspect to disclose his name in the course of a valid Terry stop is consistent with Fourth Amendment prohibitions against unreasonable searches and seizures.[196]

Thus, so long as the initial stop is based on reasonable suspicion that a suspect is committing or is about to commit a crime, a police officer can require a person to identify himself or herself—and arrest a person for failing to do so.

Although there was no mention of terrorism in the Supreme Court's decision, commentators have noted that terrorism was certainly a prevailing theme of the session in which the *Hiibel* case was decided.[197] Jamie L. Stulin has also noted that the *Hiibel* decision has definite counterterrorism implications as, with the advancement of computer database technology, a person's name can be matched against government databases, such as the National Crime Information Center (NCIC) database or the Multistate Anti-Terrorism Information Exchange (MATRIX).[198]

This can be used to determine whether he or she is currently wanted for other crimes or is involved in terrorism-related activities.[199] Stulin also noted that the *Hiibel* decision seems to broaden the *Terry* doctrine insofar as it allows more than a brief stop during which "officers who suspect criminal activity must investigate the situation in such a way as to confirm or dispel their suspicions as quickly as possible."[200] Officers may now compel identification, check to verify that name and determine if it is associated with any other untoward conduct, and—perhaps—attain probable cause for an arrest that was otherwise lacking.[201]

Hiibel does not, however, allow for an investigative stop for reasons other than those articulated by *Terry*, nor does it expand the permissible search concomitant with a Terry stop.[202] It merely allows compelled identification during the course of an otherwise valid Terry stop. The principal boundaries of the Terry stop—and the exceptions thereto—are still firmly in place. The holding in *Hiibel* merely demonstrates additional ways in which the Fourth Amendment is pliable and how its protections are reconcilable with more aggressive law enforcement initiatives.

Police Detention

Although the Fourth Amendment does not bar questioning following a lawful arrest,[203] criminal law in the United States is generally hostile to the idea of detaining an individual solely for purposes of interrogation. The Supreme Court has never "sustained against Fourth Amendment challenge the involuntary removal of a suspect from his home to a police station and his detention there for investigative purposes…absent probable cause or judicial authorization." [204] This rule was most clearly articulated in *Dunaway v. New York*, wherein the Supreme Court considered the case of a suspect who was detained by police for the sole purpose of interrogation. A murder had occurred during an attempted robbery, and an informant had supplied information to police that implicated the defendant but did not give enough information to justify a warrant. Nonetheless, the police located the defendant and took him into custody.[205] At the police station, the defendant waived his right to remain silent, waived his right to counsel, and then made incriminatory statements.[206] He was never told he was under arrest, and he was never "booked."[207]

The Supreme Court ruled that an arrest made in such a way was unlawful, as it violated the suspect's Fourth Amendment rights, and ruled that the evidence obtained during the period of investigative detention must be suppressed. In its reasoning, the Court noted that the protections of the Fourth Amendment apply to investigatory seizures of this nature and that "detention for custodial interrogation—regardless of its label—intrudes so severely on the interests protected by the Fourth Amendment as necessarily to trigger the traditional safeguards against illegal arrest."[208] Thus, by the clear language of that decision, in order to arrest and interrogate a suspect in the United States, police must have probable cause to believe that the suspect committed an offense. Detention solely for interrogation violates the Fourth Amendment and results in the loss of any evidence obtained as a result of the detention.[209] Such detention, therefore, is seemingly disallowed.

Detaining a Suspect for Investigative Purposes After Lawful Arrest

Assuming, however, that a lawful arrest has been made, the question then turns to how long police may detain a person thereafter for the purpose of investigation. To pose the question another way, after a lawful arrest based on probable cause, how long can police in the United States hold a suspect without bringing a charge or presenting him before a judge—and what are the investigative powers or limits during that period of time? To fully answer this question, it is important to first define two separate requirements of postarrest criminal procedure: the magistrate's review of a warrantless arrest, and the first (or "initial") appearance. Each of these procedural requirements serves a distinct function, and each has its own timeline, but both serve to influence the ability of police to hold and interrogate a suspect prior to the time the suspect is charged.

After a warrantless arrest, a suspect must be brought before a magistrate for a determination of whether police had probable cause to effect an arrest.[210] The Supreme Court has held that the Fourth Amendment generally requires this judicial determination of probable cause to be made within forty-eight hours of a warrantless arrest.[211] It is merely a check on police power to ensure that, where there has been a warrantless arrest, probable cause exists. In cases of warrantless arrests, therefore, a strict timeline automatically comes into play, which entails quick judicial intervention.

Of course, suspects arrested based on a warrant do not need to be presented to a magistrate within forty-eight hours due to the fact that a judicial determination of probable cause has already occurred in such cases.[212] This does not mean, however, that police may hold such a suspect for a prolonged period of time. To the contrary, all detained suspects also have a right to a "prompt appearance" before a magistrate. All suspects—whether or not arrested on a warrant—must be brought before a magistrate for an initial appearance.[213] This rule is reflected in Federal Rule 5(a)(1)(A), which states that an arrested defendant must be brought before a magistrate "without unnecessary delay."[214] Rule 5 does not define "unnecessary delay," and each case is evaluated on its own merits to determine whether the delay was necessary.[215] In any event, this hearing will have a definite impact on the nature of the ongoing investigation.

> The first appearance often is a quite brief proceeding. Initially, the magistrate will make certain that the person before her is the person named in the complaint. The magistrate will then inform the defendant of the charge in the complaint and will note various rights that the defendant may have in further proceedings. The range of rights mentioned will vary from one jurisdiction to another. Commonly, the magistrate will inform the defendant of his right to remain silent and warn him that anything he says in court or to the police may be used against him at trial. In many felony cases, the magistrate also will advise the defendant of the next step in the process, the preliminary hearing, and will set a date for that hearing unless the defendant desires to waive it.[216]

In appearing before a magistrate, a suspect will also be advised that he or she has the right to counsel and, if the suspect cannot afford one, to have counsel appointed.[217] Federal Rule 5(c) establishes the procedures for a suspect's initial appearance, during which the magistrate judge must inform him or her of the charge, of the right to remain silent, of the right to an attorney, that any statement made may be used against him or her, and of the general circumstances under which he or she may secure pretrial release. The magistrate judge must also inform the suspect of his or her right to a preliminary examination, allow the suspect reasonable time to consult with an attorney, and set or deny bail.

The effect of such an appearance and the concomitant rights advisement is multifold. The most obvious impact that the initial appearance has on the detention of a suspect is the chance that the suspect could be released (on bond or on his own recognizance). Even if retained in custody, however, the suspect will be taken out of the environment wherein police may freely interrogate him or her, and because the suspect has been advised of the right to counsel, he or she will most often either be represented by counsel or will have at least requested an attorney. Given the fact that this must happen without unnecessary delay, the potential for investigative detention of the suspect is greatly curtailed.

Statements given during this period preceding the initial appearance—and their potential use at trial—have been the subject of much judicial and legislative attention. Even before adoption of Federal Rule 5, the U.S. Supreme Court held that a defendant had a right to a prompt arraignment and that the result of a violation of this right was the exclusion of statements obtained during the period of illegal detention.[218] The early McNabb-Mallory rule was a jurisprudential rule that stated that any confession is inadmissible if obtained in violation of a defendant's right to be promptly brought before a judicial officer following arrest.[219] The basis behind this strict rule, which inhibited interrogation after arrest, was the notion that arrest was an inappropriate tool for investigation.[220] As the Supreme Court noted in *Mallory v. United States*,

> The police may not arrest upon mere suspicion but only on "probable cause." The next step in the proceeding is to arraign the arrested person before a judicial officer as quickly as possible so that he may be advised of his rights and so that the issue of probable cause may be promptly determined. The arrested person may,

> of course, be "booked" by the police. But he is not to be taken to police headquarters in order to carry out a process of inquiry that lends itself, even if not so designed, to eliciting damaging statements to support the arrest and ultimately his guilt.[221]

According to the language of this rule, there could be no real investigative detention in the United States. Unnecessary delay in arraigning an arrested defendant rendered his or her statements inadmissible, even if the statements were knowing and voluntary.[222] This rule was maintained when the Federal Rules of Criminal Procedure came into effect in 1946 and, in Federal Rule 5(a), formalized the "without unnecessary delay" standard.[223] Both the statutory rule and the then-developing jurisprudential one, thus, reflected the notion that once a suspect is arrested, police are not free to interrogate the suspect at their leisure. To the contrary, the moment the suspect is arrested, investigators are "on the clock."

The rules regarding postarrest interrogation would be altered, however, in 1968 when, in response to criticism of the McNabb-Mallory rule, Congress enacted the Omnibus Crime Control and Safe Streets Act, 18 U.S.C. § 3501. This statute states, in part, that a confession made by a person while under arrest or other detention in the custody of any law enforcement agency is not inadmissible in a federal prosecution solely because of a delay in bringing the person before a federal magistrate if such confession was made or given within six hours after the person's arrest or detention.[224] The statute further provides that delays beyond the six-hour period will not render a confession inadmissible if the court finds that the delay was reasonable. Thus, the stringent limits on postarrest detention and interrogation were somewhat eased.

Under the contemporary statutory scheme, therefore, mere delay alone is not necessarily sufficient to suppress a confession. The analysis turns on whether the confession was voluntary, and, under the relevant statute, delay is just one of five factors considered in determining voluntariness. The five factors considered are (1) the time between arrest and arraignment if the confession occurred between those two events, (2) whether the defendant understood the offense alleged,

(3) whether the defendant knew or was advised that he or she did not have to make any statements and that any statements made could be used against the defendant, (4) whether the defendant was advised of his or her right to counsel, and (5) whether the defendant had assistance of counsel when confessing.[225]

Moreover, 18 U.S.C. § 3501(c) modifies the McNabb-Mallory rule by providing a "safe harbor" zone of six hours during which confessions are still admissible so long as there are no other constitutional defects to the confession and the confession was made within six hours—or longer if such a delay is reasonable. The jurisprudence interpreting the statute has done little to illuminate the boundaries of permissible delay or what exactly is needed in order to invalidate a confession, but commentators note that the general rule in the United States today is that a constitutionally compliant confession made within six to twenty-four hours after the start of federal custody is admissible.[226] Some sources articulate the rule in a manner that seems entirely hostile to the notion of police detention for purposes of interrogation. For instance, *Moore's Federal Practice* (3rd ed.) states,

> When delay in presenting the arrestee is for the purpose of extracting a confession, the delay is considered unreasonable and any statements or confession obtained during the delay will be suppressed. If the federal arrestee is interrogated one day, lodged overnight at a detention center, and brought with due diligence for arraignment before a federal magistrate judge the next morning, or if the delay in arraigning the federal arrestee is caused solely by logistical problems in bringing him or her to the nearest available federal magistrate judge, and during the delay federal law enforcement agents do not try to secure a confession, then there is no Rule 5(a) "unnecessary delay."[227]

Another view has been articulated by the Third Circuit, which seems to indicate that holding a person for the initial six-hour period for the purpose of extracting a confession will, unless tainted by some other constitutional violation, not result in the inadmissibility of the confession or evidence obtained.[228] The Third Circuit articulated its view as follows:

> The bottom line is this: if an arrested person is detained for a substantial period of time, then the longer the delay continues, the more likely it becomes that the arrested person will feel improper pressure to confess. [§ 3501(c)] merely instructs trial courts that the inherently coercive effect of a lengthy delay in presentment is not sufficient, *standing alone*, to render a confession involuntary where the delay is either less than six hours or reasonable considering the means of transportation and the distance to be traveled to the nearest available such magistrate judge or other officer. But where there are reasons other than the length of the delay to find a confession involuntary, the fact that the delay was less than six hours (or longer because of transportation difficulties) will not prevent a court from suppressing the confession.[229]

The Second, Ninth, and D.C. Circuits have, likewise, adopted the view that confessions given within the six-hour period are only inadmissible if they are involuntary, but confessions made beyond the six-hour time period can be rendered inadmissible if either (a) involuntary or (b) voluntary but elicited after a period of "unreasonable delay."[230] The Supreme Court has recognized some dissonance in the interpretations of this rule but has yet to resolve it.[231]

Whatever the case, it is clear that section 3501(c) has carved out a period of permissible delay in detention that courts have been inclined to honor. For legislators seeking to create a form of investigative detention within the framework of ordinary U.S. criminal law, the success of this "safe harbor" zone should be of significant interest.

Rights During Police Detention

As is already evident from the discussion thus far, the U.S. Constitution, as interpreted by the U.S. Supreme Court, normally grants significant rights to suspects in criminal cases—especially those undergoing police interrogation. Aside from the previously described limits on government action, two critical rights granted to suspects under U.S. law are the right to remain silent and the right to an attorney. The U.S. Supreme Court has promulgated a set of safeguards to protect these rights, holding that police officers must inform suspects of their rights prior to custodial interrogation. Should police officers fail to comply with this warning requirement, then any statement made by the suspect while in custody cannot be admitted against him or her at trial over his or her objection—even if the statement is wholly voluntary.[232]

The Right to Remain Silent

During any period of custodial interrogation in the United States, a suspect has the right to remain silent. This is based on the Fifth Amendment of the U.S. Constitution, which states that no person "shall be compelled in any criminal case to be a witness against himself."[233] Further, in order to ensure the free exercise of this right, pursuant to the Supreme Court's holding in *Miranda v. Arizona*, if a person in custody is to be subjected to questioning, he or she must first be informed by the police (in clear and unequivocal language) that he or she has the right to remain silent.[234] The cautionary warning must be accompanied by the explanation that anything said to investigators can and will be used against the suspect in court.[235] As previously noted, the suspect is reminded of this right again at various procedural phases so that he or she is made aware of the fact that it is not necessary to talk to investigators. As a general rule, any statement given without advising a person in custodial interrogation of his or her right to remain silent cannot be used as evidence against the suspect at trial. U.S. law, therefore, emphasizes a suspect's right to remain silent and contains numerous measures to ensure suspects can exercise it. This is of great benefit to suspects and great detriment to investigators seeking information regarding the facts surrounding the suspected crime.[236]

The Right to Counsel

In addition, all criminal suspects in the United States have the right to a lawyer. Derived from the Fifth Amendment, U.S. law grants criminal suspects the right to consult with a lawyer and to have a lawyer present during interrogation.[237] This is because

> [t]he circumstances surrounding in-custody interrogation can operate very quickly to overbear the will of one merely made aware of his privilege by his interrogators. Therefore, the right to have counsel present at the interrogation is indispensable to the protection of the Fifth Amendment privilege under the system we delineate today.[238]

Prior to any interrogation, a suspect in police detention must also be unequivocally informed that he or she has this right and that, if he or she is indigent, a lawyer will be appointed for purposes of representation. Most notably, if at any time during the interrogation a suspect held by police states that he or she wants an attorney, the interrogation must cease until an attorney is present. At that time, the suspect must have the chance to confer with the attorney and to have him present during any subsequent questioning.[239] The United States Supreme Court has articulated the rule in the following manner:

> Once warnings have been given, the subsequent procedure is clear. If the individual indicates in any manner, at any time prior to or during questioning, that he wishes to remain silent, the interrogation must cease. At this point, he has shown that he intends to exercise his Fifth Amendment privilege; any statement taken after the person invokes his privilege cannot be other than the product of compulsion, subtle or otherwise. Without the right to cut off questioning, the setting of in-custody interrogation operates on the individual to overcome free choice in producing a statement after the privilege has been once invoked.[240]

Beyond the Fifth Amendment right to counsel that exists during the custodial interrogation of a suspect, an additional right to counsel derived from the Sixth and Fourteenth Amendments to the U.S. Constitution exists.[241] This right "means at least that a person is entitled to the help of a lawyer at or after the time that judicial proceedings have been initiated against him—'whether by way of formal charge, preliminary hearing, indictment, information, or arraignment.'"[242] The practical effect of this is that there can be no interrogation of a suspect (or defendant) without the presence of counsel after a preliminary hearing or arraignment.[243] This means that, in addition to the rushed timelines that law enforcement agents must struggle to meet, any person in detention who is to be interrogated has the right to have a lawyer present to give advice and protect his or her right to remain silent. Because an interrogation must cease the moment the defendant indicates he or she wants an attorney, the possibility of investigative detention is greatly diminished.

The "Public Safety" Exception

As noted, the Supreme Court's decision in *Miranda v. Arizona* held that incriminatory statements are inadmissible unless a suspect, prior to giving the statement, has been read his or her rights and has freely decided to forego them.[244] These Miranda warnings are not rights in themselves but merely measures designed to insure that the right against self-incrimination is protected.[245] The rule of *Miranda* is not, therefore, absolute. In fact, the Supreme Court has recognized an exception to this general rule in cases of "public safety."[246]

In *New York v. Quarles*, the Supreme Court faced a scenario in which a police officer went to apprehend a rape suspect who was said to be carrying a firearm.[247] The arrest took place in a crowded grocery store.[248] When the officer arrested the suspect, he frisked him and found an empty shoulder holster. The officer, thereafter, handcuffed the suspect and asked him where the gun was.[249] The suspect nodded in the direction of the gun (which was near some empty cartons) and said, "The gun is over there."[250]

At trial, the suspect successfully moved to exclude both the statement and the gun from evidence because the officer had not given the suspect his Miranda rights before asking him where the gun was. The Supreme Court, however, found that this was "a situation where concern for public safety must be paramount to adherence to the literal language of the prophylactic rules enunciated in *Miranda*."[251]

> We hold that on these facts there is a "public safety" exception to the requirement that Miranda warnings be given before a suspect's answers may be admitted into evidence, and that the availability of that exception does not depend upon the motivation of the individual officers involved. In a kaleidoscopic situation such as the one confronting these officers, where spontaneity rather than adherence to a police manual is necessarily the order of the day, the application of the exception we recognize today should not be made to depend on post hoc findings at a suppression hearing concerning the subjective motivation of the police officer.[252]

Thus, in cases where public safety is paramount, the Court has allowed for the limited interrogation of a suspect without advisement of that suspect's rights—and without a lawyer. While this exception is quite limited and case specific, given the enormous impact of *Miranda* on the prospect of investigative detention, it is worthy of attention. Professor M. K. B. Darmer has already argued that the public safety exception to *Miranda* should be applicable in terrorism cases due to the profound nature of the threat involved.[253] As I explore in the conclusion, such an expansion would greatly increase the investigative detention powers available to law enforcement in counterterrorism operations.

The Quasi-Criminal Regime

The previously outlined "strictly criminal" regime demonstrates the legal limits to detention under ordinary circumstances, as well as the rights to which criminal suspects are afforded under U.S. law. In spite of these seemingly steep barriers imposed by jurisprudence and the U.S. Constitution, however, there are some statutes that more freely permit the detention of individuals. These statutory schemes are not "strictly criminal" in that their language does not directly apply to criminal suspects. They remain, however "quasi-criminal" in that they apply to matters closely associated with criminal proceedings and can be employed for criminal purposes. The first of these to be discussed is the material witness statute, which provides for a more flexible detention regime than that normally available under U.S. criminal law. The second is the statutory scheme pertaining to the detention of noncitizens. The third is the regime of law allowing for "civil detention" of certain individuals whose confinement is necessary to prevent societal harm.

Detaining "Material Witnesses"

Perhaps the most potent weapon in the U.S. counterterrorism arsenal is 18 U.S.C. § 3144—the material witness statute. Although attention to the statute has recently increased, commentators note that the ability of federal authorities to arrest and detain a person because that person is a material witness—rather than a suspect—in a criminal case is not a new phenomenon.[254] The Federal Judiciary Act of 1789 granted such power to U.S. courts not long after the nation's founding.[255] Such powers have been reaffirmed through subsequent legislation over the past two centuries.[256] Detaining material witnesses, therefore, is an established practice in U.S. criminal law.

Under the current material witness statute, the government may detain a person in connection with a criminal proceeding if it can demonstrate that the person (a) has information which is material to a criminal matter, and (b) is a risk of flight.[257] The language of the statute reads as follows:

> If it appears from an affidavit filed by a party that testimony of a person is material in a criminal proceeding, and if it is shown that it may become impracticable to secure the presence of the person by subpoena a judicial officer may order the arrest of the person and treat the person in accordance with [the provisions of 18 U.S.C. 3142]. No material witness may be detained because of inability to comply with any condition of release if the testimony of such witness can adequately be secured by deposition, and if further detention is not necessary to prevent a failure of justice. Release of a material witness may be delayed for a reasonable period of time until the deposition of that witness can be taken pursuant to the Federal Rules of Criminal Procedure.[258]

Such an arrest still, however, requires a warrant. A material witness warrant can be obtained through a showing that, based on probable cause, the witness in question has material information relevant to a criminal matter and his or her presence cannot be obtained through a subpoena.[259]

This standard is obviously different from the standard for arresting a criminal suspect in that law enforcement need not establish probable cause that the individual actually committed a crime—only probable cause that the person has information about a crime. Thus, it reorients the inquiry from one that is more concretely focused on individual action (what he or she may have done) to one that is more abstract and epistemological in nature (what he or she might know). Commentators have noted that this makes the government's burden in arresting a material witness lower than that required to arrest an ordinary criminal suspect.[260]

After being arrested, a material witness may be further detained if, following a hearing, a judicial officer concludes that no condition or set of conditions will reasonably assure the witness' presence at trial.[261] In making such a determination, the court must consider the potential of taking of the witness' deposition rather than his or her continued detention.[262] Even after a witness is detained, the witness retains the right to file a motion requesting that the court order a deposition and, subsequently, release.[263] The government is, likewise, obligated to give a report to the court on a biweekly basis detailing the identity of any witness who has been detained longer than ten days and explaining why each witness should not be released "with or without the taking of [a deposition]."[264]

While a material witness, therefore, can be arrested based on a burden that is more easily met by the government, he or she still receives numerous procedural protections. Of note, those protections involve a judicial hearing and biweekly reporting to a judge—requirements that necessarily mean early judicial intervention in the detention process, constant judicial oversight, and repeated determinations of the validity of the detention (which—it must be remembered—is based solely on the likelihood of the witness' presence at trial). In addition, courts have noted that, although there is no Sixth Amendment right to an attorney for persons detained under 18 U.S.C. § 3144, there is a statutory right to counsel.[265] Likewise, as previously discussed, the moment that any suspect in the custody of the police is subjected to "custodial interrogation," that suspect must be advised of his or her rights and may seek counsel and/or refuse to answer questions.[266]

Nonetheless, in the final analysis, as with the burden for making the initial arrest of a material witness, the protections for material witnesses are fewer than those allowed criminal defendants.

> Unlike pretrial detention, where the length of detention is limited by the Speedy Trial Act, there are no definitive time limits on how long a material witness may be held. Unlike a criminal defendant, a witness is not a party to the proceeding and thus has no control over the schedule of the trial. Moreover, there is no similar time limitation for the scheduling of testimony in connection with grand jury proceedings. The scheduling is entirely at the whim of the prosecutor.[267]

The obvious explanation for this relative lack of procedural protection is that (as a strict reading of the statutory language reveals) the intended purpose of the statute is to allow witnesses with information about a pending case to be held long enough to testify—especially those who might disappear before trial.[268] The blurred distinction between a material witness and a criminal suspect has, however, allowed the material witness statute to be used as a limited investigative detention mechanism. Since the attacks of September 11, 2001, federal law enforcement officials have routinely relied upon 18 U.S.C. § 3144 to hold individuals for prolonged periods of time and without charge.[269] The U.S. Department of Justice has admitted to holding approximately forty to fifty people without charge as material witnesses in connection with investigations linked to September 11—roughly half of whom had been held longer than one month.[270] In spite of the rhetoric in criminal jurisprudence, which would seemingly prevent such detention, courts have found the use of the material witness statute for criminal purposes permissible.

The case of *United States v. Awadallah* provides a revealing look at how the material witness statute operates in practice, the expansive scope of the statute in its application, and the statute's limits. In *Awadallah*, the defendant was investigated following the September 11, 2001, terrorist attacks after his name and home telephone number were found in one of the hijacker's vehicles. He was subsequently arrested as a material witness pursuant to 18 U.S.C. § 3144. Roughly twenty days later, he was brought to testify before a grand jury. During his testimony, he denied knowing two of the hijackers and claimed that their names, which were contained in an examination booklet he had written for a class in September, were not written by him. Awadallah later admitted that it was his handwriting and was indicted for perjury.[271]

The district court dismissed the indictment against Awadallah, holding that section 3144 did not apply to grand jury witnesses, and therefore found that Awadallah's perjury was the result of an illegal detention. On appeal, however, the Second Circuit Court of Appeals reversed the district court's decision, noting that section 3144 allowed the arrest and detention of grand jury witnesses because, in that court's view, a grand jury proceeding is a "criminal proceeding" under section 3144. The court also held that the defendant's twenty-day detention was not unreasonably prolonged because he received two bail hearings within days of his arrest and, in both instances, judges found his continued detention to be both reasonable and necessary.[272]

In explaining the rationale for its decision, the Second Circuit noted that "the duty to disclose knowledge of crime rests upon all citizens, and that this duty is so vital that one known to be innocent may be detained, in the absence of bail, as a material witness."[273] Thus, the practice of arresting and detaining witnesses based on probable cause is a permissible one and can even be used to hold potential witnesses for testimony before a grand jury. The Second Circuit also, however, noted that the material witness statute is not a grant of uncontrolled power to the government for the purpose of detaining people indefinitely. To the contrary, the detention of material witnesses is tempered by a great deal of judicial oversight.

> While § 3144 contains no express time limit, the statute and related rules require close institutional attention to the propriety and duration of the detentions: no material witness may be detained because of inability to comply with any condition of release if the testimony of such witness can adequately be secured by deposition, and if further detention is not necessary to prevent a failure of justice. The court must "treat the person in accordance with the provisions of section 3142, which provides a mechanism for

> release. And release may be delayed only for a reasonable period of time until the deposition of the witness can be taken pursuant to the Federal Rules of Criminal Procedure. Perhaps most important, Rule 46 requires the government to make a biweekly report to the court listing each material witness held in custody for more than ten days and justifying the continued detention of each witness. These measures tend to ensure that material witnesses are detained no longer than necessary.[274]

Further, it is noteworthy that the court also found that "it would be improper for the government to use section 3144 for other ends, such as the detention of persons suspected of criminal activity for which probable cause has not yet been established."[275] In this obiter dictum, the Second Circuit recognized the distinction between impermissible investigative detention and the legitimate detention of a material witness. On that score, a Congressional Research Service report has noted the following:

> In spite of the concerns of some that the authority can be used as a means to jail a suspect while authorities seek to discover probable cause sufficient to support a criminal accusation or as a preventive detention measure, the lower courts have denied that the federal material witness statute can be used as a substitute for a criminal arrest warrant. Particularly in the early stages of a criminal investigation, however, an individual's proximity to a crime may make him both a legitimate witness and a legitimate suspect.[276]

This blurred distinction—or even logical overlap—between a suspected criminal and a suspected material witness is what allows the material witness statute to be used as a substitute for ordinary criminal procedures. U.S. jurisprudence interpreting the statute and defining its limits has, thus far, protected its use in such a fashion and has allowed U.S. law enforcement officials the ability to detain a person for a significant period of time based merely on probable cause that the person has material information to a criminal matter and is a flight risk. As further demonstrated later in this chapter, it has been a key element in U.S. counterterrorism efforts in which the ordinary criminal justice system has been utilized.

Immigration Detentions

Another governmental power that allows for a sort of investigative detention is the government's formidable ability to detain noncitizens. "In the exercise of its broad power over naturalization and immigration, Congress regularly makes rules that would be unacceptable if applied to citizens."[277] Under 8 U.S.C. § 1226(a), aliens may be "detained pending a decision on whether the alien is to be removed from the United States." Detention under section 1226(a) is discretionary; the attorney general may release the alien on bond or conditional parole. Section 1226(c) of the same statute makes detention mandatory where the alien is inadmissible or deportable based on the commission of certain offenses. Thus, in contrast to the rights afforded to U.S. citizens, aliens may be detained without probable cause of any crime—but for mere determinations as to their immigration status.

When an alien has been found to be unlawfully present in the United States and a final order of removal has been entered, the government ordinarily secures the alien's removal during a subsequent ninety-day statutory "removal period," during which time the alien normally is held in custody. During this ninety-day period, the attorney general is required to detain all aliens ordered removed until they actually depart.[278] A special provision authorizes further detention if the government fails to remove the alien during those ninety days, stating that

> [a]n alien ordered removed [1] who is inadmissible...[2] [or] removable [as a result of violations of status requirements or entry conditions, violations of criminal law, or reasons of security or foreign policy] or [3] who has been determined by the Attorney General to be a risk to the community or unlikely to comply with the order of removal, may be detained beyond the removal period and, if released, shall be subject to [certain] terms of supervision.

Thus, an alien ordered removed, who has been determined by the attorney general to be a risk to the community or unlikely to comply with the order of removal, may be detained beyond the removal period.[279] Further, if any connections with terrorism are found, the subjects may be prosecuted, removed from the United States, or held for a longer period of time.[280]

Even so, the power over noncitizens is not unlimited. Even aliens are afforded certain rights. For instance, for criminal purposes, courts have held that non-admitted aliens are entitled to Miranda warnings prior to custodial interrogations.[281] If, however, there is no desire to prosecute criminally—but only to deport—then there is no requirement to advise the noncitizen of his or her rights during such periods of detention, as deportation proceedings are civil, and not criminal, in nature. "Consequently, those Fifth and Sixth Amendment rights outlined in a Miranda-type warning are inapposite in the context of removal proceedings."[282]

There are also limits on the length of a noncitizen's detention. In *Zadvydas v. Davis*,[283] the Supreme Court considered the constitutionality of 8 U.S.C. § 1231(a)(6)—which authorizes the attorney general to detain aliens indefinitely after an order for removal if the attorney general determines the alien to be a risk or unlikely to comply with the removal order. The Court held that habeas corpus proceedings remained available to challenge post-removal-period detention and that "once removal is no longer reasonably foreseeable, continued detention is no longer authorized by the statute."[284] The Court, thus, allowed a six-month period during which there would be a presumption that removal was reasonably foreseeable. If, however, after this period, an "alien provides good reason to believe that there is no significant likelihood of removal in the reasonably foreseeable future, the Government must respond with evidence sufficient to rebut that showing."[285] Thus, detention of noncitizens beyond the point when it is "reasonably necessary to bring [about] removal" is unconstitutional.[286]

Although the holding in *Zadvydas* is now the general rule for immigration detention in the United States, it is worth emphasizing that an important aspect of the Court's ruling was the general nature of section 1231(a)(6). "The provision authorizing detention does not apply narrowly to a small segment of particularly dangerous individuals, say suspected terrorists, but broadly to aliens ordered removed for many and various reasons, including visa violations."[287] As discussed more fully in the pages that follow, this brief line of dicta could indicate the permissibility of a far greater investigative detention power vis-à-vis noncitizens than is currently allowed by U.S. statutes.

Such a legal regime—with so few limits—allows the government a great deal of power over noncitizens in its territory. These statutory tools, primarily intended for the regulation of immigration into the U.S., have also been used to approximate investigative detention. After the attacks of September 11, the Federal Bureau of Investigation (FBI) immediately initiated a massive investigation, called PENTTBOM, which sought to identify the terrorists who hijacked the airplanes and their accomplices.[288] The attorney general directed the FBI and other federal law enforcement personnel to use "every available law enforcement tool" to arrest persons who "participate in, or lend support to, terrorist activities." Law enforcement authorities quickly resorted to federal immigration laws to detain aliens suspected of having possible ties to terrorism and, within two months of the attacks, had detained more than 1,200 citizens and aliens nationwide, many of whom were questioned and subsequently released without being charged with an offense.[289]

Government efforts in this regard only intensified with the ongoing U.S. counterterrorism effort. In January of 2002, Deputy Attorney General Larry Thompson announced a new initiative to "locate, apprehend, interview, and deport" approximately 314,000 noncitizens who had failed to comply with their deportation orders. The deputy attorney general also directed federal law enforcement agencies like the FBI and the U.S. Marshals Service to focus their efforts on apprehending those most likely to have terrorist links to interview them regarding their knowledge of terrorism, and then to either prosecute them for failing to depart or reentering illegally after removal, or deport them pursuant to the existing removal order.[290]

At least one district court has concluded that such "immigration sweeps" for investigative purposes are valid. In *Turkmen v. Ashcroft*, the Eastern District of New York rejected a claim based on a violation of the Fourth Amendment resulting from such detention, noting that the plaintiff's entire detention was authorized by the "post-removal period detention statute."[291]

> That the government may have been motivated by a desire to keep terrorism suspects in jail pending further investigation does not alter the legality of the detention. It is well-established that the government's subjective intent alone...does not make otherwise lawful conduct illegal or unconstitutional. Accordingly, even accepting as true plaintiffs' allegations regarding defendants' motives, the detention of plaintiffs was authorized pursuant to the post-removal detention statute and thus did not violate the Fourth Amendment.[292]

The statutory scheme in 8 U.S.C. § 1226, et seq., therefore, provides for a legitimate means of detaining a criminal suspect for investigative purposes. So long as the suspect can be detained under the provisions of the statute, he or she can be subjected to investigative detention. It is worth noting that the logic of the *Turkmen* decision, if applied more broadly, would also validate the pretextual use of the material witness statute for investigative detention purposes.

Lastly, it must be noted that the practice of using immigration detention to effect investigative detention has been subject to some criticism—largely based on the belief that the blurring of immigration and criminal law produces disparate impact on specific races and socioeconomic groups. Professor Teresa Miller argued that the emphasis on apprehending, detaining, and removing non-U.S. citizens who are deportable because of past criminal conduct has blurred traditional distinctions between categories of deportable aliens, and, as a result, "purging the country of unwanted convicts and impoverished, low-wage workers is more achievable and more demonstrably successful than capturing Osama bin Laden, discovering weapons of mass destruction in Iraq, or preventing future terrorist attacks."[293] Thus, though the post–September 11 use of immigration laws demonstrates the potency of such an option, it is subject to criticism based on its disparate effect.

Aside from the controversy that accompanies its use, the tactic has yet another obvious drawback in that it is only effective against noncitizens. Thus, even if one were to accept the use of immigration laws for criminal purposes, it is still only a partial cure. If legislators seek to implement an investigative detention regime that applies to all suspects across the board—Timothy McVeigh and Terry Nichols, as well as members of Al-Qaeda—immigration detention can only form one part of that legal regime.

Detention in Remand

Another category of detention that approximates investigative detention is that category known as detention in remand. After a suspect is arrested and charged with a crime, this additional period of detention after arrest and charge becomes possible. Commentators note that many suspects are released or convicted within twenty-four hours of their arrest.[294] Others, however, are held in detention pending trial. Before passage of the Bail Reform Act of 1984, pretrial detention was only allowed when a judicial officer found that the suspect posed a flight risk.[295] Today, however, a suspect can be detained pending trial if the judge or magistrate finds that the suspect is dangerous.[296]

The general rule in U.S. federal court is that, upon appearance before a judicial officer, a suspect must be either (a) released on personal recognizance or upon execution of an unsecured appearance bond, (b) released with "conditions" imposed upon the suspect with which he or she is required to comply, or (c) detained.[297] Detention is authorized if, after a hearing, the judicial officer finds that "no condition or combination of conditions will reasonably assure the appearance of the person as required and the safety of any other person and the community."[298] In such circumstances, the judicial officer must order the suspect detained until trial.[299]

Federal law provides certain circumstances that create a rebuttable presumption that no condition or combination of conditions will reasonably assure the safety of any other person and the community. The first category of such presumption arises when the suspect is charged with a crime of violence, a capital offense, or a drug felony that carries at least a ten-year penalty, and the suspect was previously convicted of or released from prison for a similar crime in the past five years.[300] The second category is for suspects charged with drug crimes under Title 21 of the *United States Code*, which carry a penalty of ten years or more of confinement.[301] Thus, under U.S. federal law, a suspect may be detained until his or her trial if it is determined that he or she is a flight risk. Further, a suspect may be detained if he or she is determined to be dangerous to the community.

These provisions of the Bail Reform Act were challenged in the Supreme Court in a case entitled *United States v. Salerno, et al.*[302] In that case, the Court was required to determine whether those provisions, which allow courts to detain an arrestee pending trial, violated the substantive and procedural due process provisions of the Fifth Amendment or the Eighth Amendment's guarantee against excessive bail.[303] The defendants in *Salerno* first argued that the act violated substantive due process by punishing them prior to trial through their detention. The Court, however, noted that U.S. jurisprudence has consistently allowed "the Government's regulatory interest in community safety" to outweigh an individual's liberty interest.[304] Even outside the context of a war, the government may detain dangerous persons, such as the detention of potentially dangerous resident aliens, during detention proceedings.[305]

> On the other side of the scale, of course, is the individual's strong interest in liberty. We do not minimize the importance and fundamental nature of this right. But, as our cases hold, this right may, in circumstances where the government's interest is sufficiently weighty, be subordinated to the greater needs of society.[306]

The Court found that the detention in the Bail Reform Act was regulatory rather than punitive in nature.[307] In articulating its test for the constitutional permissibility of such detention, the Court noted that, in order to determine whether a restriction on liberty constitutes impermissible punishment or permissible regulation, it looks first to legislative intent.[308] Unless the Court finds that Congress expressly intended to impose punitive restrictions, the punitive/regulatory distinction turns on whether the restriction has a nonpunitive purpose and whether it appears excessive in relation to that purpose.[309] The Court also found that the federal government has a legitimate and compelling interest in preventing crime by such arrestees—an interest so strong it outweighs their fundamental interest in liberty.[310] The costs of the nonpunitive restriction, therefore, were not considered excessive.

> When the Government proves by clear and convincing evidence that an arrestee presents an identified and articulable threat to an individual or the community, we believe that, consistent with the Due Process Clause, a court may disable the arrestee from executing the threat. Under these circumstances, we cannot categorically state that pretrial detention "offends some principle of justice so rooted in the traditions and conscience of our people as to be ranked as fundamental."[311]

Thus, where the government can come forward with the right evidence, criminal defendants may be detained prior to trial under the regulatory scheme of the Bail Reform Act. In such circumstances, the Constitution does not prohibit the detention of criminal defendants awaiting trial so long as the statutory scheme is nonpunitive in nature, the defendant presents a demonstrable danger to society, and his or her liberty interests are outweighed by the greater needs of society.[312]

The Right to a Speedy Trial

The mere fact that a criminal defendant can be detained pending trial, however, does not mean that they may be so detained indefinitely. The Sixth Amendment of the U.S. Constitution guarantees that "in all criminal prosecutions, the accused shall enjoy the right to a speedy…trial."[313] The government cannot, therefore, unduly delay the prosecution of a suspect. The Supreme Court has held that the question of whether this provision has been violated depends on four separate enquiries: (1) whether delay before trial was uncommonly long; (2) whether the government or the criminal defendant is more to blame for that delay; (3) whether, in due course, the defendant asserted his right to a speedy trial; and (4) whether he suffered prejudice as the delay's result.[314]

> We have observed in prior cases that unreasonable delay between formal accusation and trial threatens to produce more than one sort of harm, including "oppressive pretrial incarceration," "anxiety and concern of the accused," and "the possibility that the accused's defense will be impaired" by dimming memories and loss of exculpatory evidence. Of these forms of prejudice, the most serious is the last, because the inability of a defendant adequately to prepare his case skews the fairness of the entire system.[315]

In 1974, in order to better quantify and make effective the Sixth Amendment right to a speedy trial, Congress enacted the "the Speedy Trial Act." The act provides that

> [a]ny information or indictment charging an individual with the commission of an offense shall be filed within thirty days from the date on which such individual was arrested or served with a summons in connection with such charges. If an individual has been charged with a felony in a district in which no grand jury has been in session during such thirty-day period, the period of time for filing of the indictment shall be extended an additional thirty days.[316]

An arrest, therefore, triggers the running of the "speedy trial clock" and requires that the person be charged within thirty days.

The act also requires that an accused be quickly brought to trial, mandating that

> [i]n any case in which a plea of not guilty is entered, the trial of a defendant charged in an information or indictment with the commission of an offense shall commence within seventy days from the filing date (and making public) of the information or indictment, or from the date the defendant has appeared before a judicial officer of the court in which such charge is pending, whichever date last occurs.[317]

Further, "[u]nless the defendant consents in writing to the contrary, the trial shall not commence less than thirty days from the date on which the defendant first appears through counsel or expressly waives counsel and elects to proceed pro se."[318] This entitles a criminal defendant to dismissal of the charges pending against him if he is not brought to trial within seventy days of his initial appearance or indictment.

In computing the running of this seventy-day period, the act permits certain periods of time to be excluded, such as any period of delay resulting from a continuance granted by the judge on his own motion or at the request of the defendant,[319] delay resulting from any interlocutory appeal,[320] or delay resulting from any pretrial motion.[321] As a result, the seventy-day period can be prolonged, but only for specific reasons and always with the threat of a dismissal looming on the horizon. Accordingly, there is a definite limit on the amount of time one may be detained pending trial in the U.S.

Serrin Turner and Stephen J. Schulhofer, in their work on the problems posed by secrecy in terrorism trials, have addressed the complications that arise in terrorism cases due to the Speedy Trial Act, but they have posited that the numerous bases for postponement provided in the Speedy Trial Act, as well as the provisions of the Bail Reform Act (previously discussed), may serve to palliate some of those concerns.[322]

> Incarceration before trial, without any chance to make bail, is obviously troublesome and was once widely viewed as antithetical to Anglo-American tradition. Yet in the Bail Reform Act of 1984, Congress expressly authorized pre-trial detention on grounds of dangerousness, and on review the Supreme Court upheld the statute's constitutionality. Since then, detention until trial has become commonplace not only in terrorism and violent crime cases but in nearly half of all federal prosecutions for drug and immigration offenses. Thus, by combining two tools now routinely available—postponement of trial under the Speedy Trial Act and detention until trial under the Bail Reform Act—prosecutors already have considerable power to incapacitate a dangerous terrorist suspect while they seek evidence they can safely disclose in court.[323]

Thus, Turner and Schulhofer argued that the existing legal machinery for pretrial detention in U.S. law provides a sort of foundation upon which a fortified pretrial detention mechanism could be built.[324] Such a mechanism would be of obvious value in the criminal prosecution of terrorists.

Civil Detention

Regulatory detention is not, however, limited to criminal defendants. In addition to the types of detention previously detailed, there exists another permissible form of detention, which can be described as noncriminal or "civil" detention—detention that is effected not because a person has been convicted of a crime, nor even because a person is facing a criminal proceeding, but because that person's detention is for the greater good. This sort of civil detention is derived from the state's power as *parens patriae* (father of the country) and its police powers.[325] Such detention can be effected in circumstances closely linked to the criminal process—such as detention in remand—and also for less related circumstances, such as the civil commitment of the mentally ill and the noncriminal detention of sex offenders.[326]

In *Kansas v. Hendricks*, the Supreme Court considered the constitutionality of a statute that allowed the state of Kansas to detain "any person who [had] been convicted of or charged with a sexually violent offense and who suffers from a mental abnormality or personality disorder which makes the person likely to engage in the predatory acts of sexual violence."[327] The act allowed for a procedure whereby the "custodial agency" would notify the local prosecutor of any such person's pending release. Thereafter, the prosecutor could petition in state court for that person's involuntary commitment. The prosecutor was obligated to show probable cause that the person was a "sexually violent predator" and, therefore, eligible for civil commitment under the statute.[328] This would be followed by a trial wherein the prosecutor would need to prove beyond a reasonable doubt that the person was a "sexually violent predator."[329] If the burden were met, the person would be transferred to the custody of the Department of Social and Rehabilitation Services for "control, care, and treatment until such time as the person's mental abnormality or personality disorder has so changed that the person is safe to be at large."[330]

The defendant in *Hendricks* was diagnosed with pedophilia and admitted that when "stressed out" he could not control his urge to molest children. This qualified as a "mental abnormality" under the statute.[331] He challenged the statute under various theories, including a challenge under the Fourteenth Amendment's substantive due process provisions.

In ruling that this statutory scheme was constitutional, the Supreme Court reaffirmed the principle that "the liberty secured by the Constitution of the United States to every person within its jurisdiction does not import an absolute right in each person to be, at all times and in all circumstances, wholly free from restraint."[332] Rather, the Court noted that "states have, in certain narrow circumstances, provided for the forcible civil detainment of people who are unable to control their behavior and who thereby pose a danger to public health and safety."[333] Thus, the Court stated, "[i]t...cannot be said that the involuntary civil commitment of a limited subclass of dangerous persons is contrary to our understanding of ordered liberty."[334]

The Court noted, however, that mere dangerousness was not enough to sustain such civil detention:

> A finding of dangerousness, standing alone, is ordinarily not a sufficient ground upon which to justify indefinite involuntary commitment. We have sustained civil commitment statutes when they have coupled proof of dangerousness with the proof of some additional factor, such as "mental illness" or "mental abnormality." These added statutory requirements serve to limit involuntary civil commitment to those who suffer from a volitional impairment rendering them dangerous beyond their control.[335]

The defendant in *Hendricks* argued that the government should be required to find a "mental illness" rather than a "mental abnormality" as allowed by the Kansas statute. The defendant noted that the two terms were not equivalent and that *mental abnormality* was a term coined by the Kansas legislature rather than by the psychiatric community.[336] The Court disagreed and noted that "we have never required State legislatures to adopt any particular nomenclature in drafting civil commitment statutes. Rather, we have traditionally left to legislatures the task of defining terms of a medical nature that have legal significance."[337]

The defendant in *Hendricks* also argued that the statute violated the constitutional ban on ex post facto lawmaking. The Supreme Court, however, held that the statute was not criminal in nature and, therefore, not violative of that particular ban. Key to the Court's findings in that regard were the indicia of the statute's civil nature, such as the fact that it was contained in the state's probate code rather than its criminal code, the fact that it was termed *civil commitment* in the language of the statute, and the fact that it did not require criminal liability.[338] Moreover, the court found that the statute did not implicate either of the two main purposes of criminal punishment in that it sought neither retribution nor deterrence.

Accordingly, it is within the power of states to indefinitely confine a person who is found to be dangerous—within the context of a civil (or noncriminal) detention scheme—so long as that finding of dangerousness is coupled with an additional factor, such as a finding that the person has a mental illness or mental abnormality. This is permissible completely outside the context of a criminal proceeding and can constitute a means of potentially indefinite detention based on dangerousness. Scholars, such as Professor Tung Yin and Stephanie Cooper Blum, have articulated in great detail the manner in which such governmental power could serve as a preventive detention mechanism for suspected terrorists. As detailed in chapter 6, such powers could also serve as an important investigative detention function.

TERRORISM UNDER U.S. LAW

Now that the legal regime for detention under U.S. law has been analyzed, we turn to the body of U.S. law that targets the activity referred to as "terrorism." At the outset, it is fair to ask what is meant by *terrorism*, a term subject to a variety of meanings and the subject of frequent debate.[339] Some commentators have questioned the usefulness of defining it at all.[340] Critics point out that the vocabulary used to describe political violence is underdeveloped and, thus, makes such classifications difficult and problematic.[341] Yet, there can be no doubt that there exist a number of groups in the world who seek to achieve political goals by violent means[342] and that there is at least a subset of such crime that is considered—at least by some—to be terrorism. Chaliand and Blin noted that

> [d]espite the ambiguities and disagreements…the concept of terrorism in modern usage is most commonly associated with certain kinds of violent actions carried out by individuals and groups rather than by states, and with events that take place in peacetime rather than as part of a conventional war.[343]

Although there is a core of statutes that criminalize and prohibit terrorist acts, there is no truly uniform definition of *terrorism* in U.S. law. The definitional statutes of the United States Code define an "act of terrorism" as an act of domestic or international terrorism as defined in section 2331.[344] It is to that statute, therefore, that we first look.

Under the provisions of 18 U.S.C. 2331(1), "international terrorism" was (and remains) defined as activities that: (a) involve violent acts or acts dangerous to human life that are a violation of the criminal laws of the United States or of any state, or that would be a criminal violation if committed within the jurisdiction of the United States and appear to be intended to intimidate or coerce a civilian population; (b) are designed to influence the policy of a government by intimidation or coercion or to affect the conduct of a government by mass destruction, assassination, or kidnapping; and (c) occur primarily outside the territorial jurisdiction of the United States or transcend national boundaries in terms of the means by which they are accomplished, the persons they appear intended to intimidate or coerce, or the locale in which their perpetrators operate or seek asylum.

Prior to 2001, the federal law of the United States did not have any definition of *domestic terrorism*. This changed with the USA PATRIOT Act, which, for the first time, gave a definition of domestic terrorism in U.S. criminal law. Drawing from the definition of *international terrorism*,[345] the act amended 18 U.S.C. § 2331 to create a definition of domestic terrorism that includes activities that involve violent acts or acts dangerous to human life that are a violation of the criminal laws of the United States or of any state, or that would be a criminal violation and appear to be intended (a) to intimidate or coerce a civilian population; (b) to influence the policy of a government by intimidation or coercion; or (c) to affect the conduct of a government by mass destruction, assassination or kidnapping; and occur primarily within the territorial jurisdiction of the United States.[346]

It is important to note that this provision is only definitional in nature and does not create a new federal crime. Such definitions merely exist to be incorporated into other statutory provisions that reference this specific activity.[347] For instance, 18 U.S.C. § 2333(a) grants any U.S. national injured by reason of an act of international (though not domestic) terrorism the right to sue for his or her injury.[348]

The federal crime of terrorism, on the other hand, is found in 18 U.S.C. § 2332b, which criminalizes a far more narrow range of conduct than the broader definitions in section 2331. The prohibited acts under that statute are as follows:

(a) Prohibited Acts.

(1) Offenses. Whoever, involving conduct transcending national boundaries and in a circumstance described in subsection (b)—

(A) Kills, kidnaps, maims, commits an assault resulting in serious bodily injury, or assaults with a dangerous weapon any person within the United States; or

(B) Creates a substantial risk of serious bodily injury to any other person by destroying or damaging any structure, conveyance, or other real or personal property within the United States; in violation of the laws of any state, or the United States, shall be punished as prescribed in subsection (c).

(2) Treatment of threats, attempts, and conspiracies. Whoever threatens to commit an offense under paragraph (1), or attempts or conspires to do so, shall be punished under subsection (c).

Thus, the U.S. federal crime of terrorism still requires some international nexus, in spite of the existence of a definition of *domestic terrorism* that exists elsewhere in the federal penal code. This means that, in order to consider a person a suspect for purposes of the federal crime of terrorism, some conduct transcending national boundaries must be involved.

For purposes of sentencing, the federal sentencing guidelines look to 18 U.S.C. § 2332b(g), which defines a "federal crime of terrorism" as an offense that (a) is calculated to influence or affect the conduct of government by intimidation or coercion, or to retaliate against government conduct, and (b) is a violation of any one of a long list of statutes relating to a broad range of conduct, such as destruction of aircraft or aircraft facilities, murder, destruction of communication lines, violence against maritime fixed platforms, the use of weapons of mass destruction, harboring terrorists, and receiving military-type training from a foreign terrorist organization.[349] For offenses that are felonies that involve or were intended to promote a federal crime of terrorism, the recommended sentence for the offender is dramatically enhanced.[350]

Thus, federal criminal law in the United States defines *terrorism* in multiple ways. The criminal act of terrorism requires an international nexus, while a crime that is nominally more banal can be considered an act of terrorism for sentencing purposes so long as it meets the less demanding criteria of 18 U.S.C. § 2332b(g). In this way, domestic crimes that are not technically "terrorism" under 18 U.S.C. § 2332b can be, nonetheless, punished as acts of terrorism.

A more flexible tool in the hands of prosecutors, however, is the regime of law criminalizing the provision of "material support" to terrorists and terrorist organizations. 18 U.S.C. § 2339A criminalizes the provision (or attempted provision) of material support or resources to terrorists.[351] This includes "any property, tangible or intangible, or service, including currency or monetary instruments or financial securities, financial services, lodging, training, expert advice or assistance, safehouses, false documentation or substances, explosives, personnel, and transportation, except medicine or religious materials."[352] 18 U.S.C.

§ 2339B, likewise, criminalizes the provision (or attempted provision) of material support or resources to a foreign terrorist organization.[353] 18 U.S.C. § 2339C, in turn, criminalizes the provision of direct and indirect financial support of terrorist operations.[354]

A notable absence in the current U.S. counterterrorism arsenal, however, is any law criminalizing membership in a terrorist organization.[355] Such criminalization of membership in an organization is possible so long as there is knowing membership in the organization with the specific intent to further the group's unlawful goals.[356] In other words, a conviction cannot rest on guilt by association but must be further accompanied by "the relationship of that status or conduct to other concededly criminal activity."[357] Even so, this sort of crime is currently absent, leaving a gap in the criminal law, which could be filled through appropriate legislation.

THE USE OF U.S. CRIMINAL LAW IN "TERRORIST DETENTIONS"

The analysis so far demonstrates that while the ordinary criminal law of the U.S. does not expressly allow investigative detention, certain statutes and practices exist that effect similar results. The rhetoric disallowing it, the statutes that seem to permit it, and the grey areas where it seems possible can combine into a confusing cacophony. Accordingly, it is important to see how U.S. law has been successfully employed in order to detain terrorist suspects in some rather high-profile terrorism cases. Through observing successful practices, one may discern what is considered permissible.

The Terry Nichols Case

As previously discussed, several years before the attacks of September 11, on April 19, 1995, an explosion destroyed the Alfred P. Murrah Federal Building in Oklahoma City, Oklahoma.[358] The attack killed 168 people and injured hundreds more.[359] Shortly thereafter, an Oklahoma state trooper stopped a vehicle for not displaying a license plate as required by Oklahoma state law. Its driver, Timothy McVeigh, was found to be in possession of a knife and a loaded handgun, and he was, accordingly, arrested for a misdemeanor offense.[360] McVeigh gave officers his address and also gave the name of James Nichols of Decker, Michigan, as a reference.[361] That same day, amidst the rubble of the destroyed federal building, investigators found the axle of a vehicle linked to Timothy McVeigh.[362]

Terry Nichols was quickly implicated in the crime and, upon hearing his name broadcast on television in connection with the investigation into the bombing, turned himself in at a local police station.[363] He was, thereafter, advised of his Miranda rights and interrogated by FBI agents.[364] While Nichols was still at the police station, a warrant for his arrest as a material witness was obtained pursuant to 18 U.S.C. § 3144. The affidavit stated, "Terry Nichols' renunciation of his U.S. citizenship and his association with Tim McVeigh, a person involved in such a heinous crime, indicates that his testimony cannot be secured through the issuance of a subpoena."[365]

He was arrested later that night.[366] After his arrest, Nichols gave the police information regarding his house and the location of ammunition within his home, and he gave them the names of aliases he had previously used.[367] At trial, however, Nichols challenged his arrest, arguing that there was no probable cause for his arrest as a material witness and that any statements from him following the execution of the arrest warrant should be suppressed.[368] The court found, however, that the affidavit constituted an adequate legal basis "to believe that it is or may be impracticable to rely on a subpoena to get the witness before the grand jury."[369] Accordingly, the use of the material witness statute to secure Terry Nichols' arrest was upheld.

It is worth emphasizing the timeline of the arrest in this case and the use of the material witness statute. Nichols was arrested at midnight and was then brought before a magistrate the next day.[370] He was in the process of divulging more information during his "routine processing" with a deputy marshal when his court-appointed counsel arrived and interrupted the interrogation.[371] This demonstrates the practical effects of an initial appearance, the timelines of the material witness statute, and the limits of the material witness statute.

United States v. Padilla

Shortly after September 11, 2001, a domestic court in the United States would be faced with a more complex challenge—specifically, the challenge that brought Vice Admiral Jacoby to pen his declaration, laying out the reasons for detaining a U.S. citizen and depriving him of the rights previously outlined.

José Padilla is a U.S. citizen of Puerto Rican origin who, at the age of thirty-one, had a criminal history associated with gang activity.[372] He was raised Roman Catholic, but he converted to Islam while in jail and, thereafter, left the United States for the Middle East where he made contacts with individuals associated with international terrorism.[373] Specifically, it was suspected that Al-Qaeda operatives recruited Padilla to train for jihad in Afghanistan and that Padilla subsequently met with Al-Qaeda operatives and received explosives training.[374] It was also suspected that Padilla served as an armed guard at a Taliban outpost.[375]

Padilla was arrested on May 8, 2002, at an airport in Chicago on a material witness warrant. The warrant was in connection with grand jury proceedings investigating the attacks of September 11.[376] He was then transported to New York, where he was detained for roughly a month. A week later, on May 15, 2002, counsel was appointed to represent Padilla. Thus, the status of the suspected terrorist was that of a detained "material witness" with appointed counsel.[377] On June 9, 2002, roughly a month after his apprehension, however, President George W. Bush declared Padilla an enemy combatant and transferred him to military custody at a naval brig in Charleston, South Carolina.[378] From that point onward, Padilla was not allowed to have contact with his appointed counsel or any other nonmilitary personnel.[379]

Padilla initially filed a petition for a writ of habeas corpus in the Southern District of New York. The district court judge in that initial matter, the then judge Michael B. Mukasey, concluded that Padilla's indefinite detention was a proper exercise of the president's power as commander in chief.[380] On appeal, however, the Second Circuit Court of Appeals decided that the president lacked inherent constitutional authority to detain American citizens on American soil outside a zone of combat[381] and ordered a remand of the case with instructions for the district court to issue a writ of habeas corpus directing the secretary of defense to release Padilla from military custody within thirty days.[382]

The government appealed the Second Circuit's decision to the Supreme Court, which reversed and remanded the Second Circuit's decision because Padilla's habeas petition was filed in the wrong court—it had to be filed in the district in which his immediate custodian was located. Accordingly, the decision was reversed on jurisdictional grounds.[383] Padilla, thereafter, filed a petition for a writ of habeas corpus in the District of South Carolina, claiming that his military detention violated the U.S. Constitution.[384] Finding that the president lacked authority to detain Padilla militarily, the district court in South Carolina granted the petition and held that Padilla had to be either charged with a crime or released.[385] On September 9, 2005, however, the Fourth Circuit reversed the district court, holding that the president had the congressionally sanctioned authority to detain Padilla as an enemy combatant.[386] In so holding, the Fourth Circuit found that Padilla was an enemy combatant and noted that the Authorization for Use of Military Force Joint Resolution of 2001 (AUMF) authorized Padilla's detention.[387]

> The Congress of the United States, in the Authorization for Use of Military Force Joint Resolution, provided the President all powers necessary and appropriate to protect American citizens from terrorist acts by those who attacked the United States on September 11, 2001. As would be expected, and as the Supreme Court has held, those powers include the power to detain identified and committed enemies such as Padilla, who associated with al Qaeda and the Taliban regime, who took up arms against this Nation in its war against these enemies, and who entered the United States for the avowed purpose of further prosecuting that war by attacking American citizens and targets on our own soil—a power without which, Congress understood, the President could well be unable to protect American citizens from the very kind of savage attack that occurred four years ago almost to the day.[388]

Padilla, once again, appealed this decision to the Supreme Court, but—just two business days before the government's brief in response to his petition for certiorari was due—Padilla was indicted in the Southern District of Florida on criminal charges of a less serious nature.[389] The government then moved to transfer Padilla from military custody back to civilian custody and asked the court to vacate its earlier order.

The Fourth Circuit Court of Appeals initially denied the government's motion and refused to vacate its earlier decision, noting that the government's actions had severely undermined its credibility before the court and left the impression that "Padilla may have been held for these years, even if justifiably, by mistake—an impression we would have thought the government could ill afford to leave extant."[390] Padilla, nonetheless, was eventually released from military custody and transferred to civilian custody to face charges in the Southern District of Florida—all of which related to efforts to further jihad overseas.[391]

At his criminal trial, Padilla filed a motion to dismiss for outrageous conduct in which he argued that his treatment during military custody was so violative of the Constitution that it should result in dismissal of the charges.[392] The district court, however, found that Padilla's treatment was not so outrageous as to entitle him to dismissal of the indictment and that a suitable remedy for any constitutional violations was suppression of evidence obtained by the conduct of which Padilla complained.[393]

The district court did not rule on whether the Constitution was violated during military detention as the government neatly sidestepped the issue at trial by not seeking to introduce statements elicited during Padilla's detention and interrogation in military custody.[394] The district court noted, however, that it was not deciding that Padilla's rights during his military detention were not violated, stating,

> This Court's holding does not imply that this is Mr. Padilla's only remedy with regard to any alleged mistreatment at the Naval Brig, only that it is the most appropriate remedy within the framework of this prosecution. Mr. Padilla is free to institute a Bivens action, an action for monetary damages or any other form of redress that he is legally entitled to pursue.[395]

Padilla's apprehension under the material witness statute, however, was neither a basis for legal attack nor a ground for the exclusion of evidence.

On August 16, 2007, Padilla was convicted on charges of conspiracy to murder, kidnap, and maim people overseas.[396] On January 22, 2008, he was sentenced to seventeen years and four months in prison—a sentence more lenient than the federal sentencing guidelines recommended and less than that requested by the government, which had requested the maximum penalty of life imprisonment.[397] In deciding the sentence, the judge in the case gave Padilla credit for time served during his three-and-a-half-year detention in military confinement.[398]

United States v. Al-Marri

Another example of the use of U.S. law to detain a terrorist suspect in the post–September 11 world is that of Ali Saleh Kahlah al-Marri. Al-Marri is a legal resident of the United States and a citizen of Qatar who entered the United States, along with his wife and children, on September 10, 2001.[399] Three months later, on December 12, 2001, he was arrested at his home by FBI agents and held as a material witness in the government's investigation into the attacks of September 11.[400] In February of 2002, in the Southern District of New York, Al-Marri was charged with the possession of unauthorized or counterfeit credit card numbers with the intent to defraud. A year later, he was charged with crimes related to making false statements and identity theft.[401] The material witness statute, therefore, served to hold Al-Marri for roughly two months before charges were brought.

The charges against Al-Marri were initially dismissed, however, for lack of venue.[402] New charges were, therefore, brought again against Al-Marri in the Central District of Illinois. Al-Marri pled not guilty, and a trial was set for July 21, 2003. On June 23, 2003, however, the government brought a motion to dismiss the indictment and transfer Al-Marri to military custody based on an order signed that morning by the president of the United States declaring Al-Marri to be an enemy combatant who was closely associated with Al-Qaeda.[403] Notably, there were no allegations that Al-Marri was affiliated with an enemy nation, fought alongside any nation's armed forces, or bore arms against the United States anywhere in the world.[404] Nonetheless, the government's motion was granted and, thereafter, Al-Marri was—like José Padilla—transferred to military custody in South Carolina.[405]

After his transfer to military custody, Al-Marri filed a writ of habeas corpus in the Fourth Circuit Court of Appeals, which initially reversed the judgment of the district court and ordered that his military detention cease.[406] The Fourth Circuit then vacated that decision and reconsidered the matter en banc. In contesting his military detention before the Fourth Circuit, Al-Marri argued that such detention was disallowed by the Fifth Amendment's guarantee that no person can be deprived of liberty without due process of law.[407] The en banc court found that Al-Marri could be detained but that his due process had not been adequately protected in the lower proceedings. Otherwise stated, the Fourth Circuit allowed that the government can maintain terrorist suspect in military custody if the facts, as alleged by the government, were true, but that there must be sufficient due process to determine the veracity of those allegations. Accordingly, Al-Marri was allowed to remain in military custody, although the court reversed and remanded his case for further proceedings.

The case was appealed to the U.S. Supreme Court—but the question of what process is due or even whether such military detention is legal would, however, not be answered with any degree of finality. President Obama, soon after being elected, ordered that Al-Marri be transferred from military to federal civilian custody so that he could face criminal charges related to terrorism.[408] The government then asked the Supreme Court to dismiss Al-Marri's pending appeal as moot. In spite of numerous entreaties in the media to hear the case and render a decision on the legality of such military detention,[409] on March 6, 2009, the Supreme Court dismissed the appeal and vacated the lower court decision, which had previously found that Al-Marri could be detained.[410] In so doing, the Supreme Court erased the legal authority for such detention without deciding its correctness.[411] The question of whether military detention of legal residents is legal under the U.S. Constitution is, therefore, still undecided.

Zacarias Moussaoui

Zacarias Moussaoui is a French citizen who was arrested in the United States on August 16, 2001—prior to the 9/11 attacks—on immigration violations after becoming a suspect in a terrorism investigation.[412] Although FBI and INS agents investigating Moussaoui suspected that he was planning to hijack a plane, he was not arrested for this activity nor for the terrorism-related offenses with which he was later charged.[413] He was, instead, initially arrested for overstaying his visa—and as he was in federal custody on September 11, he was not a direct part of those terrorism-related offenses.[414] Nonetheless, it was suspected that Moussaoui was involved in the 9/11 plot and was even referred to as the "twentieth hijacker."[415] After the attacks, a material witness warrant was issued, and Moussaoui was held as a material witness until he was later indicted.[416]

Moussaoui was charged with six offenses: (1) conspiracy to commit acts of terrorism transcending national boundaries (18 U.S.C. § 2332b(a)(2)); (2) conspiracy to commit aircraft piracy (9 U.S.C. § 46 502(a)(1)(A)(a)(2)(B)); (3) conspiracy to destroy aircraft (18 U.S.C. §§ 32(a)(7)); (4) conspiracy to use weapons of mass destruction (18 U.S.C.A. § 2332a(a)); (5) conspiracy to murder U.S. employees (18 U.S.C. §§ 1114, 1117); and (6) conspiracy to destroy property (18 U.S.C. § 844(f), (i), (n)).[417] The government sought the death penalty on the first four of these charges.[418] After a great deal of erratic legal maneuvering—including the firing of his attorney—Moussaoui suddenly pled guilty to all the charges against him and was, subsequently, sentenced to life imprisonment.[419]

Summary

The treatment of each of the terrorist suspects is different in certain regards. All four cases, however, share at least two common elements: a terrorist suspect, and the use of some alternative to ordinary criminal procedure to effect the arrest and detention of the suspect. In the case of Jose Padilla, the suspect was arrested under the material witness statute and held for almost a month. In the case of Al-Marri, the suspect was arrested under that same statute and held for roughly two months.

In the case of Terry Nichols, the material witness statute was used but for a much shorter time. Zacarias Moussaoui was arrested on immigration charges, held as a material witness, and then indicted.

Though there are drastic differences in how each case was handled (Nichols and Moussaoui were brought directly to federal court, while Padilla and al-Marri were subsequently transferred to military custody and their cases moved outside the ordinary criminal process), one may discern in the ubiquity of the material witness statute the fact that those seeking to bring each of these individuals to justice felt that the ordinary warrant based on probable cause of a crime was either unobtainable or problematic in some regard—thereby necessitating the need to resort to the material witness statute's more permissive provisions. Each case demonstrates both the need for a legal mechanism that can be used to easily arrest and detain terrorist suspects and the fact that such a mechanism was not readily available within the ordinary architecture of U.S. criminal law. Each case further demonstrates the acceptance of those alternatives by the courts that heard their cases. Alternative methods of detention, such as immigration detention and the material witness statute, are, therefore, a principal part of the U.S. counterterrorism arsenal—and an accepted practice.

Conclusion

The analysis of the U.S. law in this chapter demonstrates a Janus-faced relationship with investigative detention. From one point of view, it is a discouraged practice that seems anathema to the U.S. criminal justice model. This is voiced in the language of the Supreme Court in cases such as *Dunaway v. New York* and—to some degree—echoed in the cases regarding "enemy combatants."[420] Nonetheless, through legislative modifications that allow statements to be admissible in spite of minor delays after arrest, the practice of investigative detention is at least vaguely recognized as a necessary part of ordinary law enforcement. Such recognition is even more explicit in the Second Circuit, which has allowed for the continued detention of individuals for investigative purposes so long as they could be otherwise detained in accordance with the relevant statutory scheme. Likewise, with regard to material witnesses, jurisprudence within that same judicial circuit has held that such persons may be detained for the purpose of testifying before a grand jury—thus allowing a person to be arrested for the purpose of being questioned.

Where terrorism is concerned, this other face of U.S. law becomes even more dominant. An analysis of U.S. law demonstrates that, where national security concerns are implicated, the normal restrictions on detention are loosened. This is seen in the laws allowing for suspicionless stops and searches in "critical zones" and the dicta of the Supreme Court that mentions terrorism as an exceptional situation where the normal rules may not be applicable. This is also seen in the use of the material witness statute and immigration detention to effect investigative detention of terrorist suspects in the United States.

As noted, however, some dicta in recent terrorism cases and the remarks of senior officials indicate that the continued use of the material witness statute for investigative detention purposes may be in jeopardy. As a review of U.S. law and U.S. terrorism prosecutions has revealed, curtailing the use of that statute for such purposes would severely impact U.S. counterterrorism capabilities. The analysis also demonstrates, however, that there is still a great deal of flexibility in U.S. law when it comes to apprehending terrorist suspects, and moreover there is, drifting in the legal ether, enough material for the prudent legislator to grasp and sculpt a workable—if somewhat limited—investigative detention mechanism. The key is to understand how effective investigative detention regimes operate and to find how existing U.S. laws might permit this. The first step in this process is to find a model by peering across the Atlantic and observing the legal systems of our allies, which possess robust and effective forms of investigative detention, so that we may better understand how such legal regimes operate, how they are constructed, and what elements—if any—can be incorporated into a parallel regime within the United States.

CHAPTER 4

THE UNITED KINGDOM

Commentators note that "English law regulating political violence has been continuously refined in the past 300 years since the Glorious Revolution and has served as a paradigm for other countries that derive their jurisprudence from that experience."[421] That system of law has been required to adapt in significant ways over the past few decades, as the contemporary United Kingdom has endured a particularly violent struggle with terrorism. The United Kingdom's major counterterrorism challenge during the last century has been its confrontation with the Irish Republican Army (IRA).[422] In recent years, however, the United Kingdom has seen a rise in the number of terrorism-related incidents linked to foreign terrorist networks emanating from the Middle East.[423]

This chapter reviews how the United Kingdom's response to terrorism and the role of laws regulating investigative detention (and other more preventive legal devices, such as "control orders") have played into the effort to address the problem of terrorism. The analysis of criminal law and counterterrorism here is made especially complex due to the plurality of legal systems that exist under the mantle of the United Kingdom. Although Parliament passes legislation that may apply throughout the United Kingdom, there are actually three separate and distinct criminal justice systems within the United Kingdom—each with its own separate procedures and agencies.[424] To maintain focus, therefore, the comparative analysis of the criminal justice system in this chapter shall largely focus on the criminal law of England and Wales. Even so, like the threat posed by terrorism, the recently enacted counterterrorism legislation applies—with a few minor exceptions and caveats—throughout the United Kingdom.[425]

AN OVERVIEW OF THE CRIMINAL JUSTICE SYSTEM IN ENGLAND AND WALES

To understand the counterterrorism legislation in force, the scope of its impact, and the degree to which its provisions could be exported, it is important to understand how the underlying legal system operates. English criminal law is entrenched in the common-law tradition and, thus, possesses a model of criminal procedure that is characterized as adversarial or accusatorial.[426] As John Langbein has noted,

> The lawyer-conducted criminal trial, our so-called adversary system, is the defining feature of criminal justice in England and in countries like the United States that are founded on English common law. What distinguishes criminal adjudication in the Anglo-American world from the European and European-derived systems is not simply that our system allows lawyers for the prosecution and defense. The European procedure does too. The striking particularity of the Anglo-American trial is that we remit to the lawyer-partisans the responsibility for gathering, selecting, presenting, and probing the evidence. Our trial court, traditionally a jury sitting under the supervision of the judge, conducts no investigation of its own. The court renders a verdict of guilt or innocence by picking between or among the evidence that the contesting lawyers have presented to it.[427]

This sort of procedural model, which also prevails in Australia, Canada, and the United States, begins with a police investigation that is designed to gain evidence of a suspect's guilt. Once enough evidence is adduced, the case is then brought before a court where an adversarial trial is conducted. Both the accused and the government are represented at that stage by an advocate who argues their side of the matter before a neutral decision maker with no prior knowledge of the case.[428] To assist in the defense, the accused is imbued with a number of rights that he or she may invoke in defense—such as a right to remain silent, a right to counsel, a right to confront witnesses, and protections against illegal detention.[429] Procedural protections, therefore, factor largely in the English system.

There is no formal code of criminal procedure in England and Wales. Instead, criminal procedure is formed from a patchwork of diverse sources, which date back to the thirteenth century.[430] Likewise, there is no single penal code from which all substantive criminal law is derived. Criminal law in England and Wales is, rather, derived from an archipelago of sundry cases and statutes. For instance, the offenses of assault and battery are found in the Offenses Against the Person Act of 1861, while larceny and other theft-related offenses are defined in the Theft Act of 1968.[431] Substantive criminal laws and changes to substantive criminal law are, therefore, made by amendments to statutes and by the passing of new statutes, rather than through the amendment of a single code.

English Pretrial Investigation

As in the United States, criminal investigations in England and Wales are conducted by professional police.[432] Police are responsible for investigating offenses and obtaining evidence that can be used in the prosecution of the suspect.[433] There are numerous different branches and specializations within the police force in the United Kingdom, with different specialist squads and departments, different missions, and different organizations.[434] Police investigate crimes, gather evidence, question witnesses, and question the suspect. Thereafter, a custody officer within the police force makes the decision of whether to charge the suspect.[435]

Charging and Prosecuting

Before 1986, police were responsible not only for the investigation of a crime but also for its prosecution. To accomplish this function, police employed their own solicitors who appeared on behalf of the prosecution in court and instructed counsel for the Crown Court.[436] That system changed in 1986 with the introduction of the Crown Prosecution Service (CPS),[437] a prosecutorial entity that assumed the responsibility for criminal prosecutions.[438] It is composed of chief crown prosecutors, crown prosecutors, and a host of legal staff, all of which are subordinate to the director of public prosecutions.[439]

Today, public prosecutions in England and Wales are commenced when, after a police investigation, the custody officer (in consultation with the prosecutor) decides that there is enough evidence to charge the suspect with an offense.[440] Formerly, police (like private citizens) were able to make use of the procedure known as "laying an information," discussed more fully later in this chapter. After the passage of the Criminal Justice Act of 2003, however, police and prosecutors were required to issue a formal, written charge.[441] There remain certain kinds of cases that do not require coordination with the CPS in order for the police to charge a suspect, but these are minor offenses.[442] In serious or difficult cases, however, the custody officer must now coordinate with the CPS in making the charging decision. The director of public prosecutions has set out a list of offenses that require consultation with the CPS.[443]

Once a suspect has been charged, the case then moves from the realm of the police to that of the prosecutor. The evidence is brought to a lawyer within the appropriate branch office of the CPS who reviews it to determine whether charges are justified. The CPS lawyer may then discontinue the proceedings, add new charges, or decide to continue with the prosecution.[444]

Although public prosecutions are the norm in the England and Wales,[445] there are some exceptional situations in which the process for public prosecutions does not apply and another entity assumes responsibility for the prosecution. For instance, prosecutions can also be brought by private actors in England and Wales. This may be done by "laying an information," which is a means of instituting criminal action. This may be done either orally or in writing.[446] Using this procedure, the private actor tells a magistrate or a magistrate's clerk the nature of the allegation, as well as the name and address of the accused. The information is taken down and, if the information appears to be correct, a summons is issued by the magistrate requiring the accused to appear in court to answer the allegation.[447] This process has been used by private citizens to secure convictions against individuals for libel and even manslaughter.[448] The CPS, however, retains the authority to assume control over any such prosecution to carry it out or discontinue it.[449]

Those limited exceptions aside, the paradigm of police investigation and CPS prosecution represents the general model for criminal justice in the United Kingdom.[450] That basic paradigm is a relatively binary one: Police investigate and gather evidence; prosecutors review that evidence and, at their discretion, may choose to prosecute the accused.

The United Kingdom's Experience and Response

Like many countries in Europe, there are numerous examples of some form of terrorist violence throughout English history. Among the most famous is the "Gunpowder Plot" in which Guy Fawkes, along with a group of Roman Catholic restorationists from England, attempted to upend Protestant rule by planning to blow up the Houses of Parliament while King James I and the House of Lords were inside. The cover of this book depicts a dramatic scene in which Fawkes is being arrested by Thomas Knyvet in the explosive-laden cellar of the Houses of Parliament before this act of political violence could be consummated. It serves as an excellent reminder of the danger of domestic terrorism, as well as the fact that acts of terrorism (and attempts to blow up government buildings) are no recent phenomenon.

Although the modern United Kingdom, in turn, has been dealing with the threat of terrorism for some time, it was not until 2000 that the British government adopted an organized, coherent legislative scheme aimed at combating it. Prior to that legislative moment, the laws that existed were piecemeal and primarily focused on containing violence in Northern Ireland.[451] This focus on Northern Ireland was due to the fact that, until recently, the IRA was considered the predominant terrorist threat to the United Kingdom and, accordingly, the natural focus of the majority of its counterterrorism legislation.[452] It is against the backdrop of Ireland that the story of U.K. counterterrorism legislation begins. As Yonah Alexander and Edgar H. Brennar have noted,

> In the name of uniting the Irish Republic and Northern Ireland (a British territory), the IRA resorted to bombings, assassinations, kidnappings, extortion, and robberies. The IRA has taken its fight to the streets of London and other cities in England. It attacked ordinary civilians, military personnel, police, and business centers. Militant Protestant groups in Northern Ireland have also undertaken terrorist operations resulting in 3,000 fatalities, woundings, and property damage. Despite the 1994 cease-fire and the ongoing peace process, which began under the Good Friday agreement of 1998, Catholic splinter groups, such as the real IRA, as well as Protestant extremists opposing a political solution, continue their violent activities.[453]

The counterterrorism effort in Northern Ireland has, historically, been a blend of military and civilian law enforcement. Alongside the British military was the Royal Ulster Constabulary (RUC), which came into being in 1922 and served the dual role of providing law enforcement in Northern Ireland and protecting "the state from armed subversion from within and also from outside its borders."[454] The military aspect of the counterterrorism operation was an enduring one. Only recently, in 2007, did the British army's longest continuous military operation come to an end when it formally passed responsibility for security in Northern Ireland to its civilian police.[455]

Another key aspect of the United Kingdom's approach to counterterrorism was the use of the legal system and legislation aimed at restricting the physical freedom of certain individuals. As early as 1922, legislation allowed for executive orders prohibiting residence in or entry into specified areas. Such executive orders could also impose conditions requiring an individual to report to the police.[456] In 1939 the British government enacted the Prevention of Violence Act (Temporary Provisions), which allowed for legal devices known as "control orders" by which a subject could be required to register with the police, photographed, measured, and required to report regularly.[457] Such means of restriction, appearing so early in the twentieth century, would become a recurring theme.

In the late 1960s, Northern Ireland was the scene of increasing civil unrest.[458] This resulted in the deployment of British military forces to the area in 1969 in an effort to quell the unrest and allow for the reform of local security forces.[459] The aggressive British response also included the use of internment,[460] a tactic used intermittently by the British since the early 1920s.[461] The severity of these measures, however, only exacerbated the level of violence.

> From thirty-seven explosions in April 1971, forty-seven in May, fifty in June and seventy eight in July, in August the number soared to 131, followed by 196 in September and 117 in October. In order to combat the rising violence, in November the government rearmed the RUC, but by the end of the year, the number of deaths had tripled from thirty pre-internment to 174.[462]

Irish violence begat aggressive responses from Britain, which, in turn, begat an increased level of violence on the part of the IRA, thus fueling a downward spiral of instability and bloodshed. This downward spiral was characterized by incidents such as "Bloody Sunday" in 1972, in which several unarmed civilians were shot by British paratroopers.[463]

In 1972 the British secretary of state issued an order known as "the Detention of Terrorists (Northern Ireland) Order," which attempted to impose some level of legal restraint on the practice of internment. This new legal regime gave the secretary of state the power to issue an interim custody order, which could place an individual in detention for up to twenty-eight days.[464] At the end of that period of detention, the suspect would be released to a commissioner who would hear evidence to determine whether the interim custody order should be sustained.[465]

This hearing could be conducted outside the presence of the suspect and his solicitor, did not adhere to the normal rules of evidence, and could include information not available to the suspect or the suspect's solicitor.[466] A form of internment, therefore, still existed, but with some limitations and procedural requirements.

Such efforts notwithstanding, the inadequacy of the means used to address the problems in Ireland were becoming apparent, and the treatment of detainees in Northern Ireland continued to be an issue of concern. In an effort to find an alternative to internment and the other means used by Britain thus far to quell Irish violence, the Diplock Commission was appointed to review the procedures then in place and to suggest a new approach to counterterrorism in Ireland.[467] This commission sought to normalize the treatment of terrorist suspects to some degree by limiting the use of internment and transferring cases of suspected terrorists to the criminal justice system—albeit a modified one.[468] The recommendations of the commission still, however, allowed for continued internment and extrajudicial measures in certain limited circumstances.[469] In such cases, the continued use of the provisions contained in the 1972 Detention of Terrorist Order was recommended.[470]

The Diplock Commission's recommendations resulted in the enactment of the Emergency Provisions Act (EPA) in 1973. This new legislative scheme altered the way in which terrorism trials were conducted by shifting the burden of proof at trial to the accused to demonstrate that torture, or inhumane or degrading treatment, had been used to extract a confession.[471] The statute also centralized trials of terrorism cases, requiring all such trials to be conducted in Belfast.[472] One of the most striking enactments of the EPA, however, was based on the Diplock Commission's recommendation that certain kinds of offenses should be tried in the ordinary courts, but without a jury. These sorts of trials became known as "Diplock Courts."[473] Under this system, cases connected with terrorism were dealt with by a judge sitting alone.[474] Trials were held in the same courthouse where ordinary Crown Court jury trials are held, and were presided over by the same judges who conduct ordinary trials in Northern Ireland.[475] Nonetheless, there were significant differences between trial in a Diplock Court and an ordinary proceeding.

> The Diplock courts provide for trial by judge alone (without a jury) of serious "scheduled offenses" (murder, manslaughter, firearms offenses, etc.), and the great majority (86 percent) of evidence against suspects consists of statements made during interrogation, in some instances (30 percent) supported by other evidence. These confessions are generally obtained in the course of lengthy interrogations, and the admissibility of the statement or confession becomes the primary focus in contested cases rather than the ultimate question of guilt or innocence. The standard by which a statement is judged is no longer that of voluntariness, but is reduced to the international legal minimum: a statement is admissible so long as it has not been obtained by "torture, inhuman or degrading treatment."[476]

Sustained international criticism of the Diplock Courts focused on the elimination of the right to a jury trial and the admissibility of certain confessions and uncorroborated testimony.[477] Such criticism undoubtedly contributed to the decision to abolish the Diplock Courts in 2007.[478]

Another notable characteristic of the EPA was the maintenance of the internment powers that had existed prior to the Diplock Commission's report. Sections 10 and 11 of the statute authorized police to arrest without warrant any individual suspected of terrorism or any of a number of listed offenses. Where it appeared that the person was involved in the commission, or attempted commission, of either an act of terrorism or the organization and/or training of terrorist activity, the secretary of state could issue an interim custody order and the liberty of that person could be significantly curtailed in the same manner as had been done under the prior legal regime.[479]

Such measures, however, did not prove to be a panacea for the problem of Irish terrorism. Not only did the police powers and policies of internment fail to end the violence in Northern Ireland, but violence was beginning to spread beyond Irish borders and into Great Britain. In 1973 there were eighty-six explosions in Great Britain, killing one person and injuring over 380.[480] In 1974 there were ninety-nine more terrorist incidents, which resulted in seventeen more deaths and 145 injuries.[481] An infamous attack on two pubs in Birmingham resulted in twenty-one dead and 160 injured.[482] The result of these attacks was a shifting of public sentiment and a call for greater legislative action. This resulted in the 1974 Prevention of Terrorism Act (PTA)—a dramatic piece of legislation designed to counter IRA operations in Great Britain.[483]

The PTA introduced into Great Britain the notion of "extraordinary powers," which had previously been exclusive to Northern Ireland.[484] It outlawed the IRA, strengthened border control with Ireland, enhanced police powers of arrest and detention, and permitted "exclusion orders"—orders by the secretary of state that restricted the residents of Great Britain's right to travel between Great Britain and Ireland.[485] Thus, laws and tactics that had been exclusively applicable in one isolated section of the realm now found more general applicability.

The PTA remained as the exclusive statutory regime regulating terrorist offenses for decades.[486] As previously noted, its focus was on issues related to Northern Ireland rather than on the prevention and deterrence of non-Irish or international terrorism.[487] A later review of counterterrorist legislation then in force, conducted by a member of the House of Lords, Anthony Lloyd, Baron Lloyd of Berwick, concluded that this Irish focus was too narrow as—though the threat of terrorism related to Northern Ireland was in the decline—an emerging global terrorist threat was on the rise and could be expected to intensify.[488] In order to refocus U.K. counterterrorism police, Lord Berwick made a number of recommendations regarding the changing trends in terrorism and how best to address them. He also made recommendations as to how British law could better comply with the European Convention on Human Rights.[489] Many of his recommendations were enacted in a new piece of legislation known as the Terrorism Act of 2000, which sought to provide the United Kingdom with a more progressive counterterrorism scheme and to codify the myriad of the then existing counterterrorism measures into one single source.[490]

> As for the Terrorism Act of 2000, some of the most eye-catching changes are structural. For the first time ever, anti-terrorism laws are stated comprehensively in one code, which draws together what was separate legislation for Great Britain, on the one hand, and Northern Ireland on the other. The legislation is intended to be not only comprehensive, but permanent, no longer requiring renewal or re-enactment save for one part relating exclusively to Northern Ireland.[491]

The Terrorism Act of 2000, thus, replaced the Emergency Provisions Act and the Prevention of Terrorism Act.[492] It added new offenses to fill perceived gaps in existing provisions, developed the existing practice of proscribing terrorist organizations, and provided new powers of detention of suspects without charge, as well as search and seizure.[493] The 2000 act also provided a new definition of *terrorism*,[494] harmonized the laws of Great Britain and Ireland, and extended some measures to Great Britain that were previously exclusive to Northern Ireland.[495] It was not, however, a complete strengthening of the legal regime already in place. For instance, in this massive overhaul of U.K. counterterrorism legislation, the provisions allowing for exclusion orders and internment were largely abolished.[496]

As the discussion thus far demonstrates, counterterrorism legislation has been the subject of significant attention for much of the past century in the United Kingdom. The events of September 11, however, would bring this subject into even sharper focus. As Home Secretary David Blunkett remarked, "On 11 September, families lost their loved ones, and the threat of terrorism touched us all. If we fail now to take the necessary action to protect our people, future generations will never forgive us."[497] As a result, in December of 2001—on the heels of previous counterterrorism legislation—Britain passed the Anti-Terrorism, Crime, and Security Act of 2001.[498] The purpose of the act was to ensure that the United Kingdom had the necessary powers to counter the kinds of terrorist attacks that struck New York and Washington, DC.[499] This statute has a great deal of overlap with the terrorism act passed just a year prior, but it also added new provisions regarding the freezing of terrorist assets, the detention without trial of foreign persons who are denied asylum, and the retention of fingerprints in asylum and immigration cases.[500]

Although the 2000 legislation served to enhance counterterrorism capabilities in the United Kingdom, subsequent events would prompt a call for ever greater legislative action. On July 7, 2005, a terrorist cell known as the Abu Hafas al-Masri Brigade conducted a terrorist attack on the London underground by detonating explosives on three subway cars and one street-level double-decker bus.[501] The attacks resulted in the deaths of fifty-three people and roughly seven hundred injuries.[502] Just as the attacks across the Atlantic in 2001 spurred a legislative response in the United Kingdom, the terrorist bombings in London resulted in yet another piece of counterterrorism legislation—the Terrorism Act of 2006, which supplements the provisions of the Terrorism Act of 2000 by extending the period for which terrorist suspects may be detained for questioning without charge and by enhancing the police powers of search and seizure.[503] It also expands the jurisdiction of previous counterterrorism legislation by providing that there are now no geographical limits to the power of the United Kingdom to punish an act that is proscribed in either the 2000 or the 2006 legislation.[504]

The history of counterterrorism legislation in the United Kingdom is, thus, far more lengthy than that of the United States. This is due to the comparatively long and intense experience that the United Kingdom has had dealing with this threat. One sees from its experience numerous and varied attempts to deal with the issue—from internments and military engagements to specialized trials. As demonstrated in this chapter, the United Kingdom's long experience with counterterrorism has also resulted in the institutionalization of a formidable investigative detention regime. To attain a better understanding of that regime, this chapter now turns to the law of criminal detention in England and Wales.

English and Welsh Law of Detention

The Police and Criminal Evidence Act of 1984 (PACE) and supplementary Codes of Practice are, with some qualifications, the principal sources of law detailing police powers in the United Kingdom.[505] Although section 120 of PACE indicates that it is applicable only to England and Wales, numerous provisions are made expressly applicable in Scotland and Northern Ireland by that same section.[506]

Prior to the enactment of PACE, the detention of suspects and the treatment of suspects while in detention were governed by rules put forth by the King's Bench Division of the High Court.[507] Although these nine "Judges' Rules" were later pronounced by the Queen's Bench Division of the High Court, they were never ratified by Parliament or the House of Lords and were, thus, considered mere guidelines rather than rules of law.[508] The practicality of these rules was subject to debate throughout their existence, and they were characterized by the 1981 Royal Commission on Criminal Procedure as being imprecise "jigsaw pieces of two centuries of police and legal history."[509] They were, thus, later abolished in favor of PACE and the Codes of Practice, which remain in force today.

Stop and Search

Before the enactment of PACE, a police officer had the power to stop a person so long as he or she had "some grounds for suspicion."[510] Today, according to sections 1–3 of PACE, police in the United Kingdom have the general power to detain an individual without arresting him or her for the purpose of conducting a search when there are reasonable grounds for suspecting that the person has stolen or prohibited articles.[511] "Prohibited articles" are offensive weapons and articles made (or intended by those carrying them) for use in connection with burglary, theft, taking vehicles, obtaining property by deception, or criminal damage.[512] In order to effect the stop and search, however, the police officer must have a reasonable suspicion and may not simply act arbitrarily or on a whim. Sprack has noted that such reasonable suspicion can be based on the nature of the property, which is either visible or which the suspect is suspected of carrying, coupled with facts such as the time, place, and the suspect's general behavior.[513] Such reasonable suspicion may not, however, be based solely on race, religion, age, appearance, a previous conviction, generalizations, or stereotypes.[514]

The detention that can be effected by this stop and search power is brief. It may only last long enough to carry out the search at either the place the individual was stopped or nearby.[515] The police officer may search the person on the scene or take the suspect elsewhere, for example, to a nearby van or police station.[516] Likewise, the intrusion by the police officer is limited in that the most the officer may do is require the suspect to remove his or her outer coat, jacket, or gloves.[517] Some amount of reasonable force may be employed but only as a last resort.[518]

Aside from the requirement for reasonable suspicion, there are other limitations on this power. The PACE power to stop and search can only be exercised in a place to which the general public has access.[519] Although the officer may pose questions during the period of detention, the suspect is not obliged to answer them, and the officer may not detain the suspect solely for the purpose of asking questions.[520] Further, suspects so detained have certain rights, such as a right to know the name of the arresting officer and the police station to which the officer is attached, the object of the proposed search, the grounds on which it is being made, and the right to have the record of the search.[521]

Police, of course, have other powers at their disposal. In addition to the PACE power of stop and search, the Criminal Justice and Order Act of 1994 granted police the power to stop vehicles or pedestrians to search for offensive weapons or dangerous instruments without need for reasonable suspicion.[522] This power can only be exercised, however, in a prespecified place, only where serious violence may occur, and only with the written authorization of a police officer of the rank of superintendent or above.[523] Once granted, the power is valid for up to twenty-four hours but may be extended for an additional six hours.[524]

The broad ability to create a suspicionless search zone aside, like the ordinary stop and search powers in the United States, police powers in England and Wales are somewhat limited. In fact, the U.S. equivalent (the Terry stop) may be broader than its English counterpart, as—being based on the idea of protecting the officer—it permits a police officer to stop and search an individual based on reasonable suspicion that he or she is dealing with an armed and dangerous individual. The stop and search powers of police in England and Wales, in contrast, are based on a more specific belief that a person has stolen or prohibited items. Although the expanded powers allowed in the Criminal Justice and Order Act of 1994 are far broader (permitting, when authorized, searches without suspicion), such powers require authorization from higher levels and are confined to particular areas. Thus, in ordinary criminal cases, the law in England and Wales generally affords police officers comparable and, arguably, more limited powers than are afforded to police in the United States. As discussed more fully in the pages that follow, however, the ordinary powers of U.K. police in this regard increase dramatically where terrorism is concerned.

Arrest

Originally, the sole purpose of an arrest in England and Wales was to secure the suspect so that he or she could be charged and brought before a court.[525] According to Bradley, this assumed that the police would have had enough evidence to justify a charge before an arrest was made.[526] In practice, however, police began to increasingly rely on postarrest interrogation to adduce enough evidence to charge a suspect—a practice that was given sanction in the 1920s when the Judges' Rules were changed to permit such interrogation so long as suspects were first informed that they did not have to say anything and that anything they said could be used against them in evidence.[527]

Under the current law, arrests in England may be made with or without a warrant, with differing rules pertaining to both categories of arrest.[528] A police officer may lawfully arrest anyone for whom a warrant has been issued. If, however, a police officer is to effect an arrest without a warrant, certain elements must be in place. Specifically, PACE provides that police may arrest without warrant any person who is (a) about to commit an offense or who is reasonably suspected of being about to commit an offense, (b) in the act of committing an offense or who is reasonably suspected of being in the act of committing an offense, or (c) reasonably suspected of having committed an offense.[529] Such warrantless arrests can only be carried out when necessary for specific, statutorily delineated reasons, such as to enable a person's name or address to be obtained, to prevent physical injury, to prevent loss or damage to property, to allow prompt and effective investigation of the offense or of the conduct of the person in question, or to prevent hindrance of the prosecution for the offense by the person's disappearance.[530]

The kind of reasonable suspicion required in this regard has been articulated by U.K. jurisprudence as "a state of conjecture or surmise where proof is lacking [which arises] at or near the starting point of an investigation."[531] Thus, while such arrests may not be based on a mere hunch, the level of information on which such suspicion is based is certainly not a demanding one. On that score, a key item to note is that one of the conditions in which warrantless arrests are permitted is the arrest of a person suspected of preparing to commit an offence; such an arrest would allow for prompt and effective investigation of the conduct in question, potentially preventing the offence from occurring in the first place. This is indicative of the modern acceptance of arrest for investigative purposes in the United Kingdom—a characteristic that will become even more pronounced upon analysis of the rules governing detention.

Police Detention

Prior to PACE, there was little regulation of the power of police to detain and question a suspect. English jurisprudence reveals instances of suspects being held incommunicado for several days in the course of ordinary criminal investigations.[532] PACE, for the first time, gave police legally based instructions stating under what circumstances and for how long suspects could be detained in police custody.[533] Under the current legal regime, once a person is arrested, he or she may be taken to a police station and held in police custody.[534] There, the suspect is subject to police interrogation, but certain rights apply at various points throughout the course of the period of detention. J. R. Spencer has noted the following:

> The power of the police to detain a person following arrest is governed by Part IV of PACE 1984. By section 37, a person may

> be detained where the custody officer has reasonable grounds for believing that his detention without being charged is necessary to secure or preserve evidence relating to an offense for which he is under arrest or to obtain such evidence by questioning him.[535]

That period of detention can be carried out for days, depending on the seriousness of the crime and the need for further information. The process begins when a detained suspect arrives at the police station. At that time, the evidence against the suspect is reviewed by the custody officer, who considers the evidence against the suspect in order to determine whether the arrest was warranted. If the custody officer determines that the suspect should not have been arrested, then the suspect should be immediately released.[536] Should the custody officer determine that the suspect was properly arrested, then the next determination made by the custody officer is whether there is already enough information to charge the suspect. If enough evidence exists, the custody officer will require investigators to either charge the suspect with a crime or release the suspect without charge.[537] Sprack noted,

> The latter course might be taken when, for ... discretionary reasons ... the police or CPS feel that it is not in the public interest to commence a prosecution even though the evidence amply warrants it. A half-way house is to utilise the power given to the police by s 47(3)(b) of PACE to bail the detainee on condition he return to the station on a stated day. During the interim, a decision can be taken as to the desirability of prosecution and, if need be, the detainee can be released unconditionally from the police station, with a warning that consideration will be given to the question of whether to prosecute him. Proceedings may then be commenced by information and summons. Once a suspect has been charged, he may not, in general, be asked any further questions about the offense. It follows that a decision by the custody officer as to whether there is enough evidence to charge a detainee effectively prevents the investigating officers interrogating him at the police station, since he then either has to be charged (with the effect on questioning him just noted) or has to be released.[538]

If, however, the custody officer finds that there is sufficient evidence to justify the arrest but that there is not yet enough to charge the suspect with a crime, then the custody officer may authorize detention without charge. In order to do so, the custody officer must find that such detention is necessary to secure or preserve evidence relating to the offence for which the detainee is under arrest or that detention is necessary to obtain such evidence through questioning.[539] Therefore, one sees in the analysis of pretrial detention a Copernican distinction between the law of the United States and that of the United Kingdom—an individual can be detained in the course of an ordinary criminal investigation so that evidence to support a charge can be obtained. Investigative detention is, therefore, expressly permitted.

Once the custody officer authorizes detention without charge, a separate officer known as the "review officer" becomes part of the process. A review officer is a police officer of at least the rank of inspector who was not directly involved in the investigation. He or she performs similar duties to the custody officer throughout the period of detention without charge.[540]

Within the first six hours of detention without charge, a review officer must, like the custody officer, again consider whether there is enough evidence to charge the detained suspect. If there is not, then the review officer must determine whether continued detention is warranted based on the need to secure or preserve evidence relating to the offence or the need to obtain evidence through questioning.[541] The review officer must also give the suspect and/or the suspect's legal representative an opportunity to be heard on the validity of continued detention without warrant and the reasons, if any, for release. If it is decided that continued detention is necessary, the reasons for such detention must be given to the suspect orally and then entered into the custody record.[542] A second review of the detention without warrant must be held within nine hours of the first review. Reviews are then carried out in nine-hour intervals.[543]

After twenty-four hours, a detained suspect normally must be either released or charged with a crime. The twenty-four hour period begins to run from either the time that he or she arrived at the station or the time the detained suspect was informed that he or she was no longer free to leave.[544]

This twenty-four hour period is not, however, absolute. Continued detention can be authorized by the station superintendent if the superintendent determines that the detained suspect has committed an indictable offense, that continued detention is warranted based on the need to secure or preserve evidence or to obtain evidence through questioning, and that the investigation is being conducted diligently and expeditiously.[545]

After thirty-six hours, the detained suspect must be released unless charged, or unless a magistrate's court has issued what is called a "warrant for further detention."[546] Unlike the previous extensions—all of which are authorized by the police—such a warrant can only be issued by a magistrate. The magistrate will grant such an extension only after a hearing, at which the suspect is entitled to free legal representation.[547] In order to request such an extension, a police officer must apply for an extension under oath and support the request with written information that details the nature of the offense for which the suspect was arrested, the inquiries which have been and which will be made, and the reason such inquiries require continued detention.[548] The hearing should be conducted when the thirty-six hour period expires, but police may hold a suspect for an additional six hours if it is not possible for a court to hear the case at the end of the allotted period of time.[549]

In order to grant the warrant for further detention, the magistrate must find that the suspect is being held for an indictable offense, that continued detention is necessary to secure or preserve evidence of the offense or to obtain evidence by questioning the suspect, and that the investigation is being conducted diligently and expeditiously.[550] A warrant for further detention may not be for a period exceeding thirty-six hours of continued detention. Otherwise stated, with such a warrant, police may detain a suspect for up to seventy-two hours.

Finally, there is yet another opportunity to extend the period of detention by seeking an extension of that warrant of continued detention from a magistrate court, using the same procedure, which can authorize continued detention of the suspect up to a total of ninety-six hours[551]—the maximum period a suspect may be held in ordinary criminal cases.[552] At that point, the suspect must be either released or charged.[553]

The maximum amount of time one may be ordinarily detained by police for investigative purposes in the British system is, therefore, ninety-six hours (or four days). To be sure, that period is not a time of unfettered police access to the suspect. It is, rather, tempered by rights that are afforded to the suspect and which serve to limit police action. In comparison to the rights available in the United States, however, the rights afforded to criminal suspects in the United Kingdom seem a bit tepid.

Rights During Police Detention

As noted, a criminal suspect who has been arrested can be taken to the police station and held under police custody. Upon arrival at the police station, a detained suspect must be informed of his or her right to free legal advice, the right to have someone notified of the fact of his or her arrest, and the right to read the Codes of Practice.[554] Before a suspect can be questioned, the investigating officer must first obtain permission from the custody officer to transfer the suspect to the custody of the investigating officer.[555] Once such a transfer occurs, a person suspected of an offense must generally be advised of his or her rights before any questions may be posed that might be used in a prosecution.[556]

The Right to Counsel

A person who is held in police detention is entitled, if he or she requests, to consult a solicitor privately at any time.[557] This solicitor is independent and is provided free of charge.[558] A detained suspect must be told of this right when he or she arrives at the police station. Once a request to consult a solicitor has been made, the suspect should be allowed, under normal circumstances, to meet with the suspect.[559] When a detainee, therefore, has been allowed to consult a solicitor, and the solicitor is available, the solicitor must be allowed to sit in on any interview of the suspect by the police.[560]

If, during the period of detention, the suspect has not yet exercised his or her rights to consult a solicitor and to have someone informed of his or her arrest, the superintendent is obligated to remind the suspect of those rights.[561] There is a significant limitation, however, to the suspect's right to counsel. In the case of "serious arrestable offenses," the suspect can be delayed access to legal advice. Such a delay must be authorized by an officer of the rank of superintendent and is only possible where there are reasonable grounds for believing that the exercise of that right will interfere with evidence connected to a serious arrestable offense, will lead to harm to another, will lead to the alerting of other persons suspected of having committed such an offense but who are not yet arrested, or will hinder the recovery of property obtained as a result of such an offense.[562] A detained suspect's access to a solicitor may not, however, be delayed beyond thirty-six hours in ordinary cases, as that marks the point at which police must go before a magistrate to request a warrant for further detention.[563] Further, although the general rule is that police should not continue the interview until such advice has been granted, police may start questioning detained suspects before the solicitor has arrived if the situation is an emergency or if the solicitor will likely not arrive for some time.[564]

Thus, while a right to counsel exists in ordinary cases, it is by no means unlimited or inviolable. A detained suspect can be held by police and denied access to counsel for up to thirty-six hours, and questioning may, in certain circumstances, continue without counsel present. This is a vast shift in the power dynamic of the U.S. model, wherein if, during interrogation, a suspect being held by police states that he or she wants an attorney, the interrogation must cease until an attorney is present, and the suspect must be given the chance to confer with the attorney and to have him or her present during any subsequent questioning.[565] Criminal law in the United Kingdom, thus, not only affords greater police access to suspects in terms of their ability to detain them—it provides greater ability to question them.

Questioning and the Right to Remain Silent

There is no legally enforceable obligation to answer questions posed by police in the British system.[566] There is, to the contrary, a qualified right to remain silent. This right, however, is not an absolute one in that the exercise of the right to remain silent may be used against a suspect in certain circumstances. As one author has noted,

> The common law of Northern Ireland and England has always permitted the jury to draw adverse inferences from silence, especially from a defendant's refusal to testify. The common law recognizes that adverse inferences drawn from a defendant's refusal to testify are only the result of ordinary common sense.[567]

While the right to remain silent exists, it is a more limited right than that which exists in the United States in that the exercise of it can be used against you in a court of law. For instance, if, prior to a warning, a police officer makes an accusation against the suspect that an innocent person would be expected to deny, then the suspect's silence may be used against him or her as a tacit acknowledgment of the truth of the accusation.[568] In such a way, the fact that someone remains silent during the information-gathering phase of an investigation may be used against the suspect at trial.[569] This is reflected in the "caution" that must be read to the suspect before any questions are posed that might lead to information that could be incriminating: "You do not have to say anything. But it may harm your defence if you do not mention when questioned something which you later rely on in court. Anything you do say may be given in evidence."[570]

DETENTION IN REMAND

Under PACE, once a suspect is charged, the custody officer must order his or her release unless the suspect has refused to give his or her name or address, or there are reasonable grounds to believe that the name and address are not genuine. Likewise, the custody officer may detain a person after charge if (a) there is reason to believe that the detainee will not answer bail, (b) his or her detention is necessary to prevent commission of a further offense, (c) detention is necessary to prevent the suspect from causing injury to another or loss of/damage to property, (d) detention is necessary to prevent the suspect from interfering with the administration of justice or the investigation of an offense, or (e) the suspect's detention is necessary for his or her own protection.[571]

If a suspect is not released, then he or she must be brought before a magistrate's court as soon as practicable and no later than the first sitting of the magistrate's court after the suspect is charged.[572] A magistrate's court, thereafter, has the power to remand the accused suspect—either by granting the accused bail or by committing the accused to custody until the next adjournment date.[573] This is in contrast with a simple adjournment, which does not carry any restrictions for the accused.[574]

When a magistrate's court would decide to remand an accused into custody, former rules dictated that the period of remand should not exceed eight days.[575] At the end of that time, the accused was to be brought back before the court to determine whether he or she would be bailed or remanded yet again.[576] Subsequent legislation, however, extended the period of remand into custody for prudential considerations. As a result, an accused may now be remanded into custody for up to twenty-eight days without attending court.[577] In any event, regulations laying out the maximum periods during which a suspect may be kept in custody before trial dictate that, normally, no more than 182 days should elapse between the time the suspect's case is sent by the magistrate's court for trial and the start of trial—though that period of time may be extended for good cause.[578]

Bail

The term *bail* refers to the release from custody, pending a criminal trial, of an accused with the promise that the accused will surrender to custody at an appointed time and place.[579] The Bail Act of 1974 gives to accused suspects what, as Sprack noted, "may be usefully, if slightly inaccurately, be described as a right to bail."[580] Section 4 of that act provides that those individuals to whom it applies shall be granted bail except in certain enumerated circumstances—even if the accused does not apply for bail.[581] There is no such right in situations where the custody officer is considering bailing an arrestee from the police station after he has been charged; where the magistrates, having summarily convicted an offender, commit him to the Crown Court for sentencing; or where a person who has been convicted and sentenced (by magistrates or the Crown Court) is appealing against his or her conviction or sentence.[582] In such cases, the custody officer or magistrate may still grant bail, but there is not a statutory presumption in favor it.[583]

In addition, there are some situations in which a court may refuse to grant bail. For instance, when an accused has been charged with an offense punishable by imprisonment, a court need not grant bail when there are substantial grounds for believing that the accused, if released, would fail to surrender to custody, would commit an offense while on bail, or would interfere with witnesses or otherwise obstruct the course of justice.[584] The court may also refuse to grant bail where it finds that the accused should remain in custody for his or her own protection or where the accused has previously failed to answer to bail. Likewise, the court may refuse to grant bail when there has not been enough time to obtain information for the court to properly analyze the factors and considerations necessary to make a determination.[585] If an accused has not, however, been charged with an offense that carries a possible sentence of imprisonment, then bail may only be withheld if the accused has previously failed to surrender on bail and if the court finds that he or she will likely fail to surrender once again.[586]

TERRORISM UNDER THE LAW OF THE UNITED KINGDOM

Although modern counterterrorism legislation lays out a specific legal definition of *terrorism* that requires a specific terrorism-related mens rea and actus reus, until the late twentieth century, acts of terrorism in the United Kingdom were criminalized through the ordinary criminal laws.[587] From time to time, certain new offenses were created to respond to specific activity, such as the Explosive Substances Act 1883, which was enacted after anarchist bombings in London.[588] A distinct crime—or legal definition—of terrorism, however, did not exist.

The Prevention of Terrorism (Temporary Provisions) Act of 1989 defined *terrorism* as being "the use of violence for political ends and includes any use of violence for the purpose of putting the public or any section of the public in fear."[589] This rather straightforward definition was criticized for being too narrow and failing to take religious motivations into consideration.[590] It was, therefore, replaced by the Terrorism Act of 2000, which defines *terrorism* in a much more complex fashion:

1. Terrorism: interpretation

(1) In this Act 'terrorism' means the use or threat of action where –
   (a) The action falls within subsection (2),
   (b) The use or threat is designed to influence the government or to intimidate the public or a section of the public, and
   (c) The use or threat is made for the purpose of advancing a political, religious, or ideological cause.

(2) Action falls within this subsection if it –
   (a) Involves serious violence against a person,
   (b) Involves serious damage to property,
   (c) Endangers a person's life, other than that of the person committing the action,
   (d) Creates a serious risk to the health or safety of the public or a section of the public, or
   (e) Is designed seriously to interfere with or seriously to disrupt an electronic system.

(3) The use or threat of action falling within subsection (2) which involves the use of firearms or explosives is terrorism whether or not subsection (1)(b) is satisfied.[591]

Subsequent counterterrorism legislation, such as the Anti-Terrorism, Crime and Security Act 2001[592] and the Terrorism Act 2006,[593] largely refers back to this general definition in the Terrorism Act of 2000. Thus, the essence of the contemporary definition of *terrorism* is the use or threat of certain kinds of action designed to influence the government, or intimidate the public or a section of the public, when that action is made for the purpose of advancing a political, religious, or ideological cause.[594]

The actions that can qualify as terrorism are those that involve serious violence against a person, serious damage to property, endanger the life of another, create a serious risk to public health or safety, or are designed to seriously interfere with or disrupt an electronic system.[595] The use of threat of action involving firearms or explosives is considered terrorism whether or not it is designed to intimidate or influence.[596]

TERRORISM AND THE U.K. LAW OF DETENTION

A review of the counterterrorism legislation in force in the United Kingdom reveals a particularly expansive grant of power to police and prosecutors in their ability to detain and question terrorist suspects. Although these powers are impressive in their scope, they are mitigated by a cordon of legal limitations and judicial oversight, which limits their potential for abuse and renders them compatible with life in a liberal democracy. Even considering such protections, U.K. law has greatly enhanced the government's power to stop, search, arrest, and detain suspected terrorists.

Stop and Search

In contrast to the limited powers to stop and search ordinary criminal suspects, the Terrorism Act of 2000 allows a police officer to stop and search any person he or she reasonably suspects to be a terrorist in order to discover whether the suspect has possession of anything that may constitute evidence that he or she is a terrorist.[597] The act also grants to police officers the right to conduct blanket searches of specified areas, allowing police the power to stop a vehicle in an area or specified place and to search the vehicle, the driver, the passenger, and anything in the vehicle or carried by its occupants.[598]

This power to stop and search in terrorism cases is vaguely reminiscent of the pre-PACE police powers in its breadth. Unlike in ordinary cases, where the ability of police to stop and search a suspect is tied to "stolen or prohibited articles," police in terrorism cases are free to stop any person suspected of being a terrorist and conduct a search. Thus, police have far more discretionary power to stop and search terrorist suspects than in non-terrorism cases.

Arrest

The Prevention of Terrorism (Temporary Provisions) Act of 1974 gave police the power to arrest any person reasonably believed to be guilty of certain offenses or "concerned in the commission, preparation, or instigation of acts of terrorism" without a warrant.[599] Article 41 of the Terrorism Act of 2000 continues the tradition of broad grounds for the warrantless arrest of terrorist suspects, allowing that "[a] constable may arrest without warrant a person whom he reasonably suspects to be a terrorist."[600]

This is a far greater grant of power and discretion to police than is given in ordinary cases, wherein police must first suspect an offense and then determine that certain additional reasons (identification, to prevent physical injury, to prevent loss of property, protect a child, etc.) also exist.[601] The exception in U.K. law for terrorism cases does away with those requirements and replaces them with mere suspicion that a person is a terrorist. Commentators have noted that the effect of the particular formulation of this requirement in the legislation is that, in contrast with normal powers of arrest, there is no need for suspicion of any specific offense in the mind of the arresting officer.[602] As a result, with regard to suspected terrorists, an officer may effect an arrest without a warrant and without needing to state the offense of which the person is suspected.[603]

Police Custody

Under the Prevention of Terrorism (Temporary Provisions) Act of 1974, after a terrorist suspect was arrested, he or she could be detained for forty-eight hours, and the secretary of state could extend that power for another five days.[604] Today, the overall scheme for detention of terrorist suspects is placed under the judiciary, rather than the executive, but allows for far longer periods of detention for terrorist suspects.

The paradigm for police detention is tripartite: an initial arrest and a forty-eight-hour detention period, a warrant for further detention, and an extension of warrant.[605] The paradigm for the detention of terrorist suspects mirrors that ordinary model but is greatly enhanced. As previously discussed, the forty-eight-hour period of detention can be extended up to a ninety-six-hour period. Under the 2000 act, that period could be extended—in the case of a terrorist suspect—for an additional five days.[606] This period was incrementally increased to fourteen days by the Criminal Justice Act of 2003.[607] The Terrorism Act of 2006 further enhanced the power of police to detain terrorist suspects by allowing, after the initial forty-eight-hour period of detention, subsequent extensions for up to twenty-eight days.[608]

A series of checks and procedural safeguards exist, however, during that period of detention. Once a terrorist suspect is arrested, as in ordinary cases, police must periodically check on the status of the detained suspect through a "review officer," a police officer who has not been involved in the investigation that has lead to the apprehension of the suspect.[609] The first such review shall be carried out as soon as reasonably practicable after the suspect's arrest.[610] Unlike in ordinary cases, however, subsequent reviews are carried out every twelve hours but may be postponed if the review would prejudice an ongoing interview, where no review officer is readily available, or where it is not practicable for any other reason to carry out the review.[611] This is in contrast to the nine-hour reviews received by other suspects.

Further, in contrast to ordinary cases in which suspects must be normally charged or released after twenty-four hours, terrorist suspects may be detained without charge or action for forty-eight hours. In order to prolong detention beyond that initial forty-eight-hour period, a police officer of at least the rank of superintendent must apply to a "judicial authority" for a warrant prolonging the period of detention.[612] Under the 2000 act, a *judicial authority* is defined as, in England or Wales, one of the following: the senior district judge, the deputy of the senior district judge, or a district judge who is designated for the purpose of approving such warrants by the lord chancellor.[613]

After the initial period of forty-eight hours, the first extension of detention can be granted (via a warrant for further detention) for a period of seven days from the time of arrest (or five days beyond the expiration of the initial forty-eight-hour period).[614] A request for a warrant to prolong detention must be made during the initial forty-eight-hours or within six hours of the end of that period.[615] A written or oral notice to a judicial authority of an intention to make the application is considered an application for a warrant.[616] Once an application for a warrant has been made, the terrorist suspect may be detained pending the processing of that application.[617]

The differences in the handling of terrorist suspects are, thus, already evident at the outset of their period of detention. Whereas an ordinary suspect can be detained for twenty-four hours, with the police able to authorize their continued detention for up to thirty-six hours through internal mechanisms that do not involve judicial oversight, terrorist suspects can automatically be held for up to forty-eight hours (with less stringent reviews), and their detention is only subject to judicial oversight at the expiration of that period.

After the initial period of seven days from the time of arrest has been exhausted, further detention can then be authorized by an extension of warrant.[618] Applications for such extensions are made to a judicial authority by police officers of at least the rank of superintendent.[619] The initial extension of a warrant of detention can be for an additional fourteen days. Each individual extension beyond the first fourteen additional days can be for no longer than seven days each. The absolute maximum period of time such a suspect may be detained is—in the aggregate—twenty-eight days from the time of arrest.[620]

The 2006 legislation also increased the possible universe of actors who may request such an extension. As a result, a crown prosecutor (in England and Wales), a lord advocate or procurator fiscal (in Scotland), the director of public prosecutions for Northern Ireland (in Northern Ireland), and, as before, in any part of the United Kingdom, a police officer of at least the rank of superintendent may all request an extension.[621]

Rights During Police Custody

As with ordinary suspects, certain procedural rights must be observed in continuing the detention of a terrorist suspect. Before determining whether a suspect's detention may be extended, the detained suspect or the suspect's attorney may be heard on the reasons for ending the detention.[622] If the review officer decides to authorize continued detention, he or she shall then inform the detained suspect of his or her rights and of the fact that the period of detention is being prolonged.[623]

In addition, terrorist suspects have the right to have a person informed of their detention and the right to have access to a legal advisor—though there are some limitations on the latter.[624] Regarding a terrorist suspect's right to legal advice, the Terrorism Act of 2000 allows that it may be ordered that a detained suspect is only to receive legal advice in the sight and hearing of a police officer.[625] Further, delays in the exercise of both of these rights may be authorized by a superintendent for up to forty-eight hours (twelve hours more than in regular cases).[626]

The grounds for delaying the exercise of a suspect's rights are the same as those that exist in ordinary cases, with the addition of the following: the interference with the gathering of information about the commission, preparation, or instigation of acts of terrorism; the alerting of a person that could thereby make it more difficult to prevent an act of terrorism; and the alerting of a person that could thereby make it more difficult to secure a person's apprehension, prosecution, or conviction in connection with the commission, preparation, or instigation of an act of terrorism.[627] Where such a delay has been authorized, the terrorist suspect shall be told of the reason for the delay as soon as is reasonably practicable, and once that reason has ceased to exist, there should be no further delay in allowing the suspect to exercise his or her rights.[628]

Bail

The Terrorism Act of 2000 provides, vis-à-vis Northern Ireland, that there is no presumption in favor of bail for terrorist suspects and that an application for bail in terrorist cases may only be granted by a High Court judge, a court of appeal judge, or a trial judge, rather than by a magistrate. If bail is not granted, then, as with an ordinary suspect, the maximum period of remand into custody is twenty-eight days.[629] It is interesting to note, however, that the only time the issue of bail is addressed in U.K. counterterrorism legislation is in part 7 of the 2000 act. Otherwise, outside of Northern Ireland, the granting of bail is governed by ordinary criminal legislation.

Control Orders

Another aspect of U.K. counterterrorism legislation that is distinct from investigative detention but worthy of note is the use of control orders. The U.K. Terrorism Act of 2005 was designed to strengthen police powers even further and contained provisions that created a means of quasi-detention known as a "control order."[630] This is an order against an individual that imposes obligations on that person for purposes connected with protecting members of the public from a risk of terrorism.[631] Both British citizens and foreign nationals are subject to these control orders.[632] Among the most striking features of this particular device is that it is not necessarily an order issued by a court but can be, rather, an order issued by the executive branch of government.[633] Control orders are either issued by the home secretary or by a court on application of the secretary of state, depending on the level of control sought.[634] Thus, it forms a sort of "executive detention" mechanism by which terrorist suspects can be subject to certain restrictions.[635]

The obligations that can be imposed upon an individual pursuant to a control order include prohibitions or restrictions on a subject's possession, or use of specified articles or substances (such as a computer or cell phone); prohibitions or restrictions on a subject's use of specified services or specified facilities, or carrying on specified activities (such as banking); restrictions on a subject's association or communication with specified persons; and prohibitions or restrictions on a subject's movement to, from, and within the United Kingdom.[636] A person's movements may be controlled by requiring him or her to remain in a particular place or to remain at a specific place at a particular time.[637] The breach of an obligation imposed by a control order can be considered a criminal offense punishable by up to five years' confinement and a fine.[638] Thus, even though the actual control order is not considered a criminal sanction, it can lead to criminal sanctions if its terms are violated.

There are two types of control orders: "derogating control orders" and "non-derogating control orders." The first group—derogating control orders—is so named because the restrictions imposed are so onerous that they require derogation from article 5 of the ECHR. Such control orders—which involve more serious restraints on a person's movement, thus impinging upon a right guaranteed by the ECHR, such as the right to liberty—can be made only by a court on application of the secretary of state, while all others may be issued by the home secretary.[639] They are generally reserved for individuals who represent a serious risk to public safety [640] and can only be imposed upon application by the home secretary, who must be satisfied that the subject of the order is or has been involved in "terrorism-related activity." Further, the home secretary must consider that the imposition of obligations on the person is necessary for the protection of the public.[641] In addition, the court must find that the risk arises out of, or is associated with, a public emergency in respect of which there has been a derogation from article 5 of the ECHR, and that the obligations are described in the designation order.[642] Such an order ceases after six months unless renewed.[643]

Non-derogating control orders, in contrast, impose specific combinations of restrictions upon individuals that, although restrictive, do not require derogation from the ECHR—restrictions such as curfew, electronic tagging, searches of residences and other premises, restrictions on association, and restrictions on the use of telephones and Internet.[644] They may be imposed in cases where the home secretary has reasonable grounds for suspecting that an individual is or has been involved in terrorism-related activity and considers it necessary to make a control order imposing obligations on that individual in order to protect the public.[645] The home secretary must normally have the permission of the High Court to impose a non-derogating control order. The High Court then reviews the home secretary's decision. Such non-derogating control orders may last for twelve months unless renewed.[646] Even with regard to non-derogating control orders, however, a fair amount of judicial scrutiny remains.

> This means that the Home Secretary, and not the court, remains the author of the order but only if he has been granted permission to do so by the court [by way of an early judicial check in the form of an ex parte application for leave to make the order]. There are, however, two exceptional measures. By section 3(1)(b), there is the possibility that the Secretary of State has made, and included in the control order, a statement saying that the urgency of the case requires him to make the control order without permission from the court. Alternatively, it is possible under section 3(1)(c) for an order to be made on the Secretary of State's authority alone where the order is made before March 14, 2005 against a detainee under Part IV of the Anti-Terrorism, Crime, and Security Act of 2001. The argument here is that if detention was justifiable, then there was reduced urgency to check whether the lesser intrusion of a non-derogating control order was needed. For the exceptional cases under (b) or (c) above, the Secretary of State must render the control order to the court immediately, and the court must begin considering such a reference not later than seven days after the day on which the control order was made.[647]

As previously noted, in order for such an order to be granted, it must be found that there are reasonable grounds for suspecting that the person is involved in terrorism-related activity and that a control order is necessary for purposes connected with protecting members of the public from a risk of terrorism. "Involvement in terrorism-related activity" is defined as (a) the commission, preparation, or instigation of acts of terrorism; (b) conduct that facilitates or is intended to facilitate the commission, preparation, or instigation of such acts; (c) conduct that gives encouragement or is intended to give encouragement to the commission, preparation, or instigation of such acts; or (d) conduct that gives support or assistance to those known or believed to be involved in terrorism-related activity.[648] The burden of proof is based upon "the balance of probabilities" rather than beyond a reasonable doubt.[649]

It is worth noting that the advent of the control order in the United Kingdom was not without some debate. Amnesty International decried the practice early on, noting that such deprivation of liberty is violative of human rights.[650] Based on such concerns, non-derogating control orders have since been challenged in court. In *Secretary of State for the Home Department v. MB*, the court of appeal overruled a High Court decision that held that the procedure for imposing non-derogating control orders violated article 6 of the ECHR, which protects the right to a fair trial.[651] Ip has noted,

> At issue was Section 3(10) of the PTA, which states that the court is to determine whether the Home Secretary's decision to impose a control order "was flawed." The High Court Judge concluded that Section 3(10) limited the court to considering material that was available to the Home Secretary at the time the decision was made. Consequently, judicial supervision was in actuality so weak as to breach Article 6 of the ECHR. In contrast, the Court of Appeal interpreted the section to mean flawed at the time of the court hearing, which allowed consideration of a wider range of information, including the response of the individual concerned. Accordingly, the court held there was no breach of Article 6.[652]

Likewise, in *Secretary of State for the Home Department v. JJ and Others*,[653] the House of Lords ruled on the case of six controls orders. By a majority of three to two, the House of Lords rejected the secretary of state's argument that the six control orders made in those cases did not deprive the individuals of their liberty. The lower courts ruled that the effect of the restrictions, considered cumulatively, was so restrictive of the individuals' liberty in the aggregate as to amount to a deprivation of liberty and, therefore, a breach of article 5 of the ECHR. The House of Lords upheld the decisions of lower courts, and the control orders were quashed.[654]

In spite of these rulings, confusion and debate persist—even within the U.K. government—on the compatibility of control orders with applicable human rights law. Legal challenges have met with limited success but have failed to pose a significant obstacle to the use of this device by the United Kingdom. Accordingly, they remain a controversial but viable tool for the detention of terrorist suspects.

The Use of Detention in Counterterrorism

The available information from which one can measure the efficacy of the increased detention powers is limited.[655] What information has been released from the United Kingdom indicates, however, a level of success associated with the ability of police to detain suspects. A recent report presented to Parliament by the prime minister and the secretary of state for the Home Department noted that "[t]he police and the security and intelligence agencies have disrupted many attacks against the U.K. since November 2000, including four since [July 2005] alone."[656] The report noted that sixty-two people were subsequently charged with criminal offenses following arrest in 2005 under the Terrorism Act 2000 and that in the first three months of 2006, a further seven people have been charged with criminal offenses following arrests under the act.[657] This success has spurred recent calls for even longer periods of pre-charge detention.[658] Human Rights Watch noted that the British government has considered doubling the pre-charge detention period to fifty-six days—a proposition which sparked a fierce debate in the U.K. and among human rights advocates.[659] Most recently, Prime Minister Gordon Brown led a push to allow police to detain terrorist suspects without charge for up to forty-two days.[660] Such proposals, however, have received fierce criticism from human rights groups and have not succeeded in becoming law.[661]

Critics of lengthy detention argue that there is little evidence to suggest that such victories are due to lengthy periods of investigative detention or that such detention is even necessary.[662] The National Council for Civil Liberties, a U.K.-based human rights advocacy group, noted that other countries (such as the United States) do not use prolonged pre-charge detention to deal with the threats and challenges from international terrorism.[663] Reports by the Home Office, however, offer a strong counterargument to such criticism, noting that the number of people charged with an offence after arrest under the terrorist legislation grew from just over fifty in 2004 to around eighty in 2006.[664] Further, as one report noted,

> [T]he police and Security Services have a duty to intervene early, to protect the public, at a point when there may not be much evidence against suspects. This means that more work needs to be done after suspects are arrested in terrorist investigations than is the case with other crimes. In the 2004 Barot case, for example, Deputy Assistant Commissioner Peter Clarke, the National Coordinator of Terrorist Investigations said that, "there was not one shred of admissible evidence" at the point of arrest. Barot subsequently pleaded guilty and was sentenced to 40 years.[665]

Whether or not the Home Office ever succeeds in its effort to extend the length of pretrial detention, developments like the increase in people charged with a terrorist offense, the fact that terrorist investigations require postarrest evidence gathering, and the experience of successful terrorist convictions that have resulted from postarrest evidence gathering indicate that the length of pretrial detention in the United Kingdom has had a positive impact on the United Kingdom's ability to root out and prosecute terrorism.

IMPLICATIONS OF INTERNATIONAL HUMAN RIGHTS LAW

As noted, there is no prohibition on investigative detention under the ICCPR, so long as such detentions are not arbitrary, remain controlled by the judiciary, and otherwise comport with the requirements of article 9. The United Kingdom's system of investigative detention—with its extensive safeguards—certainly complies with those criteria and, thus, with the ICCPR. As noted, however, the nature of the HRC, which is the principal enforcer of the ICCPR, is considered neither a judicial nor even a quasi-judicial entity, and its decisions have no binding force—even among parties to the Optional Protocol. Therefore, member states are not legally obligated to comply with the committee's findings.[666]

The most critical international human rights instrument for the United Kingdom is the ECHR. Sprack noted that, until the passage of the Human Rights Act 1998 (HRA), the United Kingdom was one of the few members of the Council of Europe who had not made the ECHR directly enforceable in its domestic legal system.[667]

> The HRA 1998 aims to integrate the ECHR into [the British] legal system, so that all courts have an obligation to consider arguments founded upon its provisions, and to act upon the rights which formerly could only be enforced in Strasbourg. The HRA came fully into force in October 2000. Section 2 places a duty upon any court, from the magistrate's court upwards, to take into account the decisions of the European Court of Human Rights, and other bodies in Strasbourg which have interpreted the provisions of the ECHR. Section 3 lays down that primary and secondary legislation must be interpreted in a way consistent with Convention rights if that is possible. If it is impossible, the legislation will be valid and enforceable, but the higher courts (including the House of Lords, the Court of Appeal and the High Court—but not the Crown Court) may make a declaration of incompatibility (s 4). Section 6 makes it unlawful for a public authority (including a court) to act in a way which is incompatible with a Convention right, unless required to do so by provisions contained in, or made under, primary legislation.

Even so, as Spencer explained, not all aspects of the ECHR were incorporated by the Human Rights Act. Specifically, article 13 of the ECHR, which guarantees effective remedies before national authorities, was not so incorporated.[668] Likewise, when the Human Rights Act was passed, Parliament only gave courts the power to issue a declaration of incompatibility, which, in turn, gives the executive the power to amend the legislation in question if so desired.[669] Nonetheless, the ECHR and its provisions are still capable of having a profound influence on domestic law in the United Kingdom and the jurisprudence of the ECtHR is illuminative of both the challenges and the limits of state actors in the struggle against terrorism.

For instance, in *Murray v. United Kingdom*, the ECtHR considered a case which arose under section 14 of the Northern Ireland (Emergency Provisions) Act 1978. Murray challenged the reasonableness of her arrest and detention, arguing that it was not based on reasonable suspicion but, rather, was solely for intelligence-gathering purposes.[670] The ECtHR, however, found that the government had met its standard of reasonableness through a declaration that it had reliable but confidential information grounding suspicion against Murray, as well as her visits to the United States and contact with her brothers who had recently been convicted in the United States for purchasing weapons for the Provisional IRA. Given the ongoing terrorist campaign in Northern Ireland, this was enough to support the reasonableness of Murray's arrest. For purposes of the ECHR, therefore, reliable information of terrorist associations—even if confidential in nature—was sufficient to arrest and detain an individual. International human rights law posed to bar to state action under such circumstances.

Aside from the question of arrest, there is the question of the amount a time a person may be detained. The ECtHR has never articulated an exact limit on the acceptable length of pre-charge detention.[671] The court has, however, had the chance to consider the issue in the case of *Brogan and Others v. United Kingdom*.[672] In that case, a period of detention under the Prevention of Terrorism (Temporary Provisions) Act 1989 (previously discussed) lasting four days and six hours was deemed to fall below the convention standard.[673]

> The applicants argued that their arrest failed to comply with Article 5(1)(c) of the Convention on the grounds that they were not arrested on suspicion of responsibility for a specific offense. Empirical and testimonial evidence before the Court demonstrated strongly that arrests under Section 12 of the Prevention of Terrorism Act served information-gathering and counter-insurgency purposes for the state. The Court again demonstrated its reluctance to critically address the Government's assessment of fact. In this case, its avoidance mechanism was to move from a discussion of the concrete to a discussion of the abstract. The abstract discussion was grounded in a discussion of the validity of results. The Court stated that outcome per se did not determine the legitimacy of the arrest procedure. The Court's inability to respond to the general trend that arrest cases under Section 12 of the Prevention of Terrorism Act manifested in the Northern

> Ireland jurisdiction, allow the state to avoid scrutiny of the entire detention process.[674]

After this decision, the United Kingdom chose to derogate from its international obligations, under article 51 of the ECHR and article 4 of the ICCPR.[675] The ECtHR has subsequently held that a derogation involving seven days without presentment to a court was valid but emphasized that the delay was excessive by only a few days and that the suspects in question had access to counsel after forty-eight hours in detention.[676] Human rights law has therefore been an influential—but not necessarily prohibitive—force in U.K. counterterrorism law.

Conclusion

The law of the United Kingdom has been adapting to the threat of terrorism for centuries.[677] In modern times, it has served its place in the bloody struggle against the IRA[678] and international terrorists emanating from the Middle East.[679] As part of an overall strategy and as a tactic in that struggle, the law of detention has been fortified to allow greater means of detaining terrorist suspects and the ability to hold them for longer periods. It has also allowed for the preventive restraint of individuals suspected of terrorist activity. Modern counterterrorism legislation in the United Kingdom, further, greatly amplifies the investigative detention powers of the government by allowing for longer periods of detention and a longer period of time during which a suspect's access to counsel can be effectively denied. These exceptions to the ordinary criminal process are dramatic in their scope and reflect the recognition that terrorism is a special class of crime for which ordinary procedures are inadequate. It also reflects the view that, in the shadow of terrorism, some ordinary rights must sometimes bend beneath the weight of a greater societal interest—national security.

The enhancements to the ordinary legal system detailed in this chapter were facilitated—at least in part—by the fact that investigative detention already existed as a normal, accepted part of the criminal justice system in the United Kingdom. As demonstrated, the criminal law that prevails in England and Wales, for example, ordinarily allows for a period of investigative detention in which a criminal suspect can be detained and interrogated. The suspect's right to counsel can even be subjected to a form of interference insofar as it can be temporarily postponed in situations of sufficient gravity. The laws permitting prolonged investigative detention for terrorist suspects, therefore, were merely augmenting what already existed rather than fundamentally altering the United Kingdom's existing legal structure. This is in contrast to U.S. law, which, as noted, has an inherent aversion to the practice of investigative detention and has—in the jurisprudence regarding ordinary criminal suspects—erected certain fortifications against the practice.[680]

In spite of their shared legal lineage, it would not be possible to simply graft the system of investigative detention of terrorist suspects that one sees in the United Kingdom onto the U.S. legal system. The fundamental differences in the two criminal justice systems make such a transplant too problematic. What can be done, however, is to isolate those defining characteristics of the United Kingdom's system and explore ways of replicating them within the U.S. legal system in a manner that is constitutionally permissible.

In that regard, the analysis of the laws governing detention in the United Kingdom reveals a formidable legal regime that gives government broad latitude to detain terrorist suspects. This regime consists of three main elements: (1) the ability to stop and arrest a terrorist suspect based on minimal criteria, (2) the ability to hold a terrorist suspect for a prolonged period of time without charge, and (3) diminished protections for terrorist suspects during their period of detention.

Once a person in the United Kingdom is suspected of terrorism, that person can be stopped and searched by the police to discover whether he or she has possession of anything that may constitute evidence that he or she is a terrorist.[681] Should any evidence obtained in the course of that stop and search give rise to the mere suspicion that a person is a terrorist, then the suspect may be arrested.[682] Thereafter, terrorist suspects in the United Kingdom may be detained without charge for twenty-eight days from the time of arrest.[683] Further, a detained suspect is only to receive legal advice in the sight and hearing of a police officer.[684] Further, delays in the exercise of both of these rights may be authorized by a superintendent for up to forty-eight hours (twelve hours more than in regular cases).[685]

This system of investigative detention operates in a manner consistent with the legal tradition that prevails in the United Kingdom and, given the shared legal tradition, might provide some inspiration for counterterrorism legislation in the United States. There is, however, a plurality of possible models for such a regime. Another quite different model is that of the other European comparator, which is the next subject of this book—the Republic of France.

Chapter 5

France

Guillaume Parmentier noted, "France has suffered not one but several types of terrorism in which the players, demands, means, and modus operandi were different."[686] The French experience with political violence is not an altogether recent phenomenon. Some examples of such violence on French soil occurred at least as far back as the nineteenth century.[687] Modern France, however, has had a particularly intense and varied experience with terrorism. The history of the Fifth Republic demonstrates encounters with almost every variety of terrorist group, as well as almost every variety of legislative reaction. The reaction to this problem since the early 1980s has been to target terrorist activity by enhancing the powers and institutions already existing in the organic criminal justice system. In this regard, French laws governing detention have been a central subject of reform.

Overview of the French Criminal System

The French ability to detain and investigate criminal suspects is famously potent. In short, under French law, an initial contact with police through a kind of investigative stop known as a *contrôle d'identité* can lead to the discovery of a criminal offense.[688] In such cases—or where evidence has been otherwise obtained—an investigation is opened and the person may be placed in a period of prolonged police custody called *garde à vue.*[689] At that point, French police have the power to detain a witness for a prolonged period during the preliminary phase of the investigation, without ever charging the individual, before turning over the suspect to the judicial police, who may then hold the suspect for years and continue their investigation up until the time of trial.[690]

To understand how this system works, however, it is important to understand the context of the larger procedural model in which this detention regime operates. French criminal procedure is normally characterized as *inquisitorial* in contrast to the adversarial systems that prevail in the United States and the United Kingdom.[691] This implies a judicial model that assumes a more centralized and institutionalized state role.[692] While French criminal procedure has taken on a number of adversarial elements in recent years, the system nonetheless remains strongly rooted in the inquisitorial model.[693]

> Whilst the UK system focuses very much on the roles of the individual parties, the French legal process continues to have a state-centered conception of justice. During the pretrial phase in particular, the focus of investigation is the offense rather than the suspect. The judge maintains a central role during the investigation. As a *magistrat* representing the public interest (rather than that of the prosecution or defence) she is charged with searching for the truth, gathering evidence which might exculpate as well as incriminate the suspect. The defence rights of the accused have been somewhat neglected, in part because the public orientation of the *magistrat* is considered sufficient protection and also, because the accused has been traditionally seen as an object of the search for truth rather than a party to the proceedings.[694]

It is upon this pretrial phase of the French investigation, and the concomitant mechanisms for detention, that this chapter shall focus. Before thrusting headlong into the topic of French detention, however, it is prudent to briefly overview the basic parameters of that pretrial phase, its main players, and its terminology.

French Pretrial Investigation

Under French criminal law, as with other legal systems, there are different classifications of crime depending on the severity of the conduct: *crimes*, *délits*, and *contraventions*.[695] The most serious offense is known as a *crime* and is the rough equivalent of a felony in American law.[696] *Délits* carry a possible sentence of imprisonment, but are less severe than crimes. At the lowest end of the spectrum are *contraventions*, a classification reserved for petty offenses.[697] Each specific category of crime entails specific procedures and can be determinative not only of the course of the investigation, but also of the permissible parameters of detention. To avoid confusion with the term *crime*, which carries with it a specific meaning in the French context, this chapter shall use the term *offense* when referring generally to violations of the law.

There are two sorts of investigation under the French criminal system. The first is the police investigation and the second is the judicial investigation, or *instruction*. Prior to the judicial investigation, the police receive reports of crimes and conduct the initial inquiries. Depending on the type of crime, the case may remain under police investigation or may be referred to an investigative judge—the *juge d'instruction*—for further investigation.[698] In each sort of investigation, French investigators can employ investigative detention mechanisms that allow for the detention of suspects while investigators ferret out evidence of crime.

Police Investigation

There are four different classifications of investigations under the French system. The preliminary inquiry (*enquête préliminaire*) is a kind of investigation that is possible under any circumstance, regardless of the gravity of the offense.[699] This kind of investigation may be commenced by the *procureur de la République* or simply the police, though the police must thereafter report to the *procureur de la République* if they commence such an investigation on their own.[700] Richard S. Frase has noted that these inquiries are the sole form of investigation for the majority of cases involving traffic violations and other minor infractions. Until recent changes in the law, searches and seizure of evidence during such investigations could not be effected without the written consent of the suspect, and police could not summon witnesses or detain suspects.[701] Current legislation still in place requires citizens to cooperate with the preliminary inquiry and allow searches to be done in preliminary inquiries, in cases of terrorism or narcotrafficking, with judicial authorization.[702]

The investigation into flagrant offenses (*enquête de flagrance*) is a separate sort of investigation. An offense is considered "flagrant" if it is in the process of being committed or has just been committed. An offense is likewise flagrant if, at a time very close to the action of the crime, the suspect is pursued by "a public clamor" or is found in possession of objects, or presents traces or indications of evidence that leads to a belief that he or she participated in the offense.[703] In the event of an offense that is deemed "flagrant," the judicial police may search the scene and seize evidence. Officers may also search the domiciles of all persons who appear to have participated in the offense or who may have evidence and seize any evidence found. They may detain any person on the scene until completion of the investigation, and summon by force and interrogate any person capable of furnishing evidence.[704]

In the majority of French criminal cases, however, the *procureur* directs and oversees the investigation.[705] As the work of the police is placed under his or her direction, he or she may order the opening of an investigation or even delay a full investigation and order a preliminary inquiry.[706]

Judicial Investigation (Instruction)

The two main types of police in France are the administrative police (*police administrative*) and judicial police (*police judiciare*).[707] Administrative police are focused on the prevention of crimes and the maintenance of public order while judicial police are largely responsible for finding criminals once offenses have occurred.[708] Of these two groups, the *police judiciare* conduct the investigations and are granted the primary police powers of detention. The *police judiciare* act pursuant to the orders of the *procureur de la République* or on their own during the preliminary inquiry, but once a judicial investigation has begun, they must act pursuant to the orders of the investigative judge.[709]

Although the judiciary in France has an investigative role, the investigative judge may not, however, investigate on his or her own initiative.[710] Rather, once an offense is committed and evidence of it is brought before the *procureur de la République*, the *procureur* may request a judicial investigation (*instruction judiciaire*).[711] The *procureur* makes the request for an *instruction* to a separate judicial body known as the *Chambre de l'instruction*. That body may then appoint a judge to investigate the matter.[712] It is, thus, only after some evaluation and oversight that such an investigation can be initiated.

The purpose of the *instruction* is to attain enough evidence that the case under investigation can be brought to trial.[713] It generally only takes place for serious offenses such as *crimes* or *délits*. It is obligatory where a *crime* has occurred but may also be used where a *délit* is suspected. It may technically even be used in the case of a *contravention*.[714] Thus, although the judicial investigation is reserved for more serious crimes, it remains technically available for minor matters.[715] Catherine Elliott has noted that the key practical difference between the police investigation and the *instruction judiciaire* is the greater coercive powers given to the investigators in the latter.[716]

> These judges have wide powers. They can visit the scene of the crime, carry out a reconstruction of the offense (when the accused and their lawyer will normally be present), hear witnesses, search and seize property, arrest the person charged, and, most importantly, place them on remand in custody, or release them on bail with conditions imposed. [717]

In the course of the *instruction*, the investigating judge investigates the matters laid out in the *procureur*'s request and has a broad mandate to pursue all possible investigative leads and avenues of inquiry. In this quest, the judge directs a special cadre of police known as the judicial police (*police judiciaire*) who interview witnesses and seek out evidence.[718] That evidence is compiled and given to the investigating judge. If the investigating judge feels the investigation has yielded enough evidence to go forward with a prosecution, the evidence is then sent to the *procureur de la République* for prosecution.[719]

THE FRENCH EXPERIENCE AND THE FRENCH RESPONSE

Jacqueline Hodgson, professor of law at the University of Warwick, has noted that the emphasis of modern French criminal legislation has vacillated between security concerns and concerns associated with individual rights.[720] This vacillation has been motivated by events impacting the French polity at various times in its recent history, including its experience with terrorism.

In the 1950s and the 1960s, France experienced a wave of terrorist attacks linked to Organisation de l'Armée Secrète (OAS), a French anti-independence group with links to the French armed forces, French nationals in Algeria, and Algerians who were dissatisfied with French policies in Algeria.[721] France acted aggressively to counter this phenomenon of terrorism by setting up a "military justice court" to judge cases involving Algeria and terrorism. This special court operated using alternative procedures and no appeal was allowed from convictions it adjudged—even capital convictions.[722] The military justice court operated for only a brief time before encountering judicial resistance from France's Conseil d'Etat, which found its procedures lacking, annulled the *ordonnance* establishing it, and ended its operation. In response, the French government replaced the military justice court with a State Security Court (Cour de Sûreté de l'Etat) in 1963, under the direction of Charles DeGaulle. This second version contained civilian magistrates, as well as military members, and allowed for the possibility of an appeal from convictions it rendered. The Cour de Sûreté de l'Etat continued to operate in this form for decades.[723] Thus, in its early experience with terrorism, France first adopted a procedure that fell largely outside of its organic legal system.

Terrorism linked to Algeria was not, however, the only sort France would encounter. Between 1979 and 1987, France faced yet another source of terrorism from leftist groups. These groups were composed mainly of French citizens and were motivated by a plethora of diverse causes, such as opposition to capitalism, perceived American imperialism,[724] and support for immigrant laborers and workers groups.[725] The most prominent of these was Action Directe, an organization that perpetrated high-visibility attacks on government property and even conducted political assassinations.[726] The violent attacks perpetrated on French soil by this group (and splinter elements) during their existence were numerous. They included the machine-gunning and bombing of government buildings, as well as robberies designed to finance further terrorist activities.[727] The French government's response to Action Directe was quick, utilizing the State Security Court to capture and convict many of the group's leaders.[728]

The most persistent source of terrorism in modern France, however, has been separatist groups advocating independence or autonomy for specific regions.[729] Such groups have also been the least deadly, as their principal targets have been property.[730] The first separatist groups became active in France in 1969, in the form of groups like the National Liberation Front of Brittany (FLB), which focused on inflicting material damage to property that associated with the French state.[731] The FLB was responsible for such attacks as the bombing of several television transmitters in the early and mid-1970s, and the damaging of the Hall of Mirrors at Versailles in 1978.[732] As with Action Directe, most of its members were taken into custody in the early 1980s, and many were convicted by the State Security Court.[733] This course of action against the FLB was rather effective and, as a result, the FLB largely ceased its activity.[734]

Another prominent separatist movement to use terrorist tactics on French soil was the National Front for the Liberation of Corsica (FLNC), which became active in 1976.[735] The FLNC carried out bombings, conducted attacks on politically significant property, and conducted political assassinations.[736] In contrast to other groups, however, commentators note that repressive measures, such as swift police action and the use of the State Security Court, only served to radicalize this group and, thus, proved somewhat ineffective as a countermeasure.[737]

Until the 1980s, the French government combated terrorism with the same instruments and methods that had been used against the OAS in the 1960.[738] In 1981, however, with the regime of Francois Mitterrand in power, France abolished the State Security Court, which had become viewed as a symbol of political oppression.[739] Thereafter, the French government initially took the view that no special legislation was required to address terrorism.[740] Acts of terror or political violence were neither given special status nor addressed by any special procedure or mechanism. The beginning of 1980s would, however, bring a series of events that would alter that view and mark a turning point in the way the French government would deal with terrorist activity.

Notably, on October 3, 1980, a motorcycle loaded with explosives was detonated outside of a synagogue on the Rue Copernic in Paris, killing four people and wounding eleven.[741] Five other attacks on Jewish targets already had been carried out that week.[742] These attacks, which were perpetrated by terrorists from the Middle East, were accompanied by other significant terrorist activity abroad, such as the suicide bombing that killed fifty-eight French troops in Lebanon.[743] This resulted in a public outcry that demanded legislative action. First, the French government enacted the law of February 2, 1981, on Sécurité et Liberté. That law was followed by legislation in 1981 that codified and enhanced police powers to stop individuals and conduct identity checks. Nonetheless, terrorism in France continued unabated.

> An unprecedented terrorist campaign, in terms of its violence, intensity, and form, kicked off in December 1985 with explosions in two Paris department stores. In close succession came the assassination of George Besse, chief executive of Renault and the attack on Interpol, both committed by *Action Directe*, and the kidnapping of twelve French nationals in Lebanon between May 1985 and January 1987. Three waves of terror in February, March, and September of 1986, saw more than twenty attacks that targeted large Paris bookstores, shopping centers, public build-

> ings, high-speed trains, subway stations, and the Rue de Rennes in Paris, causing 230 wounded and thirteen deaths.[744]

In September of 1986, with concerns over terrorism still growing, the French government responded with dramatic counterterrorism legislation that contained fundamental reforms to the domestic French criminal justice system.[745] This legislation was remarkable in that it was the first French legislation to specifically address the concept of terrorism,[746] and, for the first time in French legal history, terrorism was recognized as a distinct criminal act.[747] These reforms also centralized all judicial proceedings relating to terrorism and created a streamlined judicial apparatus for such offenses.[748] New, specialized organs within the French government were created, centralizing all proceedings related to terrorism in the Trial Court of Paris, as well as creating a small section of prosecutors and investigating magistrates who focus exclusively on matters related to terrorism.[749] It also, as discussed more fully later in this chapter, altered the French laws of detention. This new paradigm—a specialized entity within the organic criminal justice system—would define the contemporary French approach to counterterrorism.

The concerns about the dangers of terrorism had produced a dramatic impact on the French criminal justice system. Public outrage had led to greater government power. By 1993, however, the pendulum swung away from issues of security, and the legislative emphasis returned to concerns over individual rights. The Criminal Justice and Human Rights Commission (Commission justice pénale et droits de l'homme), which was chaired by Mireille Delmas-Marty, was formed to examine ways of reconciling French criminal procedure with the European Convention on Human Rights.[750] Its proposals resulted in greater regulation of the detention of suspects by police and the weakening of the police detention powers by requiring that police inform the *procureur* of a person's detention at the beginning of the period of police detention. The 1993 legislation also granted new rights to suspects in detention, such as the right to inform another of one's detention and the right to see a doctor. French suspects were also given greater access to a lawyer during confinement.[751] The strengthening of these rights for criminal suspects represents what Jacqueline Hodgson has called the French concept of *sûreté*—a notion that finds its roots in the 1789 Declaration of the Rights of Man and which concerns the freedom from arbitrary arrest.[752]

The emphasis on *sûreté* and individual liberties would, however, be short-lived. Subsequent terrorist attacks would result in renewed emphasis on national security. In 1994 twelve French nationals were killed in Algeria by a fundamentalist Islamic terrorist group known as the Groupe Islamique Armé.[753] Shortly thereafter, that same group seized an airplane belonging to Air France at an airport in Algiers, demanding the release of two leaders of the Islamic Salvation Front.[754] Then, in 1995, a gas cylinder exploded in the Saint Michel metro station, marking the launch of a series of terrorist attacks on French soil that would kill twelve people and wound 173.[755] Islamic terrorism was making itself known in France and, in keeping with its historical pattern, the French government was, again, swift to respond with strong antiterrorist legislation, which expanded certain terrorism-related provisions of French criminal law.[756]

When the noise subsided and calm was restored, domestic affairs would impact the prevailing mood in France so that individual liberties and abuse of power were again an emergent concern. In 2000, after a number of scandals involving high-ranking politicians, President Jacques Chirac established a Commission de réflexion sur la justice, which was chaired by Pierre Truch, the president of the Cour de Cassation. This commission—and the legislation it inspired—resulted from the desire to bring French law into conformity with the ECHR. Its reforms, thus, further impacted the institution of *garde à vue* by allowing custodial legal advice at the outset of detention, requiring the police to inform the suspect of his or her right to remain silent and requiring the police to advise the suspect of the crime of which he or she is suspected.[757] The power to detain witnesses in police custody was also removed.[758] The star of individual liberties was once again in the ascendant.

Then came September 11, 2001. The reverberations of the explosions in New York would push the pendulum of public concern back toward issues related to security, where it has largely remained. In 2001, with France already experiencing rising crime figures, the shock of the September 11 attacks heightened public concern about crime and terrorism. Thus, in November of 2001, a controversial piece of legislation was passed known as the *loi relative à la sécurité quotidienne*,[759] which enhanced police powers for the purposes of targeting a broad range of crime, including terrorism.

This law would not, however, mark the apogee of this trend in French law. The appetite for greater security measures was unabated and the French political climate became increasingly dominated by national security concerns. The government, in response, focused on augmenting the country's national security apparatus.[760] Then interior minister Nicolas Sarkozy pushed forward numerous pieces of legislation that increased police power. This movement to strengthen police powers resulted in the 2003 *loi pour la sécurité intérieure*, which set out new offenses related to prostitution, begging, and threatening or hostile gatherings, but also repealed the recently enacted requirement that a suspect in detention be informed of his or her right to remain silent.[751] Most recently, in 2006, the French government passed the *loi relative à la lutte contre le terrorism et portant dispositions diverses relatives à la sécurité et aux contrôles frontaliers*, which further augmented the police powers of detention and was designed to specifically address concerns related to terrorism.[762]

Thus, a cursory overview of recent French history reveals frequent and intense confrontations with a wide variety of terrorist organizations. It also reveals France's search for an acceptable means of combating the terrorist phenomenon. The first decades were characterized by the use of a special court with military members and special rules. The last few have been characterized by augmentations of the existing tools available in ordinary French criminal law. A significant aspect of France's recent legislative initiatives has been the enhancement of the regime of law governing detention of terrorist suspects and modifications of criminal law with respect to the nature of detention in terrorist cases.

TERRORISM UNDER FRENCH CRIMINAL LAW

The French definition of *terrorism*, enacted in 1986, is extremely broad.[763] Article 421-1 of the French penal code defines *terrorism* as the commission of certain specified crimes when acting intentionally as part of an individual or collective enterprise having for its goal the disruption of public order by intimidation or terror.[764] These crimes include physical attacks against the life or physical integrity of a person,[765] as well as theft or destruction of property.[766] Crimes like production or possession of explosives and certain weapons are also included under the definition of terrorism.[767] The definition, however, also includes certain acts not normally associated with terrorism, such as certain *infractions en matière informatique* (information technology crimes). An example of the latter would be the possession of falsified identity documents by an individual participating in an organization intending to disrupt public order by intimidation or terror.[768]

As previously noted, legislation in 1996 also made it an act of terror under French criminal law to participate in a group formed with the intent to commit a terrorist act, so long as there are indications of preparation for such an act characterized by material facts.[769] Thus, with an already broad definition of conspiracy in place, the notion of conspiring to commit a terrorist offense became a part of French criminal law. Shapiro and Suzan noted that this notion of conspiracy to commit terrorism as a separate crime allowed investigating magistrates to "link suppression with prevention to ensure that terrorist actions never materialize."[770] This stands in contrast to normal French law, which requires an infraction before a judicial investigation may begin.[771]

All terrorist cases in France are handled by specialized organs within the French government, and all cases related to terrorism are centralized in the Trial Court of Paris, where a small section of prosecutors and investigating magistrates focus exclusively on matters related to terrorism.[772] Such cases are now handled by the Central Antiterrorist Service

(SCLAT) (also referred to as the 14th Antiterrorist Section) in the Cour d'Appel of Paris.[773] The SCLAT is composed of five prosecuting magistrates and four investigative judges.[774] Parmentier noted that this group has responsibility for terrorism cases throughout France and, thus, can demand to examine any matter considered sufficiently sensitive to be judged on a national level.[775] Thus, the same basic paradigm exists for the investigation of terrorist cases as exists in ordinary criminal matters, but the judicial apparatus that will engage in the matter is a specialized one and—as will be demonstrated—one that operates with far greater investigative powers at its disposal.

French Law of Detention

Detaining a person for interrogation is a critical aspect of the French criminal process, as it isolates the suspect so that he or she may be probed for information while preventing the suspect from communicating with others, such as accomplices to the suspected crime.[776] There are three principal means of detention in France of detaining individuals who have not yet been convicted of a crime. They are (1) the identity check procedure known as the *contrôle d'indentité*, (2) the period of police control known as *garde à vue*, and (3) the pretrial period of detention known as *détention provisoire*. On the one hand, the *contrôle d'identité* allows for an individual to be briefly detained for limited purposes, but it can be effected for a wide variety of reasons. *Garde à vue*, on the other hand, allows French authorities to arrest suspects and hold them without charge for a prolonged period of time (normally two days) while police gather evidence to determine whether further investigation or legal action is warranted.[777] *Détention provisoire*, thereafter, allows for detention of an individual prior to trial.[778] The result is a formidable regime of detention that provides French authorities with an effective instrument of counterterrorism.

Contrôle d'Identité

The ability to stop an individual and briefly detain that person for purposes of checking his or her identity is known as the *contrôle d'identité*.

Contemporary French criminal law states that every person found on French territory must possess a form of identification.[779] The judicial police and their agents may stop and verify the identity of any person (a) of whom there are one or more reasons to suspect of committing or attempting to commit an infraction, (b) who is preparing to commit a *crime* or *délit* (c) who seems able to furnish information useful to an investigation into a *crime* or *délit* or (d) who are the object of investigation of a judicial authority.[780] In the event that a person cannot or will not verify his or her identity, that person may be detained and brought under police control for purposes of verification.[781] If the person persists in refusing to verify his or her identity, photographs and digital fingerprints can be taken for purposes of verification.[782] The person may not be detained any longer than is strictly necessary for purposes of learning his or her identity and may not be detained longer than four hours.[783]

The *contrôle d'identité* power was originally granted to police by the *ordonnance du 2 Novembre 1945*, which gave police the authority to verify the status of foreigners in France.[784] The law of June 10, 1983, formally codified this means of detention and created in the *Code de Procédure Pénale*, for the first time, a chapter on *contrôles d'identité*.[785] The newly codified law fixed the time limit for such detention to four hours but expanded the scope of the police power by permitting judicial police to stop anyone (not merely foreigners) for the reasons now set forth in article 78-3 of the *Code de Procédure Pénale*.[786] Thus, what was once a means of verifying the status of foreigners in France was transformed into a general crime prevention tool of general applicability. This represents a considerable development in this form of detention, as it introduced a new, albeit limited, means of detaining individuals in France—including domestic citizens—for the purpose of acquiring information.

A subsequent modification to the law in 1986 enhanced that ability even further by providing that a person may be stopped and his or her identity verified to prevent a breach of public order, notably, to the security of persons and goods.[787] The amendment allowing for a person to be stopped for reasons of public order was specifically designed to eliminate the need for suspicion of some immediate threat to public safety.[788] Thus, rather than suspecting a specific crime or an immediate act, French police need only believe that there is a potential breach of public order. The result is that French law does not require individualized suspicion of a crime or immediate danger in order to stop and briefly detain people on French soil. So long as there is a belief of a potential breach of public order, persons in France can be stopped and placed under the *contrôle d'identité*.[789]

One sees in the French system a distinction from its U.S. and British counterparts in both the power granted to police and the rationale for the stop. The normal ability to stop a person under those other systems previously analyzed is somewhat more limited. U.S. police may, under normal circumstances, only briefly stop those reasonably suspected of a crime and search persons who might pose a danger to the officer. Although this power is quite broad, it still requires some particularized suspicion of criminal activity. Likewise, under PACE, police in the United Kingdom may briefly stop and perform a limited search if there are grounds for suspecting the person has stolen or prohibited articles. The French system, however, allows for someone to be stopped —absent particularized suspicion—and briefly detained by police, or, in certain circumstances, brought back to the police station for purposes of identification.

Garde à Vue

The French legal institution of *garde à vue* entails the temporary detention, surveillance, and interrogation of a suspect at a police station or with the *gendarmerie*.[790] The power to detain someone for investigative purposes was much greater prior to 1958, as there was no law regulating police custody at that time.[791] During that era, both suspects and witnesses could be placed in police custody—though witnesses could only be detained long enough to give a statement.[792] It was only with the enactment of the *Code de Procédure Pénale*, which replaced the older *Code d'Instruction Criminelle*, that a legal basis was given to this police practice.[793] Since then, in contrast to the United States, the French power to hold witnesses has suffered a degree of erosion. Legislation passed in 1993 removed the power to detain witnesses in *enquêtes preliminaries*,[794] though until 2000, witnesses could still be put into police custody for other types of investigations (*enquêtes flagrantes* and *instruction*). Today, witnesses can still be detained by force but only for up to four hours in order to take a statement.[795] This is because the true subject of modern *garde à vue* is not the witness to a crime, but the suspect. The contemporary French Code of Criminal Procedure, thus, states that an officer of the judicial police may, for purposes of an investigation, place any person in *garde à vue* where there is one or more reasons to suspect that he or she has committed or attempted to commit an offense.[796] Mere witnesses to an offense, however, can only be detained long enough for a statement to be taken by the investigating officers.[797]

The question of who a suspect is for purposes of *garde à vue* has been the subject of much legislative attention. A law of June 15, 2000, previously defined a *suspect* as one who has "indications that allows for the presumption that he or she committed or attempted to commit an offense."[798] On March 4, 2002, that definition was modified so that a police officer need only have "one or several plausible reasons to suspect that he or she committed or attempted to commit an offense."[799] This definition is more subjective and, thus, more expansive than its predecessor.[800]

Normally, a person cannot be kept under *garde à vue* more than twenty-four hours. That period of time, however, can be prolonged in ordinary cases for an additional twenty-four hours with the permission of the *procureur de la République*.[801] Thus, in certain circumstances, the normal length of detention for someone suspected of a crime may be extended to forty-eight hours.[802]

Rights During Police Detention

All persons placed under *garde à vue* are immediately informed by an officer or agent of the judicial police of the nature of the crime for which they are being investigated, as well as their right to notification of their placement in *garde à vue*, their right to be examined by a doctor, and their right to consult with an attorney.[803] These rights, discussed more fully in the following pages, constitute the principal rights of a suspect under this form of detention, but they are subject to a variety of exceptions and limitations.

Right to Inform Another of One's Status

All persons in *garde à vue* have the right to inform, via telephone, a person with whom they live, a parent, a brother, a sister, or an employer of the fact that they are in police custody. This right is not absolute and can be disregarded if the judicial officer decides to do so to for necessities of the investigation.[804] Should the judicial officer decide to deprive a suspect of this right, he or she must immediately refer the matter to the *procureur de la République*, who determines whether the right of notification may be disregarded.[805] French law enforcement can, therefore, hold a person and significantly limit the person's ability to inform another of the fact that he or she is detained. In the event the *procureur* decides to disregard this right of notification, the suspect can basically be held incommunicado.

Right to Be Inspected by a Physician

All persons in *garde à vue* have the right to be examined by either a doctor designated by the *procureur de la République* or an officer of the judicial police.[806] In the event that their period of confinement is prolonged, they may demand to be examined a second time.[807] The *procureur* or the judicial officer may also, at any time, designate a doctor to examine the suspect confined.[808] In addition, in the absence of a request to be examined (by the suspect, *procureur*, or police officer), a member of the suspect's family may request an examination to be conducted by either a doctor designated by the *procureur de la République* or an officer of the judicial police.[809]

Right to Counsel

All persons in *garde à vue* have, at the very beginning of the process, the right to consult with an attorney.[810] If there is not a way to contact a chosen lawyer at that time, then he or she may request to be provided one by the *bâtonnier*.[811] The attorney provided will be informed of the nature of the charges against the suspect and may consult with the suspect in conditions guaranteeing confidentiality. The lawyer, however, is not allowed to review the police files, attend the investigation, watch the interrogation, or tell anyone about the interview so long as the suspect is in custody.[812] In addition, the attorney may only consult with the suspect for thirty minutes.[813] If the *garde à vue* is prolonged, then the suspect may again, at the outset of the extended period, request to consult with an attorney.

Under prior legislative schemes, the French Code of Criminal Procedure contained specific time periods that triggered a suspect's right to consult with an attorney. For instance, the Act of 1 March 1993 stated that a suspect had a right to see a lawyer after twenty hours of detention.[814] This was amended by the Act of 15 June 2000, which gave the suspect the right to see an attorney within an hour, then again after twenty hours, then again after thirty-six hours.[815] This was modified again in 2004 to the current paradigm, which allows, in normal cases, for an attorney to see the suspect at the very beginning of the period of detention and then again, in cases of prolongation, after the twenty-fourth hour of detention.[816] This strengthening of the right to consult an attorney in the 2004 legislation, however, did not apply to cases involving suspected terrorism.

Right to Remain Silent

The right to remain silent technically exists under French criminal law insofar as suspects are not required to answer questions posed by law enforcement personnel. Only suspects appearing before an investigative judge, however, are informed of this right—meaning that suspects who are placed under *garde à vue* are not.[817] Exercise of this right can also lead to adverse inferences being drawn at trial:

> The law prescribes that the judges and jurors ask themselves, when deliberating upon their verdict, "what impression the means of defense made upon their reason." If an accused does not respond, or responds partially or implausibly, to incriminating evidence, the effect upon the minds of the judges and jurors is very likely to be adverse to the accused. Where the legal culture encourages responses to officials and where responses are thus expected, it is not difficult for courts to draw adverse inferences from the silence of accused persons, or more particularly the failure to respond to

> official questioning. The legal culture in France would not support a rule, as in some common law jurisdictions, prohibiting comment by a judge or a prosecutor to a jury on the failure of an accused to answer questions from the police or to give evidence. Certainly at hearings in France it is not uncommon to hear the presiding judge inform an accused who is silent on prevaricating under interrogation that the court will draw its own conclusion from such behavior.[818]

Thus, in contrast to the phalanx of rights granted the accused in the United States to shield him or her from police power, the rights of the French detainee are comparatively limited. In further contrast to the United States, where the right to a lawyer is sacrosanct and the invocation of the desire for a lawyer ends the interview, or to the British system, which allows for limited continued interrogation and a brief delay in access to counsel, the French system merely allows one to consult with an attorney prior to the interrogation—and only for thirty minutes. A suspect may access a lawyer thereafter, but only at specific points. The lawyer does not attend the interview, notice of a desire to speak with an attorney does not end the interview, and the attorney is even bound to keep the fact of the investigation confidential so long as the suspect is in custody. Further, although a technical right to silence exists, the suspect does not have to be informed of it.

It is here in the domain of police detention and the rights afforded to a suspect that one sees the greatest contrast with the U.S. and British systems. French police may detain a person so long as there are reasons to suspect a possible violation of the law—and for the express purpose of gathering information. There is no requirement for a warrant, no need for a pretext, and no requirement that the person be a danger of some sort or a flight risk. It is a detention of a suspect for the purpose of carrying out an interrogation—and it may last up to forty-eight hours. In comparison to its Anglo and American counterparts, therefore, the French law of *garde à vue* is an intimidating and potent legal device, even in its ordinary application. It is clearly designed to give police the most power to elicit information while minimizing legal protections available to the accused. It is, further, a mechanism that is well utilized. The use of *garde à vue* is already frequent and is becoming even more so. The number of incidents wherein suspects were subject to *garde à vue* in 2004 was 472,064.[819] Of that number, 386,080 were over twenty-four hours, demonstrating that the prolongation of the duration of detention is also frequent. [820]

Arrest and *Comparution Forcée*

Other means of detaining suspects available to French law enforcement authorities are the powers of arrest and what is known as *comparution forcée*. Where there has been a *crime* or a *délit* that is both flagrant and punishable by imprisonment, French law allows that any person may apprehend the offender and bring him to the nearest police officer.[821] Otherwise, a person may only be arrested on a warrant from either the investigative judge or the presiding judge of the *Chambre de l'instruction*.[822] French authorities may also detain individuals through the process of *comparution forcée* (literally, forced attendance). Pursuant to their powers of forced attendance, authorities in France have the power to have suspects detained and brought before them via the force of a legal instrument known as a *mandat d'amener*. The *mandat d'amener* is given to police, who then must bring the person before the authority that issued it.[823] This can be issued against any person suspected of having committed an offense.[824] This allows the *procureur* or investigative judge to have anyone suspected of having taken part in a flagrant *crime* to be brought immediately before him or her to face questions.[825]

In cases involving a *crime* that is flagrant, if the investigative judge has not already assumed control of the case, the *procureur* may issue a *mandat d'amener* for any person who is suspected of having participated in the offense.[826] In cases where there has been a formal decision to bring a case to trial (*mis en accusation*), an order of *prise de corps* is issued that orders the detention of any accused not already in custody.[827] Such an order can also be issued against an accused who violates the conditions of his or her bail.[828] An order of *prise de corps* can remain effective until such time as the court has reached a final decision.[829]

Détention Provisoire

The legal device of *détention provisoire* was actually known as *détention préventive* before it was renamed by legislation passed in 1970.[830] In spite of the implication of its former name, this means of detention is distinguishable from actual preventive detention in that it has always been considered to be the detention of a suspect prior to trial rather than the indeterminate detention of someone considered dangerous.[831] Its new name, therefore, was an apt redesignation. In spite of its name change, the essence of the device has remained the same—the detention of a suspect under investigation pending trial.[832]

Prior to the 1958 Code of Penal Procedure, French law allowed detention in cases where it was necessitated by "frequent exigencies of public policy or the quest for the truth."[833] The 1958 Code of Penal Procedure formalized this rule of law, stating that "preventative detention is an exceptional measure."[834] Nonetheless, the law of that time still allowed a rather sweeping power of detention in which any suspect facing a term of imprisonment could be placed in detention.[835] That period of detention could not ordinarily exceed a period of two months, but it could be extended for an additional two months if the *procureur de la République* requested an extension from an examining judge.[836] There was no limit to the number of extensions that could be granted.[837]

Not all suspects were, however, doomed to such a fate. For instance, those suspected of only petty offenses could not be placed in detention.[838] In cases where the maximum penalty was less than two years and the suspect was domiciled in France, the suspect could not be detained for longer than five days after his or her first appearance before the examining judge.[839] Likewise, the 1958 Code of Penal Procedure mandated that suspects be released from detention when the suspect was domiciled in (or had a de facto residence in) France and had never been convicted of a *crime* or a *délit correctionel* for which the penalty was imprisonment for a term exceeding three months.[840] Those not entitled to mandatory release could still request release but were not entitled to it.[841]

The current law in France reaffirms that a person under investigation is presumed innocent, but that, in exceptional cases, for the necessity of the investigation or for reasons of security, a person can be placed in *détention provisoire*.[842] Legal reforms in 2000 largely allocated the power to order such detention to the *juge des libertés et de la detention*.[843] This kind of detention is limited to a person being investigated for a *crime* or a *délit correctionel* for which the penalty is three years' imprisonment or more.[844] Further, such detention cannot be ordered unless it is shown that lesser measures (such as *contrôle judiciare*) would be insufficient for the attainment of one of the following objectives: to preserve evidence; to prevent the influencing of witnesses; to prevent confederation between the person under investigation and coconspirators or accomplices; to protect the person under investigation; to guarantee the presence of the person for judicial proceedings; to stop an infraction or prevent its recurrence; and to stop exceptional and persistent threats to public order provoked by the gravity of the infraction, the circumstances of its commission, or the importance of the prejudice caused by the offense.[845] The judge will issue the order for detention after an adversarial hearing in which he or she hears the submissions of the prosecutor, the observations of the person under investigation, and (if applicable) the accused's lawyer.[846]

For cases involving *délits correctionels*, the period of detention may not exceed four months if the person is only being investigated for a crime that carries a maximum penalty of five years and has not been previously convicted and sentenced to over a year in prison.[847] In all other cases, the period of detention may be prolonged by the *juge des libertés et de la détention* after an adversarial hearing (*débat contradictoire*) for an additional four months.[848] The period can still be prolonged thereafter, though the total length of detention should not normally exceed one year.[849] In all cases, the law states that the duration of *détention provisoire* may not exceed a reasonable time. What is considered reasonable depends on the seriousness of the crime and the complexity of the investigation.[850]

Prior to legislation passed in 2000, there was no limit on the period of *détention provisoire* for cases considered *crimes*.[851] Under current law, for cases involving *crimes*, a person may not ordinarily be kept in *détention provisoire* for more than one year, though that period may be prolonged for six months by the *juge des libertés et de la détention* after an adversarial hearing (*débat contradictoire*).[852] This period of detention may be prolonged again but may not exceed two years if the maximum penalty faced by the person being investigated is less than twenty years' imprisonment. Otherwise, the period of detention may be extended to three years—and four if the offense took place outside of French territory.[853] In cases of both *délits correctionels* and *crimes*, the period of detention can be extended even further in certain cases.

In is important to emphasize that *détention provisoire* is a power of the *juge des libertés et la detention* and is linked to the conduct of the judicial investigation. Thus, suspects are not merely warehoused during this period. While in *détention provisoire*, suspects are interrogated and an active investigation into their suspected crime takes place outside their cell walls. Investigators are actively gathering evidence while the suspect is kept under lock and key.[854] This makes *détention provisoire* a powerful investigative device, as it allows for law enforcement to detain the suspect for far longer periods than police may in *garde à vue* and carry on an active investigation without risk of spoliation of evidence. In addition, while a person may generally receive visits and communicate with the outside world while in *détention provisoire*, a suspect may be denied communication with anyone other than an attorney for a period of ten days. This period can be renewed for an additional ten days.[855]

In the area of interrogation, however, the investigative powers of the state during *détention provisoire* become rather limited. Once an investigation is opened, the investigating judge will question the suspect but will first advise the suspect of his or her right to remain silent and that he or she has a right to have his or her attorney present.[856] Thus, *détention provisoire* enables the investigative judge to detain a person for a longer period of time pending trial—but in circumstances in which the detainee has greater rights.

Counterterrorism Enhancements in the French Law of Detention

Contrôle d'Identité

As previously discussed, the *contrôle d'identité* was augmented in 1986 by allowing that a person may be stopped and his or her identity verified to prevent a breach of public order, notably, to the security of persons and goods.[857] This was specifically designed to eliminate the need for suspicion of some immediate threat to public safety and, instead, allow police to briefly detain an individual with only suspicion of a potential breach of public order.[858] Although this broadening of police power occurred during a period of time when the French government was specifically concerned with terrorism and its effects,[859] still no special provision exists for *contrôle d'identité* in cases of terrorism. The length of *contrôle d'identité* and reasons for effecting a stop under its auspices have not been enhanced for terrorism cases, and no special set of rules applies in such matters. Thus, while this is certainly a police power that can be effectively employed for counterterrorism purposes, there is no true augmentation for counterterrorism purposes in the regime of law governing the *contrôle d'identité*.

Garde à Vue

A review of *garde à vue*, however, reveals wide derogation from the general rule. The 1986 antiterrorist legislation expanded *garde à vue* for individuals suspected of terrorist crimes, allowing for an additional forty-eight-hour extension of detention on top of the ordinary forty-eight-hour period that a suspect could already be held without charge.[860] Thereafter, the law of March 9, 2004, enlarged the range of exceptions for *garde à vue* and allowed for prolonged detention for a larger group of offenses. Currently, according to article 706-88 of the French Code of Criminal Procedure, the length of *garde à vue* can be extended for two periods of twenty-four hours each in cases of particularly severe crimes, such as terrorism, torture, and narcotrafficking, after the initial maximum period of police detention has been exhausted.[861] There now exists, therefore, a category of diverse crimes—including terrorism—for which an exception to the forty-eight-hour limit exists and for which the period of *garde à vue* can be extended for an additional forty-eight-hour period.

Although the "exceptional" category of offenses was broadened so that terrorism was no longer the unique trigger for such prolonged detention, the specter of terrorism would still prompt French legislators to expand the length of police detention for terrorist suspects beyond the ranks of other crimes and again grant it its own special status. The legislation of 2006 (*Loi relative à la lutte contre terrorism et portant dispositions diverses relatives à la sécurité et aux contrôles frontaliers*) further augmented the police powers of detention by allowing for another additional forty-eight-hour period of detention in specific terrorism cases.[862] Under current French law, therefore, if the preliminary investigation reveals a serious risk of an imminent act of terrorism on French soil or elsewhere, or if the investigation reveals that that the necessities of international cooperation make it imperative, the *juge des libertès* can prolong the period of *garde à vue* in terrorist cases for an additional twenty-four hours. This twenty-four-hour period can be extended once. Thus, two decades after the initial forty-eight-hour extension of *garde à vue* in terrorism cases, the current regime of French law allows for a terrorist suspect to be held in *garde à vue* for a period of up to 144 hours (six days).[863]

Rights During Police Custody

Another aspect of *garde à vue* that is exceptional insofar as terrorism is concerned is the manner in which a suspect is afforded his or her right to counsel. As previously noted, the right to consult with an attorney during *garde à vue* is a recent innovation that was introduced into the French criminal process in 1993.[864] In normal cases, an individual in *garde à vue* has a right to consult with an attorney at the very beginning of the period of detention and then again, in cases of prolongation, after the twenty-fourth hour of detention.[865] In cases of terrorism and narcotrafficking, however, the individual may not consult with an attorney until the seventy-second hour (after the second prolongation of detention.)[866] Thus, terrorism suspects will not be afforded the same rights as ordinary suspects in this regard for at least three days.

It is also worth noting a certain change that does not apply specifically to terrorism, but which has been effected in recent national security legislation. The 2003 *loi pour la sécurité intérieure* had a much broader impact than crimes involving terrorism, setting out new offenses related to prostitution, begging, and threatening or hostile gatherings.[867] The most significant aspect of this law vis-à-vis detention, however, is that it repealed the requirement that a suspect be informed of his or her right to remain silent.[868] Hodgson elaborated on the effect of this reform:

> In the vast majority of cases, this means that there is no requirement to inform the suspect of her right to remain silent during the investigation against her. In the small minority of cases (less than 5 percent) where suspects are investigated under the *instruction* procedure, they will be informed of their right to silence once brought before the *juge d'instruction*, but only after having been detained and interrogated by the police for up to 48 hours, or four days in very serious cases.[869]

Accordingly, the right to remain silent under French law exists, but suspects will not, in the majority of cases, be notified of it. The obvious implication of this is that suspects will be more likely to speak to investigators when questioned and provide information about criminal activity.

Détention Provisoire

As noted, legislation passed in 2000 actually curbed detention in remand in France by imposing limits on the amount of time a person could be detained prior to trial.[870] French authorities still, however, have broad latitude to hold suspects in terrorism cases. Although, under current law, for cases involving *crimes*, a person may not ordinarily be kept in *détention provisoire* for more than one year, and that period may be prolonged for six months by the *juge des libertés et de la détention* after an adversarial hearing (*débat contradictoire*).[871] This period of detention may be prolonged again but may not exceed two years if the maximum penalty faced by the person being investigated is less than twenty years' imprisonment. Otherwise, if the maximum penalty faced by the person being investigated is twenty years' imprisonment or more, the period of *détention provisoire* may be extended to three years. The delay may then be extended to four years if the offense took place outside of French territory, as well as for certain enumerated crimes, including narcotrafficking and terrorism.[872]

Thus, as with *garde à vue*, expanded governmental powers exist for *détention provisoire* in terrorism cases—but along with a host of other crimes that are deemed significant. Unlike *garde à vue*, however, the period of time a suspect may remain in *détention provisoire* undergoing investigation is startling. A suspect may remain in French detention for years while investigators work to unearth evidence of an offense. It is, therefore, arguably the most potent (and most alarming) feature of the French detention regime.

Vigipirate

Lastly, one cannot ignore the French national security legislation called "Vigipirate." This legislation, which was conceived during the wave of left-wing terrorism in the 1970s, allows the French government to mobilize law enforcement, customs, intelligence agencies, and—if required—the military in order to better respond to threats to national security and provide security for critical infrastructure.[873] It also increases the ability of law enforcement agents to search for evidence related to terrorism. As W. Jason Fisher explained,

> Vigipirate allows authorities to conduct bag and body searches and limited forms of inquiry at designated public places, and to extend such search power to private security firms and national rail service employees. The Vigipirate plan also grants the *procureur de la République* the power to authorize the judicial police—the law enforcement division tasked with assisting the judiciary—to search vehicles in public areas where no criminal offense is being perpetrated, so long as such searches are tied to an investigation relating to terrorism. Moreover, under Vigipirate, the judicial police may search a vehicle in a public area without authorization from the *procureur de la République* if "plausible grounds" exist to suspect persons inside the vehicle of attempting, having attempted, or having already carried out a criminal offense.[874]

French authorities also possess enhanced abilities to conduct searches in times of heightened risk. This, of course, may lead to evidence that can trigger the robust detention provisions at the disposal of French law enforcement. Together with the investigative detention regime detailed in this chapter, it creates a formidable counterterrorism tool.

THE USE OF DETENTION IN COUNTERTERRORISM

The French laws of detention have found direct application in counterterrorism operations and have been used to great effect. The ability to easily detain and freely interrogate terrorist suspects has had the dual effect of bringing terrorists to justice and supplying useful intelligence for the continuing struggle against other terrorists. An example of the use of their detention regime is Operation Chrysanthemum, which was the French government's response to the abduction of three consular officials in Algeria.[875] Over a period of two days, 110 people in France were questioned and eighty-seven were taken into custody. This operation, which only resulted in the incarceration of three people, was denounced by some as an overaggressive reach by the French government.[876] However, the interior minister at the time, Charles Pasqua, regarded the interrogations as sending a message to extremists that the French government was aggressively seeking to suppress the activity of Islamic terrorists in France.[877]

Another example of the use of French detention laws in a counterterrorism effort is the operation against the Chalabi network, a critical support cell for Algerian fighters.[878] In the effort to cripple this group, French law enforcement arrested ninety-three people, released fifteen, and held the remaining seventy-eight for trial. The impact of this effort was the dismantling of the Chalabi network in a very short time.[879] Jeremy Shapiro and Bénédicte Suzan noted that such arrests were possible due to the French laws that allow authorities to arrest suspects and hold them at their disposition without charge while evidenceis gathered.[880]

The ability to arrest and detain individuals not only assisted in the targeting of those individuals but also informed French law enforcement's understanding of the threat they faced, and it allowed French authorities to "connect the dots" and understand the relationship between various terrorist cells operating on their soil and abroad.[881]

> In this regard, arresting a large number of people, in view of the magistrates, makes it possible to carry out corroborated interrogations to maintain knowledge of perpetually evolving networks. Thus, for example, the arrests in 1998 permitted authorities to prevent the attacks planned on the Football World Cup, one of which was intended for State de France, the new and highly visible stadium built for the World Cup Final.[882]

French laws of detention, therefore, have played an important role in their counterterrorism effort, allowing for the targeting and prosecution of specific terrorist organizations, as well as allowing for the gathering of intelligence vital to stopping future attacks.

Implications on International Human Rights Law

Unlike the United States and the United Kingdom, which require the enactment of legislation in order to incorporate international law, France has a "monist" constitutional system under which conventions like the ICCPR and the ECHR are automatically enforceable in domestic courts.[883] Nonetheless, the incorporation of the ECHR has not served to displace the French regime of investigative detention.[884] As noted, the ECtHR has never articulated an exact limit on the acceptable length of pre-charge detention, nor has it elaborated an exhaustive list of grounds for which such detention is permissible.[885] The practice of investigative detention, therefore, is not foreclosed by the ECHR or its jurisprudence.

Likewise, neither the ECHR nor its jurisprudence disallows the drawing of an adverse inference from a suspect's silence. Commentators note, "It is clear, therefore, that the Court does not consider that the drawing of inferences from an accused's silence is in itself incompatible with article 6, as long as judicial safeguards operate to ensure fairness."[886] Nonetheless, Hodgson has noted that France's criminal procedure is the frequent subject of condemnation by the ECtHR for various reasons, including, but not limited to, the length of detention pending trial and inadequate legal aid.[887] For instance, in *Tomasi v. France*, the ECtHR considered the case of a terrorist suspect accused of involvement in an attack linked to the Corsican

National Liberation Front, which led to the death of a French soldier.[888] The suspect's pretrial detention lasted for five years and seven months.[889] In finding such a delay violative of the ECHR, the court noted that, not only had the reasons for denying requests for release largely lost their relevance and importance as time went by, but also the French authorities had failed to handle the proceedings expeditiously. Specifically, the court found that there were two instances of unjustified delay during the preliminary investigation—one for fourteen months and another for twenty-three months.[890] The ECtHR articulated its approach as follows:

> The persistence of reasonable suspicion that the person arrested has committed an offence is a condition *sine qua non* for the validity of the continued detention, but, after a certain lapse of time, it no longer suffices; the Court must then establish whether the other grounds given by the judicial authorities continued to justify the deprivation of liberty. Where such grounds were "relevant" and "sufficient", the Court must also ascertain whether the competent national authorities displayed "special diligence" in the conduct of the proceedings.[891]

Thus, in finding that France had violated article 5(3) of the ECHR, the ECtHR has held—while specifically looking at the French system—that mere suspicion is not enough to continue holding a person beyond an initial arrest. Further, even when continued detention is valid, national authorities must proceed expeditiously with the criminal proceedings.[892] "Consequently, Article 5(3) requires that there must be a 'special diligence' in bringing the case to trial if the accused is detained. A detained person is entitled to have the case given priority and conducted with particular expedition."[893]

The impact of the *Tomasi* case was the institution of reforms in France, such as the introduction of the *juge des libertés et de la détention* to decide issues of detention during investigation.[894] As previously noted, prior to legislation passed in 2000, there was no limit on the period of *détention provisoire* for cases considered *crimes*.[895] After the *Tomasi* case, reforms were instituted so that, for cases involving *crimes*, a person may not ordinarily be kept in *détention provisoire* for more than one year, though that period may be prolonged for six months by the *juge des libertés et de la détention* after an adversarial hearing (*débat contradictoire*).[896] This period of detention may be prolonged again but may not exceed two years if the maximum penalty faced by the person being investigated is less than twenty years' imprisonment. Otherwise, the period of detention may be extended to three years—and four if the offense took place outside of French territory.[897]

Another key case involving the French system was brought by a Moroccan/Dutch national named Ahmed Selmouni, who was arrested on drug charges and held in custody on the outskirts of Paris for four days.[898] During his period of *garde à vue*, Selmouni was physically abused and eventually had to be hospitalized.[899] During the course of his detention, he was severely beaten, forced to run along a corridor with police officers on either side tripping him, was invited to suck a police officer's penis, was urinated upon, and was threatened with a syringe.[900] The ECtHR unanimously held that this constituted torture, making France only the second country in Europe (the first was Turkey) to be so condemned for torture.[901] Thus, it is not only the length of detention that has aroused the ire of the ECtHR, but the conduct of police during those periods of detention.

France does take action in response to decisions (and condemnation) of the ECtHR—and such condemnation has been frequent.[902] Those actions have served to accommodate the provisions of the ECHR to an extent, but, as seen from the analysis in this chapter, France retains an impressively potent investigative detention regime. The extent of the pretrial detention power in such a regime is likely to produce continued conflict with the ECHR. As Hodgson noted,

> It is this pre-trial state of the criminal process that we see most clearly the tension between the demands of conformity with the principles and guarantees of the ECHR and the desire to retain a broadly inquisitorial structure which has at its centre the ideal of the judicially supervised investigation.[903]

CONCLUSION

French legislation has consistently recognized the need for special rules to combat the phenomenon of terrorism, even as its domestic criminal courts took the lead in the fight. In that struggle, the law of detention has occupied a significant place and has been continuously enhanced to form a powerful weapon for law enforcement. Suspects can be detained, held, and interrogated for prolonged periods of time without being charged, without access to an attorney, and without being advised of any eventual right to access an attorney. The laws governing detention in France contain exceptional rules allowing for greater governmental power in the pursuit of terrorist suspects, the cumulative effect of which is a potent counterterrorism tool.

Although *garde à vue* stands as the only variety of detention for which a "counterterrorism exception" exists, a discernable trend toward enhancement of detention powers is evident in France. These enhancements were motivated by concerns over terrorism—a fact evident from the review of French events at the time, as well as by the express mention of terrorism in the enacted laws. The strengthening of these three distinct yet interrelated forms of detention creates an overall effect that is significant in the aggregate, creating a rather formidable detention regime. The effect can be a long and seamless period of detention. Consider Bron McKillop's description of the detention process in a French homicide case:

> The prosecutor, having been notified of the garde à vue had come to an end and that the suspect was being brought to his office at the court house (cite judiciare) requested, by a requisitoire introductif, that the investigating judge on duty that week (also with an office in the courthouse) investigate the "serious presumptions" of pre-meditated homicide against the suspect and issue a warrant for his detention. The suspect was accordingly taken directly before the investigating judge for a "first appearance interrogation" (interrogatoire de premiere comparution). Also present at this interrogation were an assigned lawyer (avocat) representing the suspect and a recording clerk (greffier). The gendarmes, who had been involved in the garde à vue and who had escorted the

> suspect to the courthouse, were excluded from the interrogation. The investigating judge first confirmed the identity of the suspect. He then informed him that he was being charged (inculpe) with the offenses specified by the gendarmerie. He also advised him that he was free not to make any statement.
>
> . . .
>
> The defendant's statement, in a form agreed upon between the defendant and the investigating judge, was typed up by the greffier and signed by the defendant, the investigating judge and the greffier. The defendant was then taken to the local gaol where he remained, under an order of the investigating judge for his "provisional detention", renewed after the first twelve months, until the hearing of the case more than 21 months later.[904]

In such a case, the initial stop that triggered the twenty-one-month period of detention prior to trial could have been effected merely because a policeman suspected a potential breach of public order.[905] This emphasizes not only the length one may be detained prior to trial in France but also the ease with which such lengthy detentions can be initiated. Had McKillop's example been a terrorism case, rather than a homicide case, the periods of detention could have been far longer. Nonetheless, and in spite of the profound procedural dissimilarities, the regime of counterterrorism law in France reflects the same basic elements found in the U.K.'s investigative detention regime: the ability to stop and arrest a terrorist suspect based on minimal criteria, the ability to hold a terrorist suspect for a prolonged period of time without charge, and diminished protections for terrorist suspects during their period of detention.

Interestingly, the British government has taken a hard look at ways of incorporating elements of the French system into its own. Part of the allure to the British is the role that magistrates play and the significant powers of investigative detention concomitant to the French paradigm. An article in *The Economist* noted that

> [s]ome British officials have been looking with envy at civil-law countries like France, where the criminal-justice system allows

> detention for months, even years, after a suspect has been formally "placed under investigation", but not yet charged. Police can also continue to interrogate suspects during that time.[906]

A 2007 report on the subject for the Home Office, however, noted the following:

> There are significant cultural and constitutional differences between the French and English criminal justice systems, but one is not necessarily more effective than the other. A fundamental conclusion of this study is that if we were to try and emulate the magistrate system here, we would need to import the system in its entirety rather than borrow and graft certain elements on to our [criminal justice system]. This would require fundamental changes to our adversarial, common law tradition.[907]

The same is true of importing such methods to the United States, making use of French criminal procedure as a model problematic. As with the United Kingdom, this seeming incompatibility is cause for both regret and relief. Such significant government power to detain is not necessarily desirable in all societies. Some feel that incorporating such power would be deleterious to legal traditions that center on the freedom of the individual.[908] There is, further, room for concern when examining the French experience. Exceptions made for purposes of counterterrorism were soon adopted for other crimes, such as drug trafficking, thus normalizing the exception to a degree. This could be seen as proof that, once the decision is made to erode rights to a small degree, the torrent soon opens to encompass a greater range of freedom than was originally anticipated.

TABLE 1. Comparative analysis of investigative detention powers.

	United States	United Kingdom	France
Ability to stop and search ordinary suspect	Need reasonable suspicion of criminal activity	Need reasonable grounds for believing suspect has stolen or prohibited articles	Need one or more reasons to suspect criminal activity, the ability to furnish useful information, or potential breach of public order
Ability to stop and search terrorist suspect	Need reasonable suspicion of criminal activity	Need reasonable suspicion suspect is a terrorist	If suspect cannot verify identity, he or she may be brought back to station to have identity verified
Other special abilities to stop and search	Suspicionless searches authorized in "critical zones" and where "special needs" apply	With written authorization, can stop and search vehicles or pedestrians without suspicion in specified places for up to 30 hours	Vigipirate searches of bodies and private vehicles without need for approval of procureur
Ability to arrest without warrant	Need probable cause of a crime	Need reasonable suspicion suspect is in the process of committing an offense, is about to commit an offense; or has committed an offense,	Need one or several plausible reasons to suspect that he or she committed or attempted to commit an offense
Maximum period of pre-charge detention in ordinary cases	48 hours, but must proceed to magistrate without unnecessary delay	Normally 48 hours, extendable up to 96 hours (4 days)	48 hours
Maximum period of pre-charge detention in terrorism cases	48 hours, but must proceed to magistrate without unnecessary delay	Extendable up to 28 days	144 hours (6 days)

(*continued on next page*)

TABLE 1. (*continued*)

	United States	United Kingdom	France
Maximum period of detention in remand in ordinary cases	70 days, but can be extended or prolonged	182 days, but prosecution may apply for an extension	Normally 1 year
Maximum period of detention in remand in terrorism cases	70 days, but can be extended or prolonged	182 days, but prosecution may apply for an extension	4 years
Other alternative forms of detention	Material witness statute	Control orders	None
Right to remain silent	Exists with few exceptions	Exists, but adverse inferences can be drawn from silence	Exists, but suspect need not be informed of it
Right to counsel	Exists and is absolute	Exists, but in cases of serious arrestable offenses can be delayed for 36 hours	Exists, but limited to brief and intermittent consultation
Detention rights in terrorism cases	Unchanged	Advice of counsel can be subject to monitoring and can be delayed for 48 hours	Right to counsel can be delayed for 72 hours

Chapter 6

Conclusion

The practice of questioning and examining a source to obtain the maximum amount of usable, reliable information in the least amount of time is a fundamental element of counterterrorism.[909] As such, detention and interrogation of terrorist suspects are considered critical to the gathering of timely, reliable information—information that is of key importance for national security purposes.[910] The ability to hold a suspect for a period of time while minimizing the external influences on the interrogation process serves to maximize the quality and quantity of information obtained.[911] While this is important for intelligence-gathering purposes, it is equally important for law enforcement agencies, which must complete an investigation and attain enough evidence to convict a suspect, disrupt ongoing terrorist operations, and avert further attacks. A review of the experiences and legislative responses of the United States, the United Kingdom, and France demonstrates that the ability to detain terrorist suspects has been central to each country's counterterrorism efforts.

On the international plane, while there are generally accepted due process requirements, there is no objection to the practice of investigative detention as a part of a nation's criminal procedure. Investigative detention is not incompatible with the U.S. obligations under the ICCPR per se,[912] nor is there a general trend against it under international human rights law. Such detention is permissible so long as it is not arbitrary, it is based on grounds and procedures established by law, information of the reasons for detention are given to the suspect, courts are in control of the detention, and compensation is available in the case of a breach.[913] Further, delays before presentment to a judge must not exceed "a few days."[914] Given those guidelines, the task before policy makers and legislators, therefore, is to build a legal framework that allows for such interrogation within the context of domestic law without transgressing international human rights law or offending domestic standards, which would thereby jeopardize the possibility of criminal punishment for the suspect.

This task is especially challenging in the United States, where contemporary jurisprudence indicates that investigative detention is anathema to U.S. criminal law. An analysis of the existing legal apparatus, however, calls such blanket assertions into doubt—especially when taking into account much of the legal maneuvering in post–September 11 America. Even so, the laments of its foremost law enforcement officials, such as Mukasey—a district court judge with experience in terrorism cases who became a U.S. attorney general—express the need for a legal architecture that provides U.S. law enforcement with a more capable investigative detention mechanism. Simultaneously, one hears a gnawing uncertainty regarding the continued application of statutes which have been used to approximate one.

> Perhaps the world's greatest deliberative body (the Senate) and the people's house (the House of Representatives) could, while we still have the leisure, turn their considerable talents to deliberating how to fix a strained and mismatched legal system, before another cataclysm calls forth from the people demands for hastier and harsher results.[915]

Mukasey, in his public plea for change, expressly noted that part of the problem in the United States is that its criminal law lacks "a statute that authorize[s] investigative detention on reasonable suspicion, of the sort available to authorities in Britain and France, among other countries."[916] The analysis of those two systems reveals a multitude of differences in the way criminal justice is conceived, how suspects are detained, and how suspects are questioned. In spite of those differences, however, one can discern from them some basic elements of a regime of investigative detention: the ability to stop and arrest a terrorist suspect based on minimal criteria, the ability to hold a terrorist suspect for a prolonged period of time, and diminished protections for terrorist suspects during their period of detention.

Regarding the ability to stop and arrest a suspect based on minimal criteria, the analysis demonstrates that in the United Kingdom a terrorist suspect can be stopped and searched by the police based upon mere suspicion that the person is a terrorist, in order to discover whether he or she has possession of anything that may constitute evidence that he or she is a terrorist.[917] Should any evidence that was obtained in the course of that stop and search (or any evidence independent of that event) give rise to the mere suspicion that a person is a terrorist, the suspect may then be arrested.[918] Likewise, across the Channel in France, the procedures for *contrôle d'identité* allow that a person may be stopped and his or her identity verified based solely upon suspicion of a potential breach of public order.[919] This initial contact with police through a *contrôle d'identité* can easily lead to the discovery of a criminal offense.[920] Moreover, in order to place a suspect in *garde à vue*, a French police officer need only have "one or several plausible reasons to suspect that he or she committed or attempted to commit an infraction."[921]

Thus, one sees in the investigative detention regimes of both the United Kingdom and France the ability of law enforcement to take some degree of physical control over terrorist suspects (in both the initial stop and the actual arrest) based upon minimal criteria—a degree of permissiveness that makes detaining terrorist suspects easier.

The second element of the analyzed investigative detention regimes is the ability to detain a terrorist suspect for a prolonged period of time for the purpose of investigation. In the United Kingdom, for instance, after being stopped, the terrorist suspect may be detained without charge for twenty-eight days from the time of arrest—purely for investigative purposes—during which time the police conduct an investigation while holding the suspect safely under their guard.[922] A plethora of oversight and safeguards are built into this system to prevent abuse and to assuage concerns of government abuse.[923] French counterterrorism legislation, likewise, allows police to place any suspect in *garde à vue* for six days—held without charge and subject to interrogation without the presence of an attorney.[924] At that point, French police have the power to detain a witness for a prolonged period during the preliminary phase of the investigation, without ever charging the individual, before turning over the suspect to the judicial police. Thereafter, for the necessity of the investigation or for reasons of security, a person can be placed in *détention provisoire.*[925] For cases involving serious offenses, such as terrorism, a person may be kept in *détention provisoire* for up to three years—and up to four years if the offense took place outside of French territory.[926] All the while, investigative judges may actively investigate the suspect's case. This gives French authorities enormous investigative latitude and enables them to isolate the suspect and disrupt his or her operations while building a case that will lead to criminal punishment. Thus, in both the United Kingdom and France, law enforcement authorities may hold an individual in police custody for a prolonged period of time for the purpose of conducting an investigation.

The third common element of the investigative detention regimes outlined in this book is the diminished level of the protections given to terrorist suspects while in custody. For instance, U.K. legislation grants terrorist suspects the right to a legal advisor, but this right can be suspended for up to forty-eight hours and, when it is allowed, it can be ordered that a detained suspect is only to receive legal advice in the sight and hearing of a police officer.[927] In France, similarly, an individual in *garde à vue*—under normal circumstances—only has a right to consult with an attorney at the very beginning of the period of detention and then again, in cases of prolongation, after the twenty-fourth hour of detention.[928] In cases of terrorism and narcotrafficking, however, the individual may not consult with an attorney until the seventy-second hour (after the second prolongation of detention).[929] Further, criminal suspects in France do not have to be informed of their right to remain silent. In both the United Kingdom and France, therefore, terrorist suspects have diminished legal protections while in custody—granting investigators greater access to them and increasing the ability of investigators to conduct effective interrogations.

Existing U.S. Law in Direct Comparison

The laws of the European comparators, which are the subject of this book, are impressive in the amount of investigative power they grant. But how potent are those powers in comparison to the ability of U.S. law enforcement to detain and interrogate terrorist suspects? The assessment of the relative capability of U.S. criminal law demonstrates that the ability of U.S. law enforcement to detain terrorist suspects, while not insignificant, is appreciably weaker.

The Ability to Stop and Arrest Terrorist Suspects Based on Mere Suspicion

Initial Stops and Searches

As previously noted, police in the United States normally have the power to stop individuals they suspect of criminal activity for brief questioning and a limited search. This ability to stop and search—in the ordinary case—is based on reasonable suspicion of a crime and the need to protect the officer from harm.[930] Jurisprudence has required that the stop and search be temporary, last no longer than is necessary to effect the purpose of the stop, and employ the least intrusive means available to verify or dispel the officer's suspicion.[931] An analysis of U.S. case law governing initial stops and searches, however, demonstrates that police in the United States are given a great degree of latitude in this regard—and so long as a police officer can articulate some reason for suspicion that a person might be engaged potentially illegal activity (remember that the suspects in *Terry* were merely pacing back and forth in front of a store, peering into the window, and periodically conferring with one another), that person may be stopped, questioned, and even subjected to a cursory search. Thereafter, police in the United States may arrest a suspect without a warrant—but only if the initial stop and cursory search has revealed probable cause to believe that the suspect has committed a crime.[932]

The limitations on U.S. law enforcement in this regard are even more elastic in circumstances involving matters of national security. For instance, suspicionless searches and seizures have been allowed in "critical zones" and in those "special circumstances" cases involving a "closely guarded category of constitutionally permissible suspicionless searches."[933] Moreover, terrorism is a consistently recurring example of that extraordinary class of criminal activity for which such suspicionless seizures are appropriate.[934] U.S. criminal law, therefore, while containing limits and restraints on police action, actually grants law enforcement authorities a rather generous amount of power to stop and question individuals—especially where issues like terrorism are concerned.

To be sure, these U.S. police powers are different from those of their European counterparts. The laws of the United Kingdom allow a person to be stopped and searched based on the suspicion that the person is a terrorist—a stop based on a suspicion regarding the status of the individual rather than the person's activities. France, on the other hand, allows police to briefly stop a person based on the potential breach of public order, rather than the suspicion of a specific act that U.S. law requires.[935] Neither U.K. nor French law, therefore, requires suspicion of a particular crime in order to briefly detain a terrorist suspect. Nonetheless, the rather low level of suspicion required under U.S. law, the manner in which criminal suspicion can be built upon rather vague criteria, and the latitude afforded to police officers under the jurisprudence makes this almost a distinction without a difference. Further, the permissibility of investigative stops without particularized suspicion in "critical zones" and in situations where "special needs," such as national security, are implicated gives U.S. law enforcement as much authority as that given to police in the United Kingdom to conduct limited, suspicionless searches under PACE. It is, therefore, reasonable to conclude that, in the area of initial stops and searches, U.S. law is roughly on par with its European counterparts.

Arrest

It is in the area of arrest (actually putting on the handcuffs and taking the suspect into custody) that the comparative weakness of U.S. law begins to become more evident. While, as discussed, law enforcement agents in the United Kingdom and France can conduct an arrest of a terrorist suspect based on reasonable suspicion, U.S. law still requires probable cause to effect and arrest—a higher standard than reasonable suspicion and one that requires more evidence.[936]

As demonstrated, U.S. law has found an adaptation that allows it to somewhat approximate a lower standard for arrest via the material witness statute, which allows for the detention of an individual when it can be shown that, based on probable cause, the witness in question has material information relevant to a criminal matter and his or her presence cannot be attained through a subpoena.[937] As noted, this changes the inquiry from "what has he or she done?" to "what might he or she know?" and, therefore, lessens the burden of requiring probable cause to effect an arrest. Otherwise stated, the "material witness" can be picked up based on probable cause that he or she has information of an ongoing criminal matter rather than actual involvement in the crime.

While a true comparison of these various standards is difficult, it is worth noting that—even under the material witness statute—law enforcement agents in the United States are required to show probable cause of *something.* In contrast, police in the United Kingdom and France are able to arrest a terrorist suspect based on reasonable suspicion. Not even the more permissive provisions of the material witness statute allow such action in the United States. In the realm of effecting an arrest, therefore, U.K. and French law still grants greater power to law enforcement agents than that available under U.S. law.

The Ability to Hold Terrorist Suspects for the Purpose of Investigation

In this second category—holding terrorist suspects for the purposes of investigation—U.S. law becomes appreciably weaker than that of the United Kingdom or France. Aside from the generally more onerous requirements for arrest, U.S. law further complicates detention of suspects by requiring early judicial intervention. Arrested suspects in the U.S. must be promptly brought before a magistrate after arrest to be arraigned, and "[w]hen delay in presenting the arrestee is for the purpose of extracting a confession, the delay is considered unreasonable and any statements or confession obtained during the delay will be suppressed."[938] Even if a suspect is arrested as a material witness, he or she may only be detained thereafter if, following a hearing, a judicial officer concludes that no condition or set of conditions will reasonably assure the witness' presence at trial.[939] This is obviously in contrast to the ability of police in the United Kingdom to detain terrorist suspects without charge for twenty-eight days from the time of arrest purely for investigative purposes[940] or the French ability to hold a person in *garde à vue* for six days before judicial intervention.[941]

Nonetheless, there are some exceptions to the U.S. rule—even in the context of criminal law. For instance, the Omnibus Crime Control and Safe Streets Act carved out a safe harbor that protects the admissibility of those statements made during a six-hour delay prior to bringing an arrestee before a magistrate, [942] thus making it permissible to delay presentment to a magistrate for at least six hours. The effect of this is to allow, in the context of a normal federal criminal investigation, a legitimate six-hour investigative period. Even so, this period of time is obviously far shorter than that granted to investigators in the United Kingdom and France—and there is no law in place allowing for its prolongation in cases involving national security or other exigencies. Accordingly, U.S. law is considerably less accommodating in the area of holding terrorist suspects for the purposes of investigation.

What About the Material Witness Statute?

The issue of judicial intervention aside, U.S. law might be seen as giving law enforcement greater ability to detain terrorist suspects than that allowed by U.K. law (under which a terrorist suspect may only be detained without charge for twenty-eight days from the time of arrest)[943] or that allowed by the French power of *garde à vue*, under which the *juge des libertès* can only authorize police detention for up to 144 hours (six days).[944] This is because such time constraints are routinely surpassed under the material witness statute.[945] It is also worth noting that, to the extent it can be used against mere witnesses, it gives greater power to detain witnesses than is found even in France, where witnesses can be detained by force, but only for up to four hours, in order to take a statement.[946] This might be seen as reason to believe the material witness statute has short-circuited the strictures of U.S. criminal law and has even surpassed those powers granted under European law.

As previously noted, however, early judicial intervention—even for material witnesses—prevents the statute from being a true approximation of the investigative detention regimes in Europe. Further, as Attorney General Mukasey has opined, the use of the material witness statute is problematic, as the government only has a limited time after the apprehension of the suspect to choose to allow the suspect to testify, prosecute him or her, or release him or her.[947] As discussed, the procedural rules that govern the use of the material witness statute keep a steady stream of pressure on federal authorities to release material witnesses through the requirement of a hearing, the ability of material witnesses to motion for their release, and the requirement of biweekly reports stating why such witnesses cannot be released or deposed. Moreover, as discussed, there is also the subtle hint from the Second Circuit that courts will not permit the misuse of the material witness statute if it is found that the person is being detained for suspected criminal activity for which probable cause has not yet been established.[948] This could expose the government to the argument that its use of the material witness statute to effect investigative detention is a sort of shadow play—a pretence supported only by an artificial architecture that is too tenuous to sustain convictions.

Accordingly, U.S. law, in the realm of holding terrorist suspects for the purposes of investigation—even when taking the material witness statute into consideration, does not grant to U.S. law enforcement agents the sort of power available to those in the United Kingdom or France. And while the material witness statute grants U.S. authorities a certain degree of flexibility, it is far from being a true investigative detention regime of the sort found in Europe.

Diminished Protections for Terrorist Suspects

Furthermore, there are drastic differences in the relative powers of police during the periods of detention insofar as U.K. and French police have far greater access to their detainees and the ability to interact with them (to varying degrees) without the presence of counsel.[949] In contrast, under U.S. law, there are no diminished protections for terrorist suspects—even those being detained under the material witness statute. In U.S. jurisprudence, the right to remain silent and the privilege against self-incrimination have been lauded in the most beatifying terms, described as "a hallmark of our democracy."[950] As previously noted, the Fifth Amendment to the U.S. Constitution gives every suspect in custodial interrogation the right to remain silent, and, in order to ensure the free exercise of this right, if a person in custody is to be subjected to questioning, he or she must first be informed by the police (in clear and unequivocal language) that he or she has the right to remain silent.[951] The cautionary warning must be accompanied by the explanation that anything said to investigators can and will be used against the suspect in court.[952] Similarly, suspects in the United States have the right to consult with a lawyer and to have a lawyer present during interrogation.[953] The moment a suspect requests a lawyer, the interrogation ends. Such rights are even given to noncitizens against whom U.S. law enforcement seeks to bring criminal action.

This robust set of rights and privileges—which serve to inhibit interrogation—mark a departure from the United Kingdom, which allows adverse inferences to be drawn from one's silence and allows suspension of one's right to an attorney for up to forty-eight hours.[954] In addition, the adherence to such a rights-based system differs significantly from the French system, which does not require a suspect to be advised of his or her right to remain silent and allows only intermittent consultation with an attorney.[955] Accordingly, where the rights of suspects are concerned, the United Kingdom and France have far more potent legal regimes.

Immigration Detention

There is, however, one area of U.S. law in which the abilities of law enforcement agents are greatly enhanced—the regime of law applicable to noncitizens. In the event the terrorist suspect is a noncitizen, then the power of U.S. law to scoop up, detain, and interrogate the suspect is at its zenith. Under 8 U.S.C. § 1226(a), an alien may be "detained pending a decision on whether the alien is to be removed from the United States."[956] Detention under section 1226(a) is discretionary; the attorney general may release the alien on bond or conditional parole. Detention is mandatory when the alien is inadmissible or deportable based on the commission of certain offenses. Thus, in contrast to the rights afforded to U.S. citizens, aliens may be detained without probable cause of any crime—but for mere determinations as to their immigration status. Further, it allows continued detention for a prolonged period of time—though not without some constraints. For instance, the Supreme Court has held that habeas corpus proceedings remain available to challenge post-removal-period detention and that "once removal is no longer reasonably foreseeable, continued detention is no longer authorized by the statute."[957] The Court has further held that there is a six-month period during which there is a presumption that removal is reasonably foreseeable. If, however, after this period, an "alien provides good reason to believe that there is no significant likelihood of removal in the reasonably foreseeable future, the Government must respond with evidence sufficient to rebut that showing."[958] Attempts to detain a noncitizen beyond the point when it is "reasonably necessary to bring [about] removal" are, therefore, unconstitutional under U.S. law.[959]

These protections notwithstanding, the protections for noncitizens under U.S. law are—overall—much weaker. For instance, for criminal purposes, courts have held that non-admitted aliens are entitled to Miranda warnings prior to custodial interrogations.[960] If, however, there is no desire to prosecute criminally—but only to deport—then there is no requirement to advise the noncitizen of his or her rights during such periods of detention, as deportation proceedings are civil, and not criminal, in nature. "Consequently, those Fifth and Sixth Amendment rights outlined in a Miranda-type warning are inapposite in the context of removal proceedings."[961] At least one district court has expressly found that this sort of detention can be used for investigative purposes.[962]

In many ways, therefore, immigration detention in the United States meets the elements common to the investigative detention regimes in the United Kingdom and France. Accordingly, so long as the terrorist suspects in question are noncitizen aliens, the United States does have a rather robust investigative detention regime at its disposal. Suspects can be arrested so long as there is probable cause to believe they are in the country illegally, and, thereafter, they can be detained for months. Its drawback, of course, is its inapplicability to terrorist suspects generally and its unique application to noncitizens. Thus, the U.S. immigration detention regime is of no use in cases where the terrorist suspects are of a more domestic variety.

Is Legislative Modification Really Needed?

At the core of this analysis is the question of whether further legislative modification of U.S. law is needed in order to give the United States the same advantages in counterterrorism as its European counterparts. The answer depends as much on one's point of view as it does the facts of the individual case. What is not subject to serious debate, however, is the need for U.S. law enforcement to be able to detain terrorist suspects before an act of terrorism can be committed. In that regard, as noted in chapter 3, the primary detention tool in terrorism cases in the United States is the material witness statute. Its flexibility and easier burden have made it a ubiquitous presence in counterterrorism cases. As discussed, it contains many restrictions that prevent it from serving as a full investigative detention mechanism. Most notably, however, continued use of the statute in the same manner seems somewhat uncertain. Jurisprudence has already signaled that courts may not tolerate the use of the material witness statute for the detention of persons for criminal activity for which probable cause has not yet been established[963]—which is precisely the purpose of investigative detention. Though only dicta, such language could be seen as an omen that portends an uncertain future for the continued use of the material witness statute in the same manner. In the words of former attorney general Mukasey, "The material witness statute has its perils."[964] Should the material witness statute cease to function in the same way or face judicial curtailment, then the ability of U.S. law enforcement to effect investigative detention would be dramatically impacted. It is, therefore, prudent to consider possible modifications of U.S. law that would—within the limits imposed by the Constitution and international human rights law—allow for greater powers similar to those available in the United Kingdom and France.

Possible Modifications of U.S. Law

Having analyzed the restrictions in U.S. criminal law, the exceptions to its limitations, and the areas of permissibility in the quasi-criminal realm, the focus now turns to what modifications could be made to U.S. criminal law in order to incorporate the elements of investigative detention one sees in Europe. Among the most promising modifications in that regard are the enhancement of the ability of police to stop and identify terrorist suspects thought the enactment of a federal "stop and identify" law and the criminalization of membership in terrorist organizations. In addition, laws should be enacted to maximize the "public safety" doctrine—the rather limited area identified by the Supreme Court in which law enforcement agents are not required to advise a suspect of his or her rights prior to interrogation. Further, the six-hour "safe harbor zone" created in the Omnibus Crime Control and Safe Streets Act should be doubled in order to give police a full day in which to hold suspects prior to presentment before a magistrate. Finally, in those instances where the permissible periods of detention have still not yielded enough evidence to charge a suspect, a civil detention law should be enacted—modeled on that proposed by Professor Yin—which would allow for preventive and investigative detention of terrorist suspects while the investigation into that suspect's conduct continues.

Criminalizing Mere Membership in a Terrorist Organization

As previously discussed, 18 U.S.C. § 2339A and § 2339B provide a flexible tool for law enforcement by criminalizing the provision of material support or resources (to include services, personnel, advice, etc.) to a foreign terrorist organization.[965] Currently, however, merely belonging to a terrorist organization is not a crime.[966] Otherwise stated, U.S. criminal law prohibits conduct in support of a terrorist organization but not the membership therein. As one court has noted, "Section 2339B does not prohibit membership in Al Qaeda, nor does it prohibit persons from espousing or sympathizing with the views of Al Qaeda, however unpopular those views might be."[967] As a result, law enforcement agents in the United States seeking to arrest or otherwise detain terrorist suspects need to attain evidence of more than just active membership. Evidence of some act of support must be also be found.

Such a membership-based crime is not, however, completely antithetical to U.S. law. Although it is a violation of the First Amendment to punish an individual for mere membership in an organization that has a mix of both legal and illegal goals, a statute may lawfully prohibit association with such an organization so long as that statute also requires evidence that the defendant specifically intended to further the organization's unlawful goals.[968] Criminalizing membership in an organization is, therefore, possible so long as there is knowing membership in the organization along with the specific intent to further the group's illicit purpose.[969] In other words, a conviction cannot rest on guilt by association but must be coupled with "the relationship of that status or conduct to other concededly criminal activity."[970]

This rule of law comes from a case entitled *United States v. Scales*. The statutory provision at issue in that case (the Smith Act) provided in relevant part that

> [w]hoever organizes or helps or attempts to organize any society, group, or assembly of persons who teach, advocate, or encourage the overthrow or destruction of any such government by force or violence; or becomes or is a member of, or affiliates with, any such society, group, or assembly of persons, knowing the purposes thereof

is guilty of a crime.[971] David Henrik Pendle, explaining the Court's decision, writes,

> [T]he Supreme Court provided a test to determine what types of relationships with criminal organizations can serve as the basis for criminal liability. The test requires a court to analyze the substantiality of the relationship between a person's status or conduct and an organization's concededly criminal activity. Where that relationship is tenuous, personal guilt is required in order to convict someone on the basis of that relationship; however, if the relationship between the accused's involvement and the underlying substantive illegal conduct is strong, personal guilt is not required.[972]

The Supreme Court in *Scales*, thus, required the government to prove more than the defendant's mere membership; the government had to prove that the defendant "knew that the organization engages in criminal advocacy, and that it was his purpose to further that criminal advocacy."[973] Membership combined with purpose to further the activity, therefore, was sufficient to create criminal culpability. No material support was required.

By enacting legislation criminalizing the active membership in a terrorist organization with the specific intent to further that group's goals, Congress could make it far easier to develop reasonable suspicion of criminal activity on the part of certain known suspects. Any evidence of active membership in a terrorist organization under such circumstances should be sufficient to subject a suspect to lawful arrest.

The Smith Act (18 U.S.C. § 2385) is still a part of Title 18 and could simply be amended to include not only membership in organizations that seek to overthrow a government but also organizations that seek to engage in terrorist activity. The language for the statute could be based on those parts of the Smith Act that have already survived constitutional attack. In so doing, Congress could create a status-based offense and give federal law enforcement officials powers akin to those available in the United Kingdom, where a terrorist suspect can be stopped and searched by the police based upon mere suspicion that the person is a terrorist.[974]

A Federal Stop and Identify Statute

As noted, the procedures for *contrôle d'identité* in France allow that a person may be stopped and his or her identity verified based solely upon suspicion of a potential breach of public order.[975] In contrast, there is not yet a federal "stop and identify" statute—meaning that a suspect in the United States may currently refuse to identify himself or herself to federal law enforcement without penalty.[976] As previously noted, the Supreme Court has held that suspect in the United States can be compelled to identify himself or herself to police during an otherwise valid investigatory stop and can even be prosecuted for failure to do so.[977] This gap in law enforcement ability could, accordingly, be closed by the passage of a law permitting the stop and search of terrorist suspects similar to that available under French law. Such a statute could be based on the Nevada statute, which has been constitutionally tested and now bears the Supreme Court's seal of approval. To assuage the concerns of those opposed to too dramatic a grant of federal power, however, the statute could be more narrowly tailored so that it applies specifically to terrorism and terrorism-related activity.

By enacting such a statute, legislators could grant federal law enforcement agents the ability to stop any person suspected of terrorism or terrorism-related activity—based only on reasonable suspicion—and have them either choose to identify themselves or face prosecution. This would enhance the ability of federal law enforcement to identify those suspected of terrorism and ferret out terrorist activity. It would also enhance the investigative detention powers of U.S. law enforcement agents in terrorism cases by strengthening their ability to stop and question suspected terrorists.

Extending the "Public Safety" Doctrine

Diminishing the legal protections available to terrorist suspects in the same way that the British and French governments have done is problematic in the context of the U.S. legal system. This is because the U.S. Supreme Court's decision in *Miranda v. Arizona*, holding that police must provide a suspect with specific warning prior to interrogating the suspect, is a constitutional decision that may not be overruled by an act of Congress.[978] The Supreme Court has expressly held that "Congress may not legislatively supersede our decisions interpreting and applying the Constitution."[979] Accordingly, legislative attempts to allow statements to be obtained without such warnings have been overturned.[980] This indicates that walls surrounding *Miranda* and the rights afforded to suspects in police custody are too high to allow for extensive legislative intrusion. The right against self-incrimination, the right to counsel, and the prophylactic warnings mandated by the Supreme Court, are simply far too resistant to legislative alteration.

As discussed, one of the few narrow exceptions to the requirements of the *Miranda* decision is the "public safety" doctrine. Professor Darmer, noting the difficulties of legislative modification of *Miranda*, has argued that the public safety doctrine should be judicially extended to terrorism cases based on a balance of the competing societal interests inherent in counterterrorism:

> One possible way to deal with the more speculative public safety cases would be to balance the likelihood that the suspect has the information with the importance of the information. The more potentially important the information, the less tolerable it seems to formulate rules that require authorities to bypass questioning a detainee. If there were even a .0001 percent chance that a [terrorist] had information about another terrorist plot akin to the World Trade Center and Pentagon attacks, does it make sense to say that he must first be given Miranda warnings?[981]

Aside from the possibility of such a judicial extension of the doctrine, the possibility exists for legislative modification within the narrow confines of the existing, judicially recognized zone of permissive "unadvised" interrogation. Given the enormous danger terrorists pose to national security and the lives of citizens (a clear issue of public safety), a statute could be drafted declaring that information of a terrorist attack is a matter of utmost public safety, which would allow on-the-scene interrogation of terrorist suspects immediately upon their apprehension without rights advisement in order to determine what attacks are being planned, where other terrorists are located, and similar information.[982]

Such a statutory provision would admittedly push the envelope of the "public safety" doctrine and carve new ground in U.S. counterterrorism law, but it would have the advantage of operating within an area of exception already recognized and defined by the Supreme Court. It, therefore, would not curb existing rights any more than U.S. jurisprudence currently allows. As a result, it would avoid running afoul of any constitutional boundaries. Further, it would allow for police to extract information and evidence during a critical period of time and without the need to "Mirandize" a terrorist suspect or await the arrival of his attorney.

Extending the "Safe Harbor Zone"

As previously discussed, once a suspect has been arrested, as a general matter, federal officials must take persons they arrest before a magistrate or other judicial official without unnecessary delay.[983] The Omnibus Crime Control and Safe Streets Act carved out a six-hour period during which confessions would not be excluded solely because of delay.[984] The effect of this statute is the creation of a period of time during which the inherently coercive effect of a lengthy delay in presentment is not sufficient, standing alone, to render a confession involuntary.[985] The Supreme Court has considered this statute and—though noting confusion as to its meaning—has yet to strike it down or in any way indicate that it is contrary to any established constitutional principle.

A statute could be implemented, therefore, increasing the six-hour period to a greater length of time. Such a statute has yet to be attempted and, therefore, there is no jurisprudence to assist the legislator in knowing how long a period could be established without triggering concerns of undue coercion. The suggestion of any time period, therefore, would be somewhat arbitrary. Nonetheless, a statute could be drafted that doubles the existing time period to create a twelve-hour period during which delay in presentment does not render a confession involuntary. Such a modest enhancement would do nothing more than extend the existing period by six hours, but, in so doing, this would give investigators a full day in which to work to obtain additional evidence in select cases. Moreover, this twelve-hour period would fall well within the forty-eight-hour window for presentment in cases of a warrantless arrest and would move the United States closer to allowing prolonged detention of terrorist suspects for investigative purposes.

Allowing for Prolonged Detention for Alien Terrorist Suspects

As previously noted, aliens are not afforded all of the rights U.S. citizens are granted under U.S. law. As a result, they may be detained far more easily than citizens. A notable limit on the detention of aliens, however, was articulated in *Zadvydas v. Davis*,[986] in which the Supreme Court found that "once removal [of a detained alien] is no longer reasonably foreseeable, continued detention is no longer authorized."[987] In accordance with that finding, the Court found that there would be a six-month period during which there would be a presumption that removal was reasonably foreseeable. After this period, however, if an "alien provides good reason to believe that there is no significant likelihood of removal in the reasonably foreseeable future, the Government must respond with evidence sufficient to rebut that showing."[988] Thus, in normal circumstances, the government will face significant resistance when attempting to hold an alien in detention beyond six months.

The *Zadvydas* decision, however, contained indicia of an exception in terrorism cases, noting that 8 U.S.C. § 1231(a)(6) had to be so limited, as it did "not apply narrowly to a small segment of particularly dangerous individuals, say suspected terrorists, but broadly to aliens ordered removed for many and various reasons, including visa violations."[989]

Such language indicates that a statute that would allow indefinite detention of a narrow class of dangerous aliens—such as terrorist suspects—would pass constitutional muster. Such a statute could be based off of the language of 8 U.S.C. § 1231(a)(6).

By enacting such a statute, legislators could empower federal law enforcement agents to detain alien terrorist suspects for prolonged periods of time while investigation into their terrorist activities continued along with lawful attempts at continued interrogation. As the most dramatic U.S. experience with terrorism has largely consisted of attacks conducted by noncitizens, such a detention regime would effectively provide for an investigative detention regime similar to that available to French authorities under *détention provisoire*, which allows the French to detain such a suspect for up to three years—and four years if the offense took place outside of French territory—while their investigative judges actively investigate the suspect's case.[990]

A Hybrid Civil-Criminal Approach

Once the ability to stop and hold terrorist suspects for investigative purposes is enhanced in the ways described, it will become increasingly possible to obtain evidence of the suspect's terrorist activities at an early investigative stage. This is because law enforcement will have greater ability to stop, interrogate, and investigate terrorist suspects against whom little evidence existed prior to their detention. This evidence may then be enough to both prove the suspect's guilt beyond a reasonable doubt and, therefore, move forward with a criminal prosecution. In such instances, pursuant to the Bail Reform Act, the suspect could be detained pending trial because of the threat a terrorist poses to the community.

Alternatively, even if there is not enough evidence for a prosecution at that time, it may then be possible to subject the terrorist suspect to civil detention. It is here that the synergy between "preventive" detention and investigative detention becomes salient. As noted, in certain circumstances, U.S. law permits the forcible civil detainment of people who are unable to control their behavior and who thereby pose a danger to public health and safety.[991] Such involuntary civil commitment of a limited subclass of dangerous persons has been found to be compatible with the American judiciary's understanding of "ordered liberty."[992] It is, therefore, within the power of the U.S. government to indefinitely confine a person who is found to be dangerous—within the context of a civil (or noncriminal) detention scheme—so long as that finding of dangerousness is coupled with an additional factor, such as finding that the person has a "mental illness" or "mental abnormality."[993]

Professor Tung Yin has argued for this "noncriminal detention" model to be used as a means of detaining terrorists in the more limited context of those captured and imprisoned by the U.S. military at Guantanamo Bay, Cuba.[994] Yin argued that, assuming the individuals in question have been classified as terrorists or enemy combatants, those persons could be proven dangerous at a hearing and, thereafter, similarly detained.[995]

> By synthesizing common elements from domestic forms of noncriminal detention, the proposed model creates a process whereby nonstate actors captured during authorized military campaigns can be detained as long as the United States can demonstrate their continued dangerousness. The burden of proving such dangerousness rests with the United States, and the detainee is to be provided counsel to assist him in defending himself at the hearing. This approach is consistent with the nature of detention pursuant to military force, and is more flexible than the "prosecute or release" mindset.[996]

Thus, Yin argued that a terrorist or enemy combatant could be detained so long as the government could continue to demonstrate that person's continued dangerousness.[997] Yin, accordingly, articulated the use of "civil detention" to effect preventive detention. A critical component in Yin's formulation of a terrorist detention model (as well as the civil detention models in *Hendricks* and *Salerno*) is a hearing at which the government puts forward evidence to prove the suspect's dangerousness. For instance, in *Salerno*, the government was required to demonstrate more than probable cause alone to believe that the charged crime was committed by the arrestee—it was required to put forth clear and convincing evidence of dangerousness: "[B]ut that is not enough. In a full-blown adversary hearing, the Government must convince a neutral decisionmaker, by clear and convincing evidence, that no conditions of release can reasonably assure the safety of the community or person."[998]

That requirement by the government to prove dangerousness by clear and convincing evidence was a principal factor in the Supreme Court's upholding the constitutionality of the Bail Reform Act.[999] Civil detention, therefore, requires that the government put forth evidence demonstrating the reasons the individual in question must be detained. The entire point of investigative detention, in contrast, is the need to obtain evidence for prosecution because, at the time of the detention, such evidence is lacking. In other words, as demonstrated in the cases of the United Kingdom and France, investigative detention regimes allow the government to detain a person when there is not yet clear and convincing evidence of that person's dangerousness or involvement in terrorist activity.

That said, the possibility exists for a hybrid civil-criminal approach whereby select terrorism cases—in which there is some evidence, but not yet enough to convict—are brought before a tribunal for a hearing at which the government puts forward evidence to prove the suspect's dangerousness and, thereafter, detain the suspect while investigators complete the investigation. Such civil detention would be permissible so long as the initial detention of the terrorist suspect is regulatory rather than criminal in nature. As the Supreme Court's ruling in *Salerno* demonstrates, such regulatory detention can be closely intertwined with the function of criminal prosecution without crossing the line and losing its regulatory character.[1000] As with the Bail Reform Act, the key is to conceive of "terrorist detention" as regulatory in nature, based on the dangerousness of the terrorist suspect and separate from the investigation that would proceed during the suspect's period of detention. In such a way, the regime of law allowing preventive detention in the United States could be harnessed for investigative purposes.

From a civil commitment perspective, such a statutory model would serve the important societal goal of separating dangerous fanatics from the societies they seek to harm. From a criminal justice perspective, it would also allow for limited investigative detention in more developed investigations—but it would do little for those where evidence is lacking. While the U.S. law of civil detention may, therefore, play a central role in facilitating continued detention of terrorist suspects at a later stage in an investigation, it is, acting alone, insufficient to enable a full and effective investigative detention regime.

Conclusion

The need for a comprehensive, effective means of effecting investigative detention has been articulated by highly placed individuals within the national security apparatus of the United States.[1001] In calling out for greater ability in this regard, the legal systems of the United Kingdom and France have been specifically highlighted as potential models.[1002] An analysis of the investigative detention regimes in those two countries reveals three common elements: (1) the ability to stop and arrest a terrorist suspect based on minimal criteria, (2) the ability to hold a terrorist suspect for a prolonged period of time, and (3) diminished protections for terrorist suspects during their period of incarceration.

A comparative analysis of U.S., U.K., and French law reveals that U.S. law contains many limitations not encountered by our European allies, which serve to inhibit any sort of true investigative detention. Even so, there is, drifting in the legal ether, enough material for the prudent legislator to grasp and sculpt a workable (if extremely limited) investigative detention scheme in the United States, primarily through enhancement of the ability of police to conduct "stop and frisks" though (a) the enactment of law criminalizing membership in terrorist organizations; (b) the creation of a federal "stop and identify" statute; (c) maximization of the "public safety" doctrine; (d) doubling the six-hour "safe harbor zone" created in the Omnibus Crime Control and Safe Streets Act; and (e) enacting a civil detention law such as that proposed by Yin.

Such measures may push the envelope of existing law, but it must be recalled that U.S. jurisprudence has allowed a certain degree of elasticity when national security concerns are implicated—and specifically where terrorism is concerned. It is in that malleable zone that these statutes would strictly operate. As such, they should be juridically viable and capable of withstanding legal challenges. Even then, however, the counterterrorism capabilities these statutes would create in U.S. law would still fall short of the robust investigative detention regimes that exist across the Atlantic. Nonetheless, they would provide U.S. law enforcement authorities with useful tools—all within the framework of the existing criminal law system—by which terrorist suspects across the spectrum (citizen or noncitizen) could be lawfully detained and investigated. This, of course, is not an endeavor that should be undertaken lightly. As Turner and Schulhofer noted,

> Any expansion of existing pre-trial detention laws would—and should—be controversial. The point relevant here, however, is that any such measures—if they are indeed justifiable and are crafted to meet constitutional requirements—can readily be incorporated into the federal court system. The courts are already equipped with considerable pre-trial detention hardware. If special measures are needed for terrorism suspects, then this existing hardware can be upgraded. Such a step should not be taken without careful congressional consideration, and perhaps should not be taken at all. But if expanded detention is determined to be acceptable, adjusting the machinery already available within the federal court system is infinitely preferable to the government's current use of military detention to hold terrorism suspects indefinitely, beyond the reach of any judicial review.[1003]

For now, as nothing else currently exists, the material witness statute and immigration detention will continue to supply the primary means of detention in domestic U.S. counterterrorism operations. Should that legal artifice begin to crumble, however, legislators will need to act to give U.S. law enforcement reliable investigative detention powers of some sort. Looking across the Atlantic to the elements of the investigative detention regimes in the United Kingdom and France, positive steps can be taken to move ordinary U.S. criminal law closer to this goal. By implementing the changes detailed, legislators could preserve existing constitutional guarantees while placing investigative detention in the United States into a normalized legal framework. This would also give to those charged with U.S. counterterrorism operations, such as former attorney general Mukasey and Vice Admiral Jacoby, at least some modicum of what they seek—the ability to ensnare the rattlesnake before it strikes.

NOTES

1. *See* Franklin D. Roosevelt, *Fireside Chat of September 11, 1941*, *quoted in* DICTIONARY OF MILITARY AND NAVAL QUOTATIONS 247 (1966).
2. *See* Declaration by Vice Admiral Lowell E. Jacoby, United States Navy 1 (Jan. 9, 2003) [hereinafter Jacoby Declaration], *available at* http://www.pegc.us/archive/Padilla_vs_Rumsfeld/Jacoby_declaration_20030109.pdf.
3. *Id.*
4. *Id.* at 4.
5. *Id.* at 4–5.
6. *Id.* at 6.
7. *See* Michael B. Mukasey, Op-Ed., *Jose Padilla Makes Bad Law: Terror Trials Hurt the Nation Even When They Lead to Convictions*, WALL ST. J., Aug. 22, 2007.
8. Jacoby Declaration, *supra* note 2, at 5.
9. *See* CHRISTOPHER L. BLAKESLEY, TERRORISM, DRUGS, INTERNATIONAL LAW, AND THE PROTECTION OF HUMAN LIBERTY 33 (1992).
10. *See* Doug Cassel, *Pretrial and Preventive Detention of Suspected Terrorists: Options and Constraints Under International Law*, 98 J. CRIM. L. & CRIMINOLOGY 811, 816 (2008).
11. *See* Doug Cassel, *International Human Rights Law and Security Detention*, Notre Dame Law School Legal Studies Research Paper No. 08-32, at 2, *available at* http://www.ssrn.com/link/notre-dame-legal-studies.html. *See also* ANDREW HARDING, PREVENTIVE DETENTION AND SECURITY LAW: A COMPARATIVE SURVEY 266 (1993).
12. *See* Christopher Slobogin, *A Jurisprudence of Dangerousness*, 98 NW. U. L. REV. 1, 2 (2003).
13. Cassel, *supra* note 10, at 816.
14. Mukasey, *supra* note 7.
15. *See, e.g.*, Kam C. Wong, *Legalism and Constitutionalism in the People's Republic of China*, 1 INT'L J. CRIM. JUST. SCI., Issue 2 (July 2006).
16. Cassel, *supra* note 10, at 830.
17. *Id.*
18. *See* United Nations Office on Drugs and Crime (Terrorism Prevention Branch), *Preventing Terrorist Acts: A Criminal Justice Strategy Integrating Rule of Law Standards in Implementation of United Nations Anti-Terrorism*

Instruments (2006) [hereinafter *Preventing Terrorist Acts*], *available at* http://www.unodc.org/pdf/terrorism/TATs/en/3IRoLen.pdf.

19. *See* Jeremy Shapiro, *Detention of Terrorism Suspects in Britain and France*, BROOK. INST. (July 15, 2008).
20. *Id.*
21. *See*, e.g., BENJAMIN WITTES, LAW AND THE LONG WAR (2008); STEPHANIE COOPER BLUM, THE NECESSARY EVIL OF PREVENTIVE DETENTION IN THE WAR ON TERROR: A PLAN FOR A MORE MODERATE AND SUSTAINABLE SOLUTION (2008); see also Tung Yin, *Ending the War on Terrorism One Terrorist at a Time: A Noncriminal Detention Model for Holding and Releasing Guantanamo Bay Detainees*, 29 HARV. J.L. & PUB. POL'Y 149, 211 (2005).
22. *See* Kenneth Roth, *After Guantanamo: The Case Against Preventive Detention*, FOREIGN AFFAIRS (May/June 2008).
23. Shapiro, *supra* note 19.
24. *See* KONRAD ZWEIGERT & HEIN KOTZ, AN INTRODUCTION TO COMPARATIVE LAW 15 (Tony Weir trans., 3d rev. ed. 1998).
25. *See* Adam Roberts, *Transformative Military Occupation: Applying the Laws of War and Human Rights*, 100 AM. J. INT'L L. 580, 590 (2006).
26. *See* JEFFREY L. DUNOFF, STEVEN R. RATNER & DAVID WIPPMAN, INTERNATIONAL LAW, NORMS, ACTORS, PROCESS: A PROBLEM-ORIENTED APPROACH, 441–43 (2d ed. 2006).
27. *See* Richard B. Bilder, *An Overview of International Human Rights Law, in* GUIDE TO INTERNATIONAL HUMAN RIGHTS LAW PRACTICE 3 (3d ed. 1999).
28. *See* HENRY J. STEINER & PHILIP ALSTON, INTERNATIONAL HUMAN RIGHTS IN CONTEXT: LAW, POLITICS, MORALS 137 (2d ed. 2000).
29. Cassel, *supra* note 10, at 816–17. In addition to the ICCPR and the ECHR, Cassel noted that international law regarding detention can also be derived from the Universal Declaration of Human Rights and the United Nations Convention Against Torture and Cruel, Inhuman, and Degrading Treatment or Punishment (CAT), as well as from regional instruments, such as the American Convention on Human Rights, the American Declaration of the Rights and Duties of Man, the Principles of Best Practices on the Protection of Persons Deprived of Liberty in the Americas, and the African Charter on Human and People's Rights. Cassel also referenced numerous international humanitarian law instruments, such as the Geneva Conventions. *Id.*
30. *See* Marian Nash (Leich), *Contemporary Practice of the United States Relating to International Law*, 89 AM. J. INT'L L. 96 (1995).
31. *See* DUNOFF, RATNER & WIPMAN, INTERNATIONAL LAW: NORMS, ACTORS, PROCESS 449 (2d ed. 2006).

32. *See* Brenda Sue Thornton, *The New International Jurisprudence on the Right to Privacy: A Head-On Collision with* Bowers v. Hardwick, 58 ALB. L. REV. 725, 734–35 (1995).
33. *Id.*
34. Thornton, *supra* note 32, at 734.
35. *See* International Covenant on Civil and Political Rights art. 9(1) [hereinafter ICCPR].
36. *Id.* art. 14(1).
37. *Id.* art. 14(2)–(5).
38. *Id.* art. 14(1).
39. Thornton, *supra* note 32, at 736.
40. *See Optional Protocol to the International Covenant on Civil and Political Rights*, Mar. 23, 1976 [hereinafter *ICCPR Optional Protocol*], *available at* http://www.ohchr.org/english/law/pdf/ccpr-one.pdf.
41. *See International Covenant on Civil and Political Rights New York*, Dec. 16, 1966 (List of Signatories), *available at* http://www2.ohchr.org/english/bodies/ratification/4.htm.
42. *See Optional Protocol to the International Covenant on Civil and Political Rights New York*, Dec. 16, 1966 (List of Signatories), *available at* http://www2.ohchr.org/english/bodies/ratification/5.htm.
43. *See* Sean D. Murphy, *Canadian Deportation to United States of Death-Penalty Convict*, 98 AM. J. INT'L L. 180, n.7 (2004) (noting, "The first optional protocol...allows states to submit themselves to a system of investigation and quasi-adjudication of individual complaints by the Human Rights Committee. Canada is a party to the first optional protocol, whereas the United States is not."); *See also* Colm Campbell & Ita Connolly, *A Deadly Complexity: Law, Social Movements and Political Violence*, 16 MINN. J. INT'L L. 265, 307 (2007).
44. *See* ALEX CONTE, SCOTT DAVIDSON & RICHARD BURCHILL, DEFINING CIVIL AND POLITICAL RIGHTS 6 (2005).
45. *See* William J. Aceves, *Actio Popularis? The Class Action in International Law*, 2003 U. CHI. LEGAL F. 353, 361, (citing KIRSTEN A. YOUNG, THE LAW AND PROCESS OF THE U.N. HUMAN RIGHTS COMMITTEE 176 (2002)).
46. *See, e.g.*, United States v. Duarte-Acero, 208 F.3d 1282, 1287 (11th Cir. 2000) (looking to HRC's guidance as "most important" component in interpreting ICCPR claim [brackets omitted]); Richard B. Lillich, *The Growing Importance of Customary International Human Rights Law*, 25 GA. J. INT'L & COMP. L. 1 (1995) (referring to the Human Rights Committee as "the authoritative and prestigious body of experts from 18 countries

established to monitor compliance with the International Covenant on Civil and Political Rights"). *See also* Celina Romany, *Black Women and Gender Equality in a New South Africa: Human Rights Law and the Intersection of Race and Gender*, 21 BROOK. J. INT'L L. 857, 884 (1996) (noting that the Human Rights Committee is "an authoritative interpreter of the ICCPR").

47. *See* Diane Marie Amann, *International Law Weekend Proceedings: The Rights of the Accused in a Global Enforcement Arena*, 6 ILSA J. INT'L & COMP. L. 555, 565 (2000).
48. CONTE, DAVIDSON & BURCHILL, *supra* note 44, at 6.
49. *See* Christyne J. Vachon, *Hong Kong's 1997 Transition: U.N. Enforcement Mechanisms to Guarantee Hong Kong's Human Rights Will Endure After the Transition*, 28 DENV. J. INT'L L. & POL'Y 97, 120 (1999); *see also Declarations recognizing the competence of the Human Rights Committee under article 41*, Office of the United Nations High Commission for Human Rights (last updated Jan. 5, 2009), *available at* http://www2.ohchr.org/english/bodies/ratification/docs/DeclarationsArt41ICCPR.pdf.
50. Nash (Leich), *supra* note 30, at 111.
51. Thornton, *supra* note 32, at 737.
52. STEINER & ALSTON, *supra* note 28, at 786.
53. *Id.* at 787.
54. *See* OVEY & WHITE, THE EUROPEAN CONVENTION ON HUMAN RIGHTS 7 (4th ed. 2006).
55. *Id.*
56. *See* European Convention on Human Rights art. 5(1) [hereinafter ECHR] (noting, "everyone has the right to liberty and security of the person").
57. *Id.* art. 5.
58. OVEY & WHITE, *supra* note 54, at 134.
59. ECHR, *supra* note 56, art. 5(1)(c).
60. *See* Fox, Campbell, and Hartley v. United Kingdom, Series A no. 182, ¶ 32 (1990).
61. ECHR, *supra* note 56, art. 5(3).
62. OVEY & WHITE, *supra* note 54, at 134.
63. *Fox, Campbell, and Hartley*, *supra* note 60, at ¶ 32.
64. ECHR, *supra* note 56, art. 15(1).
65. STEINER & ALSTON, *supra* note 28, at 797.
66. *Id.*
67. OVEY & WHITE, *supra* note 54, at 10.
68. *Id.* at 11.
69. Cassel, *supra* note 10, at 850.

70. *Id.*
71. *See* U.N. Human Rights Committee, *General Comment 8: Right to Liberty and Security of Persons (Art. 9): 30/06/82* (June 6, 1982) [hereinafter *General Comment 8*].
72. *Id.*
73. *Id.*
74. *Preventing Terrorist Acts*, *supra* note 18.
75. *Id.*
76. United Nations Commission on Human Rights, The Working Group on Arbitrary Detention, Fact Sheet No. 26, *available at* http://www.ohchr.org/english/about/publications/docs/fs26.htm.
77. *Id.*
78. *Id.*
79. *See* Dunaway v. New York, 442 U.S. 200, 212 (1979).
80. *See* Mary Clifford, *The Criminal Justice in the United States: General Overview*, *in* COMPARATIVE AND INTERNATIONAL CRIMINAL JUSTICE SYSTEMS: POLICING, JUDICIARY, AND CORRECTIONS 11 (2000).
81. *Id.* at 12.
82. *Id.*
83. *See* WAYNE LAFAVE, JEROLD H. ISRAEL & NANCY J. KING, PRINCIPLES OF CRIMINAL PROCEDURE: INVESTIGATION 2 (2004).
84. *See* CRAIG M. BRADLEY, CRIMINAL PROCEDURE: A WORLDWIDE STUDY 519 (2007).
85. LAFAVE, ISRAEL & KING, *supra* note 83, at 3.
86. *See* JAMES BECKMAN, COMPARATIVE LEGAL APPROACHES TO HOMELAND SECURITY AND ANTI-TERRORISM 28 (2007).
87. LAFAVE, ISRAEL & KING, *supra* note 83, at 4 (noting, "While the Federal Rules are applicable only in the general federal system, they almost always reflect the basic position adopted in a substantial number of states").
88. CLIFFORD, *supra* note 80, at 17.
89. *Id.*
90. *Id.* at 21.
91. LAFAVE, ISRAEL & KING, *supra* note 83, at 4.
92. *Id.* at 8.
93. *Id.* at 8–9.
94. *See Law & Order* (NBC television broadcast, 1990 to present).
95. BECKMAN, *supra* note 86, at 13.
96. *Id.* at 13.
97. *See* GERARD CHALIAND & ARNAUD BLIN, THE HISTORY OF TERRORISM: FROM ANTIQUITY TO AL QAEDA 401 (2007).

98. *Id.* at 403.
99. *Id.* at 401.
100. *See* Yonah Alexander, *United States*, *in* COUNTERTERRORISM STRATEGIES: SUCCESSES AND FAILURES OF SIX NATIONS 16 (Yonah Alexander ed., 2006).
101. CHALIAND & BLIN, *supra* note 97, at 401.
102. Alexander, *supra* note 100, at 17.
103. *Id.*
104. *Id.*
105. *Id.*
106. *Id.* at 18.
107. BECKMAN, *supra* note 86, at 24.
108. CHALIAND & BLIN, *supra* note 97, at 409.
109. *Id.*
110. *Id.*
111. Alexander, *supra* note 100, at 19.
112. *See* Richard A. Clarke, *Al Qaeda, the Organization: A Five-Year Forecast*, 618 ANNALS 14, 27 (2008).
113. Alexander, *supra* note 100, at 20.
114. BECKMAN, *supra* note 86, at 25.
115. Alexander, *supra* note 100, at 20.
116. BECKMAN, *supra* note 86, at 25 (noting that the Los Angeles Times reported that, in April of 1995, approximately 48 percent of the individuals polled thought that civil liberties should generally give way to law enforcement in fighting terrorism).
117. *Id.* at 25.
118. *Id.*
119. *Id.* at 26.
120. CHALIAND & BLIN, *supra* note 97, at 413.
121. *Id.*
122. *Id.*
123. *Id.*
124. BECKMAN, *supra* note 86, at 27.
125. *Id.*
126. Alexander, *supra* note 100, at 37.
127. *See* U.S. CONST. amend. IV.
128. *See* Gerstein v. Pugh, 420 U.S. 103, 111 (1975).
129. Terry v. Ohio, 392 U.S. 1 (1968).
130. *See* United States v. Cortez, 449 U.S. 411, 417–18 (1981).

131. *See* STEPHEN A. SALTZBURG & DANIEL J. CAPRA, AMERICAN CRIMINAL PROCEDURE: CASES AND COMMENTARY (5th ed. 1996).
132. *See* United States v. Brignoni-Ponce, 422 U.S. 873 (1975).
133. *See Terry*, 392 U.S. at 20–21; United States v. Sharpe, 470 U.S. 675, 682 (1985).
134. *See* Florida v. Royer, 460 U.S. 491 (1983).
135. *See Sharpe*, 470 U.S. at 682.
136. United States v. Sokolow, 490 U.S. 1, 6 (1989).
137. *See* Illinois v. Wardlow, 528 U.S. 119, 124 (2000).
138. *Id.* at 125.
139. United States v. Place, 462 U.S. 696, 709 (1983), noting,

> [T]he brevity of the invasion of the individual's Fourth Amendment interests is an important factor in determining whether the seizure is so minimally intrusive as to be justifiable on reasonable suspicion. Moreover, in assessing the effect of the length of the detention, we take into account whether the police diligently pursue their investigation.

140. *See Royer*, 460 U.S. at 502–03.
141. *See Dunaway*, 442 U.S. at 207–08.
142. *Id.*
143. *See* United States v. Watson, 423 U.S. 411, 417–18 (1976).
144. *Id.*
145. *Id.*
146. *See* Atwater v. City of Lago Vista, 532 U.S. 318, 341 (2001).
147. *Id.*
148. *See* Payton v. New York, 445 U.S. 573, 590–91 (1980).
149. *See Gerstein*, 420 U.S. at 114–15.
150. *See* Gramenos v. Jewel Co., 797 F.2d 432, 437 (7th Cir. 1986).
151. *Dunaway*, 442 U.S. at 216; *see also* Brown v. Illinois, 422 U.S. 590, 605 (1975).
152. United States v. Ramsey, 431 U.S. 606, 616–17 (1977).
153. LAFAVE, ISRAEL & KING, *supra* note 83, at 192.
154. *Id.*
155. *Id.* at 193.
156. *Id.*
157. *Id.*
158. *See Ramsey*, 431 U.S. at 616–17.

159. *See* United States v. Skipwith, 482 F.2d 1272, 1276 (5th Cir. 1973).
160. *Id.*
161. *Id.* at 1274.
162. *See* United States v. Moreno, 475 F.2d 44 (5th Cir. 1973)
163. *Id.* at 44–46.
164. *Id.* at 46.
165. *Id.*
166. *Id.*
167. *Id.* at 47.
168. *Id.* at 51.
169. *Id.* at 48.
170. *Id.* at 49.
171. *See* New Jersey v. T. L. O., 469 U.S. 325, 351 (1985) (Blackmun, J., concurring).
172. *Id.*
173. *See* United States v. Martinez-Fuerte, 428 U.S. 543, 556 (1976).
174. *See* Michigan Dep't of State Police v. Sitz, 496 U.S. 444, 453–55 (1990).
175. *See* Chandler v. Miller, 520 U.S. 305 (1997).
176. *Id.* at 309.
177. *Id.*
178. *Id.*
179. *Id.*
180. *See* City of Indianapolis v. Edmond, 531 U.S. 32, 42 (2000).
181. *Id.*
182. *Id.* at 44.
183. Illinois v. Caballes, 543 U.S. 405 (2005).
184. *Id.* at 417 n.7 (Souter, J., dissenting).
185. *See T. L. O.*, 469 U.S. at 351.
186. *See Caballes*, 543 U.S. at 417.
187. *See* Hiibel v. Sixth Judicial Dist. Court of Nevada, 542 U.S. 177 (2004).
188. *See* NEV. REV. STAT. § 171.123 (2009).
189. *See Hiibel*, 542 U.S. at 182.
190. *Id.* at 181.
191. *Id.* at 180.
192. *Id.* at 180–81.
193. *Id.* at 181.
194. *Id.* at 183.
195. *Id.*

196. *Id.* at 187–88.
197. *See* Jamie L. Stulin, *Does* Hiibel *Redefine* Terry*? The Latest Expansion of the* Terry *Doctrine and the Silent Impact of Terrorism on the Supreme Court's Decision to Compel Identification*, 54 AM. U. L. REV. 1449, 1478–79 (2005).
198. *Id.* at 1462.
199. *Id.*
200. *Id.*
201. *Id.* at 1468.
202. *See Hiibel*, 542 U.S. at 187–88.
203. *See* Gordon Van Kessel, *The Suspect as a Source of Testimonial Evidence: A Comparison of the English and American Approaches*, 38 HASTINGS L.J. 1, 35–36 (1986).
204. Hayes v. Florida, 470 U.S. 811, 815 (1985).
205. *See Dunaway*, 442 U.S. at 200–01.
206. *Id.*
207. *Id.* at 212.
208. *Id.*
209. *Id.*
210. *See Gerstein*, 420 U.S. at 114–15.
211. *See* County of Riverside v. McLaughlin, 500 U.S. 44, 57 (1991).
212. *See* WAYNE LAFAVE, JEROLD H. ISRAEL & NANCY J. KING, PRINCIPLES OF CRIMINAL PROCEDURE: POST-INVESTIGATION 10 (2004).
213. *See* FED. R. CRIM. P. 5(a)(1)(A).
214. *Id.*
215. *See* Walton v. United States, 334 F.2d 343, 346 (10th Cir. 1964).
216. LAFAVE, ISRAEL & KING, *supra* note 212, at 10.
217. *Id.*
218. *See* United States v. Mitchell, 322 U.S. 65, 67 (1944); Upshaw v. United States, 335 U.S. 410, 413–14 (1948).
219. LAFAVE, ISRAEL & KING, *supra* note 83, at 282.
220. *Id.* at 283.
221. Mallory v. United States, 354 U.S. 449, 454 (1957).
222. *See* United States v. Loc Tien Nguyen, 313 F. Supp. 2d 579 (E.D. Va. 2004).
223. *See* FED. R. CRIM. P. 5(a).
224. *See* 18 U.S.C. § 3501(c) (2009).
225. *Id.* at § 3501(b).

226. *See* MOORE'S FEDERAL PRACTICE—CRIMINAL PROCEDURE § 605.03(2)(a)(i) (3d ed. 2007).
227. *Id.* at § 605.03(2)(c).
228. *See* United States v. Corley, 500 F.3d 210, 218 (2007).
229. *Id.* (italics original).
230. *See* United States v. Alvarez-Sanchez, 511 U.S. 350, 361 (1994); *see also* United States v. Perez, 733 F.2d 1026, 1031 (2d Cir. 1984).
231. *See Alvarez-Sanchez*, 511 U.S. at 351.
232. *See* Michigan v. Tucker, 417 U.S. 433, 443 (1974).
233. *See* U.S. CONST. amend. V.
234. *See* Miranda v. Arizona, 384 U.S. 436, 467–68 (1966).
235. *Id.* at 469–70.
236. *See* M. Katherine B. Darmer, *Miranda Warnings, Torture, the Right to Counsel and the War on Terror*, 10 CHAP. L. REV. 631, 633 (noting, "While Miranda may impose tolerable limits on ordinary law enforcement efforts, those same limits may be intolerable for a society facing very real threats of terrorism").
237. *See Miranda*, 384 U.S. at 469.
238. *Id.*
239. *Id.* at 473–74.
240. *Id.* at 473–74.
241. *See* U.S. CONST. amends. VI, XIV.
242. Brewer v. Williams, 430 U.S. 387, 436 (1977)
243. *Id.*
244. *See Miranda*, 384 U.S. at 467–68.
245. *See Tucker*, 417 U.S. at 444.
246. *See* New York v. Quarles, 467 U.S. 649, 655–56 (1984).
247. *Id.* at 651–52.
248. *Id.*
249. *Id.* at 652–53.
250. *Id.* at 651–52.
251. *Id.* at 653.
252. *Quarles*, 467 U.S. at 655–56.
253. *See* M. K. B. Darmer, *Lessons from the* Lindh *Case: Public Safety and the Fifth Amendment*, 68 BROOK. L. REV. 241, 286 (2002), noting,

> While the *Lindh* court never had the opportunity to address the question whether the public safety exception applied to that case, or should be expanded, other courts will inevitably face such questions in the near term. And nowhere does the need for a robust public safety

exception appear so justified as in those cases dealing with terrorism and national security.

254. *See* Roberto Iraola, *Terrorism, Grand Juries, and the Federal Material Witness Statute*, 34 St. Mary's L.J. 401, 406–07 (2003).
255. *Id.*
256. *Id.*
257. *Id.* at 403.
258. 18 U.S.C. § 3144 (2009).
259. Iraola, *supra* note 254, at 410.
260. *See* Ronald L. Carlson, *Distorting Due Process for Noble Purposes: The Emasculation of America's Material Witness Laws*, 42 Ga. L. Rev. 941, 973–74 (2008), noting,

> It is much easier to establish probable cause to detain a material witness than a suspect. In the context of a criminal arrest, probable cause requires the existence of reasonable grounds to believe a crime has been committed and that the accused committed it. Probable cause for arrest and detention of a witness simply requires the judicial officer to find that a person who is a flight risk has material information about a crime. The different burdens for establishing probable cause to arrest a criminal suspect and a material witness create the opportunity for abuse in the form of pretextual detention under the lower material witness standard in place of arrest as a criminal suspect. (internal quotes and citations omitted)

261. *Id.* at 411.
262. *Id.* at 412.
263. *Id.* at 406–07.
264. *See* Fed. R. Crim. P. 15(a).
265. *See* Abdallah Higazy v. Templeton, 505 F.3d 161(2d Cir. 2007).
266. *See Miranda*, 384 U.S. at 467–68.
267. Katherine Nesbitt, *Preventative Detention of Terrorist Suspects in Australia and the United States: A Comparative Constitutional Analysis*, 17 B.U. Pub. Int. L.J. 39, 61 (2007).
268. Beckman, *supra* note 86, at 33.
269. *Id.*
270. *Id.*
271. *See* United States v. Awadallah, 349 F.3d 42, 56 (2d Cir. 2003).
272. *Id.* at 56.

273. *Id.* at 59.
274. *Id.* at 62.
275. *Id.* at 42, 56.
276. Congressional Research Service ("CRS") Report for Congress, *Arrest and Detention of Material Witnesses: Federal Law in Brief and Section 12 of the USA PATRIOT and Terrorism Prevention Reauthorization Act*, H.R. 3199 (Sept. 8, 2005), *available at* https://www.policyarchive.org/bitstream/handle/10207/2557/RL33077_20050908.pdf?sequence=1.
277. Mathews v. Diaz, 426 U.S. 67, 79–80 (1976).
278. *See* 8 U.S.C. § 1231(a)(2) (2009).
279. *Id.* at § 1231(a)(6).
280. *Id.* at §§ 1158(b)(2)(A)(v), 1182(a)(3)(B)(i)(I).
281. *See, e.g.*, United States v. Moya, 74 F.3d 1117, 1119 (11th Cir. 1996); United States v. Henry, 604 F.2d 908, 914 (5th Cir. 1979).
282. Vasquez-Trujillo v. Gonzales, 151 F. App'x 509 (9th Cir. 2005) (citing Trias-Hernandez v. INS, 528 F.2d 366 (9th Cir. 1975)); *see* United States v. Alderete-Deras, 743 F.2d 645 (9th Cir. 1984).
283. *See* Zadvydas v. Davis, 533 U.S. 678 (2001).
284. *Id.* at 701.
285. *Id.*
286. *Id.*; *see also* Teresa Miller, *Blurring the Boundaries Between Immigration and Crime Control After September 11th*, 25 B.C. THIRD WORLD L.J. 81, n.94 (2005), noting that

> [a]lthough Zadvydas restricted the government's authority to hold immigration detainees indefinitely, it did not overrule [Shaughnessy v. United States,] which authorized the indefinite detention of immigration detainees determined by Congress or the Executive to pose a threat to national security.

287. *Zadvydas*, 533 U.S. at 690.
288. *See* Office of the Inspector General, United States Department of Justice, *The September 11 Detainees: A Review of the Treatment of Aliens Held on Immigration Charges in Connection with the Investigation of the September 11 Attacks* (Apr. 2003) [hereinafter OIG Report], *available at* http://www.usdoj.gov/oig/special/0306/full.pdf.
289. *Id.*
290. *See* Miller, *supra* note 286, at 87–88.

291. *See* Turkmen v. Ashcroft, 2006 U.S. Dist. LEXIS 39170 (E.D.N.Y. June 14, 2006).
292. *Id.* at *128 (citing Whren v. United States, 517 U.S. 806, 813 (1996)) (internal quotation marks omitted).
293. Miller, *supra* note 286, at 112.
294. Saltzburg & Capra, *supra* note 131, at 728.
295. *See* Michael Harwin, Note, *Detaining for Danger Under the Bail Reform Act of 1984: Paradoxes of Procedure and Proof*, 35 Ariz. L. Rev. 1091, 1091–92 (1993).
296. *Id.*
297. *See* 18 U.S.C. § 3142 (2009).
298. *Id.*
299. *Id.*
300. Harwin, *supra* note 295, at 1109–10.
301. *Id.*
302. *See* United States v. Salerno, 481 U.S. 739 (1987).
303. *Id.* at 746.
304. *Id.* at 747.
305. *Id.* at 747–48.
306. *Id.* at 750–51.
307. *Id.* at 746–47.
308. *Id.* at 747.
309. *Id.*
310. *Id.* at 749.
311. *Id.* at 750–51.
312. *Id.*
313. *See* U.S. Const. amend. VI.
314. *See* Doggett v. United States, 505 U.S. 647, 651 (1992).
315. *Id.* at 654.
316. *See* 18 U.S.C.S. § 3161(b)(1) (2009).
317. *Id.* at § 3161(c)(1).
318. *Id.* at § 3161(c)(2).
319. *Id.* at § 3161(h)(7)(A).
320. *Id.* at § 3161(h)(1)(C).
321. *Id.* at § 3161(h)(1)(D).
322. *See* Serrin Turner & Stephen J. Schulhofer, The Secrecy Problems in Terrorism Trials 37–40 (2005).
323. *Id.* at 37 (citations omitted).

324. *Id.* at 40, also noting that

> Professors Philip Heymann and Juliette Kayyem have proposed that Congress enact a statute permitting detention of dangerous terrorism suspects for up to two years when proceeding promptly to trial would be impossible without a severe loss of national security secrets. Their proposal would allow parts of the detention hearing to be held outside the defendant's presence, provided that cleared counsel representing the defendant was afforded the opportunity to review and contest any classified evidence.

325. *See* JUDITH LYNN FAILER, WHO QUALIFIES FOR RIGHTS? HOMELESSNESS, MENTAL ILLNESS, AND CIVIL COMMITMENT 68 (2002).
326. *See* Kansas v. Hendricks, 521 U.S. 346, 352 (1997).
327. *Id.*
328. *Id.*
329. *Id.* at 353.
330. *Id.*
331. *Id.* at 359–60.
332. *Id.* at 357 (citing Jacobson v. Massachusetts, 197 U.S. 11, 26 (1905)).
333. *Id.*
334. *Id.*
335. *Id.* at 358.
336. *Id.* at 358.
337. *Id.* at 359.
338. *Id.* at 361–62.
339. *See* STEPHEN DYCUS, WILLIAM C. BANKS & PETER RAVEN-HANSEN, COUNTERTERORISM LAW 5(2007) (noting, "Although everyone who uses the term today agrees that terrorism is bad, the inevitable politicization of terrorism renders any search for a consensus definition futile").
340. *See* Richard Baxter, *A Skeptical Look at the Concept of Terrorism*, 7 AKRON L. REV. 380 (1974) (noting, "We have cause to regret that a legal concept of 'terrorism' was ever inflicted upon us. The term is imprecise; it is ambiguous; and above all, it serves no operative legal purpose.").
341. *See* MICHAEL Y. DARTNELL, ACTION DIRECTE: ULTRA-LEFT TERRORISM IN FRANCE, 1979–1987, at 1–13 (1995).
342. DYCUS, BANKS & RAVEN-HANSEN, *supra* note 339, at 5 (noting, "Although Al Qaeda and its affiliates remain the most prominent terrorist threat, the general trends in terrorism show that micro-actors—small autonomous

cells and individuals enabled by technologies and international commerce—are increasingly worrisome and difficult to counter").

343. CHALIAND & BLIN, *supra* note 97, at 16.
344. *See* 18 U.S.C. § 3077(1) (2009).
345. DYCUS, BANKS & RAVEN-HANSEN, *supra* note 339, at 8.
346. BECKMAN, *supra* note 86, at 27.
347. *See* Tasia E. McIntyr, *Protecting Against Terrorism or Symbolic Politics? Fatal Flaws in Ohio's Criminal Terrorism Statute*, 56 CASE W. RES. L. REV. 203 (2005).
348. *See* Boim v. Quranic Literacy Institute, 291 F.3d 1000, 1008 (7th Cir. 2002).
349. *See* 18 U.S.C. § 2332b(g)(5) (2009).
350. *Id.* at app. 3A1.4 (Terrorism) (noting that for such offenses, the offense level is to increase by 12 levels, but if the resulting offense level is less than level 32, increase to level 32; further, in each such case, the defendant's criminal history category shall be Category VI).
351. *Id.* at § 2339A.
352. *Id.* at § 2339A(b)(1).
353. *Id.* at § 2339B.
354. *Id.* at § 2339C.
355. DYCUS, BANKS & RAVEN-HANSEN, *supra* note 339, at 491 (noting, "Congress has not made it a crime to be a member of a [foreign terrorist organization]").
356. *See* Scales v. United States, 367 U.S. 203, 224–25 (1961).
357. *Id.*
358. *See* United States v. Timothy McVeigh and Terry Lynn Nichols, 940 F. Supp. 1541, 1545 (D. Colo. 1996).
359. *Id.*
360. *Id.* at 1546.
361. *Id.*
362. *Id.*
363. *Id.* at 1547–48.
364. *Id.* at 1548.
365. *Id.* at 1562.
366. *Id.* at 1550.
367. *Id.* at 1549–51.
368. *Id.* at 1562.
369. *Id.*
370. *Id.* at 1550.

371. *Id.* at 1551.
372. *See Profile: Jose Padilla* (BBC News television broadcast Aug. 16, 2007), *available at* http://news.bbc.co.uk/1/hi/world/americas/2037444.stm.
373. *Id.*
374. *See* Padilla v. Hanft, 423 F.3d 386, 389–90 (4th Cir. 2006).
375. *Id.* at 390.
376. *Id.*
377. *See* Sean D. Murphy, *Second Circuit Rejection of Presidential Power to Declare U.S. National "Enemy Combatant"*, 98 AM. J. INT'L L. 186, 186 (2004).
378. *See Padilla*, 423 F.3d at 390.
379. Murphy, *supra* note 377, at 186.
380. *See generally* Padilla v. Bush, 233 F. Supp. 2d 564 (S.D.N.Y. 2002).
381. *See* Padilla v. Rumsfeld, 352 F.3d 695, 718–19 (2d Cir. 2003).
382. *Id.* at 734.
383. *See generally* Rumsfeld v. Padilla, 542 U.S. 426 (2004).
384. *See generally* Padilla v. Hanft, 389 F. Supp. 2d 678 (D.S.C. 2005).
385. *Id.*
386. *See* Padilla v. Hanft, 423 F.3d 386, 397 (4th Cir. 2005).
387. *Id.*
388. *Id.*
389. *See* Padilla v. Hanft, 432 F.3d 582, 584 (4th Cir. 2005).

> The government has held Padilla militarily for three and a half years, steadfastly maintaining that it was imperative in the interest of national security that he be so held. However, a short time after our decision issued on the government's representation that Padilla's military custody was indeed necessary in the interest of national security, the government determined that it was no longer necessary that Padilla be held militarily. Instead, it announced, Padilla would be transferred to the custody of federal civilian law enforcement authorities and criminally prosecuted in Florida for alleged offenses considerably different from, and less serious than, those acts for which the government had militarily detained Padilla. The indictment of Padilla in Florida, unsealed the same day as announcement of that indictment, made no mention of the acts upon which the government purported to base its military detention of Padilla and upon which we had concluded only several weeks before that the President possessed the authority to detain Padilla,

namely, that Padilla had taken up arms against United States forces in Afghanistan and had thereafter entered into this country for the purpose of blowing up buildings in American cities, in continued prosecution of al-Qaeda's war of terrorism against the United States.

Id.

390. *Id.* at 587.
391. *See* United States v. Padilla, 2007 U.S. Dist LEXIS 26077, at *4 (S.D. Fla. Apr. 9, 2007).
392. *Id.* at *5.
393. *Id.*
394. *Id.* at *17.
395. *Id.* at *18.
396. *See* Abby Goodnough, *Jose Padilla Convicted on All Counts in Terror Trial*, N.Y. Times, Aug. 16, 2007.
397. *See* Kirk Semple, *Padilla Sentenced to 17 Years in Prison*, N.Y. Times, Jan. 22, 2008.
398. *Id.*
399. *See* Al-Marri v. Pucciarelli, 2008 U.S. App. LEXIS 14979, at *13–*14 (4th Cir. S.C. 2008).
400. *Id.* at *14.
401. *Id.*
402. *Id.*
403. *Id.* at *15.
404. *Id.* at *9–*10.
405. *Id.* at *17.
406. *Id.* at *5.
407. *Id.* at *20.
408. *See* David Johnston & Neil A. Lewis, *U.S. Will Give Qaeda Suspect a Civilian Trial*, N.Y. Times, Feb. 26, 2009.
409. *See, e.g., A Necessary Supreme Court Showdown*, N.Y. Times, Mar. 5, 2009 ("We do not expect Mr. Obama will follow Mr. Bush's dismal lead in fashioning an ultra-imperial presidency. Nevertheless, the court should not feel comfortable about dismissing Mr. Marri's case at this late date, especially when the government has not renounced its claimed power to engage in this unconstitutional conduct. To do so would undermine the remedy of habeas corpus, as well as trust in the judicial process.").

410. *See* Al-Marri v. Spagone, 2009 U.S. LEXIS 1777, 77 U.S.L.W. 3502 (U.S. Mar. 6, 2009).
411. *See* Adam Liptak, *Justices Erase Ruling That Allowed Detention*, N.Y. TIMES, Mar. 6, 2009.
412. *See* Tung Yin, *Coercion and Terrorism Prosecutions in the Shadow of Military Detention*, 2006 BYU L. REV. 1255, 1268 (2006).
413. *Id.*; *see also* United States v. Moussaoui, 382 F.3d 453, 457 (4th Cir. 2004).
414. *See* Tung Yin, *supra* note 412, at 1268; *see also Moussaoui*, 382 F.3d at 457.
415. *See* Nina H. B. Jorgensen, *The Right of the Accused to Self-Representation Before International Criminal Tribunals*, 98 AM. J. INT'L L. 711, 711 (2004). *See also* Heidee Stoller, Tahlia Townsend, Rashad Hussain & Marcia Yablon, *Developments in Law and Policy: The Costs of Post-9/11 National Security Strategy*, 22 YALE L. & POL'Y REV. 197, n.17 (Winter 2004) ("Although Moussaoui was originally arrested on immigration charges, news reports indicate that he was subsequently held as a material witness until his indictment") (internal quotations and citations omitted).
416. *See* University of Missouri-Kansas Law School, *The Zacarias Moussaoui (September 11) Trial: A Chronology*, *available at* http://www.law.umkc.edu/faculty/projects/ftrials/moussaoui/zmchronology.html.
417. *See Moussaoui*, 382 F.3d at 457.
418. *Id.*
419. *See* Neil A. Lewis, *Moussaoui Given Life Term by Jury over Link to 9/11*, N.Y. TIMES, May 4, 2006.
420. *See* Hamdi v. Rumsfeld, 542 U.S. 507 (2004).
421. *See* YONAH ALEXANDER & EDGAR H. BRENNER, THE UNITED KINGDOM'S LEGAL RESPONSES TO TERRORISM xii (2007).
422. *Id.*
423. *Id.* at xiii.
424. *See* MALCOLM DAVIES, HAZEL CROALL & JANE TYRER, CRIMINAL JUSTICE: AN INTRODUCTION TO THE CRIMINAL JUSTICE SYSTEM IN ENGLAND AND WALES 6 (1995).
425. *See* CLIVE WALKER, BLACKSTONE'S GUIDE TO THE ANTI-TERRORISM LEGISLATION xi (2002).
426. BRADLEY, *supra* note 84, at xvii.
427. JOHN H. LANGBEIN, THE ORIGINS OF ADVERSARY CRIMINAL TRIAL 1 (2003).
428. BRADLEY, *supra* note 84, at xviii.
429. BRADLEY, *supra* note 84, at 154.

430. J. R. Spencer, *The English System*, *in* EUROPEAN CRIMINAL PROCEDURES 142 (Mireille Delmas-Marty & J. R. Spencer eds., 2002).
431. *See* J. DAVID HIRSCHEL & WILLIAM WAKEFIELD, CRIMINAL JUSTICE IN ENGLAND AND THE UNITED STATES 24 (1995).
432. DAVIES, CROALL & TYRER, *supra* note 424, at 96.
433. *See* JOHN SPRACK, A PRACTICAL APPROACH TO CRIMINAL PROCEDURE 67 (2006).
434. DAVIES, CROALL & TYRER, *supra* note 424, at 95–96.
435. SPRACK, *supra* note 433, at 41.
436. *Id.* at 67.
437. *Id.*
438. *Id.*
439. *Id.* at 69.
440. *Id.* at 30.
441. *Id.* at 75–76.
442. *Id.* at 40.
443. *See* FRASER SAMPSON, GLENN HUTTON & DAVID JOHNSTON, BLACKSTONE'S POLICE INVESTIGATORS' MANUAL 284–85 (2007).
444. *See* Lissa Griffin, *The Correction of Wrongful Convictions: A Comparative Perspective*, 16 AM. U. INT'L L. REV. 1241, 1256 (2001).
445. SPRACK, *supra* note 433, at 30.
446. *Id.* at 37.
447. *Id.* at 74.
448. *Id.* at 73.
449. *Id.* at 71.
450. *Id.*
451. BECKMAN, *supra* note 86, at 59.
452. *Id.* at 51.
453. ALEXANDER & BRENNER, *supra* note 421, at xii.
454. *See* Fionnuala Ni Aolain, *Legal Developments: The Fortification of an Emergency Regime*, 59 ALB. L. REV. 1353, n.48 (1996) (citing CHRIS RYDER, THE RUC: A FORCE UNDER FIRE (2d ed. 1992)).
455. *See* Matthew Weaver & James Sturcke, *British Army Ends Northern Ireland Operation*, THE GUARDIAN, July 31 2007, *available at* http://www.guardian.co.uk/uk/2007/jul/31/northernireland.military/print.
456. *See* Clive Walker, *Keeping Control of Terrorists Without Losing Control of Constitutionalism*, 59 STAN. L. REV. 1395, 1415 (2007).
457. *Id.* at 1403 (2007).

458. *See* LAURA K. DONOHUE, COUNTER-TERRORIST LAW AND EMERGENCY POWERS IN THE UNITED KINGDOM 1922–2000, at 117 (2001).
459. *Id.*
460. *Id.* at 118.
461. *Id.* at 44–63.
462. *Id.* at 118.
463. *Id.*
464. *Id.* at 132.
465. *Id.* at 133.
466. *Id.*
467. *Id.* at 122–23.
468. *Id.* at 124.
469. *Id.*, quoting Diplock Report, ch. 4, para. 27.

    We are driven inescapable to the conclusion that until current terrorism by the extremist organizations of both factions in Northern Ireland can be eradicated, there will continue to be some dangerous terrorists against whom it will not be possible to obtain convictions by any form of criminal trial which we regard as appropriate to a court of law…The only hope of restoring the efficiency of criminal courts of law in Northern Ireland to deal with terrorist crimes is by using an extra-judicial process to deprive [terrorists] of their ability to operate in Northern Ireland.

470. *Id.*
471. *Id.* at 129.
472. *Id.*
473. *See* Sean Doran, John D. Jackson & Michael L. Seigel, *Rethinking Adversariness in Nonjury Criminal Trials*, 23 AM. J. CRIM. L. 1, 11 (1995).
474. *Id.* at 6.
475. *Id.* at 11.
476. Hurst Hannum, *Ten Years On in Northern Ireland. The legal control of political violence. By Kevin Boyle, Tom Hadden, and Paddy Hillyard*, 75 AM. J. INT'L L. 705, 706 (1981) (book review).
477. *See, e.g.*, John D. Jackson, *Making Juries Accountable*, 50 AM. J. COMP. L. 477, 510 (2002); Michael P. O'Connor & Celia M. Rumann, *How to Avoid Getting Burned by the Same Mistakes Made Fighting Terrorism in Northern Ireland*, 24 CARDOZO L. REV. 1657, 1698 (2003).
478. *See Diplock Courts*, BBC NEWS, Jul. 3, 2007, *available at* http://news.bbc.co.uk/1/hi/programmes/law_in_action/6265734.stm.
479. *See* 1973 Northern Ireland (Emergency Provisions) Act, 11(1) and 12.
480. *See* DONOHUE, *supra* note 458, at 207.

481. *Id.*
482. *Id.*
483. *Id.* at 216.
484. Fionnuala Ni Aolain, *supra* note 454, at 1353, noting,

> The primary emergency laws in force in the jurisdiction are the Northern Ireland (Emergency Provisions) Act of 1991 (EPA) and its counterpart, the Prevention of Terrorism (Temporary Provisions) Act of 1989 (PTA). The EPA operates only in Northern Ireland, while the PTA operates throughout the entire United Kingdom, but both statutes are designed to obtain convictions in cases involving those suspected of paramilitary activity, based on confessions obtained through prolonged detention and intense interrogation. (citations and internal quotations omitted)

485. Donohue, *supra* note 458, at 221–22.
486. *See* Alun Jones, Rupert Bowers & Hugo D. Lodge, Blackstone's Guide to the Terrorism Act 2006, at 2–3 (2006).
487. Beckman, *supra* note 86, at 55.
488. Jones, Bowers & Lodge, *supra* note 486, at 3.
489. *Id.*
490. Beckman, *supra* note 86, at 57–58.
491. Walker, *supra* note 425, at xi.
492. *Id.* at 37.
493. Jones, Bowers & Lodge, *supra* note 486, at 3.
494. Walker, *supra* note 425, at 30.
495. *Id.*
496. *Id.* at 31.
497. *Id.* at 7 (citing Home Office Press Release 250/2001, Oct. 15, 2001).
498. *Id.* at 266.
499. Jones, Bowers & Lodge, *supra* note 486, at 3.
500. Walker, *supra* note 425, at 33.
501. Beckman, *supra* note 86, at 51.
502. *Id.*
503. Jones, Bowers & Lodge, *supra* note 486, at 1.
504. *Id.* at 5.
505. Sprack, *supra* note 433, at 22–23.
506. *See* Police and Criminal Evidence Act 1984 § 120.
507. Van Kessel, *supra* note 203, at 35–36.

508. *Id.* at 35–37.
509. *Id.* at 38.
510. HIRSCHEL & WAKEFIELD, *supra* note 431, at 92–93.
511. *See* Police and Criminal Evidence Act 1984 § 1(2), (3).
512. *Id.* at § 1(7)–(9).
513. SPRACK, *supra* note 433, at 52.
514. *See* Police and Criminal Evidence Act code A (Stop and Search), par. 2.2.
515. SPRACK, *supra* note 433, at 52.
516. *Id.*
517. *See* Police and Criminal Evidence Act 1984 § 2(9)(a).
518. SPRACK, *supra* note 433, at 52.
519. *See* Police and Criminal Evidence Act 1984 § 1(1).
520. *Id.* at § 2(1).
521. SPRACK, *supra* note 433, at 52–53.
522. *Id.* at 53.
523. *Id.*
524. *Id.*
525. BRADLEY, *supra* note 84, at 154.
526. *Id.*
527. *Id.*
528. *Id.* at 154–55.
529. SPRACK, *supra* note 433, at 26.
530. *Id.* at 27.
531. *Id.* (quoting Lord Devlin in *Hussien v. Chong Fook Kam* [1970] AC 942, 948).
532. Van Kessel, *supra* note 203, at 17–18 (citing Regina v. Mackintosh, 76 Crim. App. 177, 178–80 (C.A. 1982)); Regina v. Dodd, 74 Crim. App. 50, 54–57 (C.A. 1981).
533. *See* Mike Maguire, *Effects of the "P.A.C.E." Provisions on Detention and Questioning: Some Preliminary Findings*, 28 BRIT. J. CRIMINOL., No 1, at 20–21 (Winter 1988).
534. SPRACK, *supra* note 433, at 27.
535. Spencer, *supra* note 430, at 206.
536. SPRACK, *supra* note 433, at 30.
537. *Id.*
538. *Id.*
539. *Id.*
540. *Id.* at 31.

541. *Id.*
542. *Id.*
543. *Id.*
544. *Id.*
545. *Id.*
546. *Id.*
547. *Id.*
548. *Id.*
549. *Id.* at 32.
550. *Id.*
551. *Id.*
552. *Id.*
553. *Id.*
554. *Id.* at 29.
555. *Id.* at 44.
556. *Id.* at 42.
557. GARY SLAPPER & DAVID KELLY, THE ENGLISH LEGAL SYSTEM 427 (2004).
558. SPRACK, *supra* note 433, at 46.
559. *Id.*
560. SLAPPER & KELLY, *supra* note 557, at 428.
561. SPRACK, *supra* note 433, at 31.
562. SLAPPER & KELLY, *supra* note 557, at 431.
563. SPRACK, *supra* note 433, at 47.
564. SLAPPER & KELLY, *supra* note 557, at 434.
565. *See Miranda*, 384 U.S. at 473–74.
566. SPRACK, *supra* note 433, at 42.
567. *See* Brian P. Lenihan, *Unsound Method: Judicial Inquiry and Extradition to Northern Ireland*, 34 B.C. L. REV 591, 631 (1993).
568. Van Kessel, *supra* note 203, at 10–12.
569. SPRACK, *supra* note 433, at 42.
570. *Id.*
571. *Id.* at 33.
572. SLAPPER & KELLY, *supra* note 557, at 426.
573. SPRACK, *supra* note 433, at 98.
574. *Id.*
575. *Id.*
576. *Id.* at 99.
577. *Id.*
578. *Id.* at 106.

579. *Id.* at 98.
580. *Id.* at 101.
581. SLAPPER & KELLY, *supra* note 557, at 486.
582. SPRACK, *supra* note 433, at 102–03.
583. *Id.* at 103.
584. SLAPPER & KELLY, *supra* note 557, at 486.
585. *Id.* at 486.
586. *Id.* at 486.
587. JONES, BOWERS & LODGE, *supra* note 486, at 1.
588. *Id.*
589. *See* PREVENTION OF TERRORISM (TEMPORARY PROVISIONS) ACT 1989 § 20(1).
590. WALKER, *supra* note 425, at 21.
591. *See* Terrorism Act of 2000 pt. I, § 1.
592. WALKER, *supra* note 425, at 21.
593. JONES, BOWERS & LODGE, *supra* note 486, at 1 (noting that expressions used in part 1 of the 2006 act have, by virtue of § 20, the same meaning as those in the 2000 act).
594. *See* Terrorism Act of 2000 § 1(1).
595. *Id.* at § 1(2).
596. *Id.* at § 1(3); *see also* Lenihan, *supra* note 567, at 621 (noting, "In 1984, Parliament enacted the Police and Criminal Evidence Act ["PACE"] throughout most of the United Kingdom, and in 1989 extended it to Northern Ireland").
597. WALKER, *supra* note 425, at 146.
598. *Id.* at 147.
599. JONES, BOWERS & LODGE, *supra* note 486, at 61.
600. *See* Terrorism Act of 2000 § 41(1).
601. SPRACK, *supra* note 433, at 27.
602. WALKER, *supra* note 425, at 121.
603. *Id.*
604. JONES, BOWERS & LODGE, *supra* note 486, at 64.
605. *Id.*
606. *See* Terrorism Act of 2000 § 41(3), (7).
607. BECKMAN, *supra* note 86, at 80.
608. *See* Terrorism Act of 2006 § 25(3).
609. *Id.* at sched. 8, §21(1).
610. *Id.* at sched. 8, §21(2).
611. *Id.* at sched. 8, §22.
612. *Id.* at sched. 8, §29(1).

613. WALKER, *supra* note 425, at 124 (noting that in Scotland, in contrast, a "judicial authority" is the sheriff. In Northern Ireland, the "judicial authority" who may approve such warrants is a county court judge, or a resident magistrate who is designated for such a purpose by the lord chancellor.).
614. JONES, BOWERS & LODGE, *supra* note 486, at 64.
615. *See* Terrorism Act of 2000 sched. 8, §30(1)(a), (b).
616. *Id.* at sched. 8, §30(2).
617. *Id.* at § 41(6).
618. JONES, BOWERS & LODGE, *supra* note 486, at 64.
619. *Id.* at 66.
620. *Id.* at 64.
621. *See* TERRORISM ACT OF 2006 § 23(2).
622. WALKER, *supra* note 425, at 129.
623. *Id.*
624. *See* Terrorism Act of 2000 sched. 8, §§6–7.
625. WALKER, *supra* note 425, at 138.
626. *Id.*
627. *Id.*
628. *Id.*
629. *Id.* at 190.
630. BECKMAN, *supra* note 86, at 73.
631. *Id.* at 80.
632. *Id.* at 74.
633. *See* Daniel Moeckli, *The Selective War on Terror: Executive Detention of Foreign Nationals and the Principle of Non-Discrimination*, 31 BROOK. J. INTL'L L. 495, 508 (2006).
634. Walker, *supra* note 456, at 1415.
635. Moeckli, *supra* note 633, at 508.
636. Walker, *supra* note 456, at 1412–13.
637. *Id.* at 1413.
638. JONES, BOWERS & LODGE, *supra* note 486, at 4.
639. Walker, *supra* note 456, at 1415.
640. *See* John Ip, *Comparative Perspectives on the Detention of Terrorist Suspects*, 16 TRANSNAT'L L. & CONTEMP. PROBS. 773, 801 (2007).
641. *Id.*
642. *Id.*
643. *Id.*
644. *Id.*
645. *Id.*

646. *Id.*
647. Walker, *supra* note 456, at 1421–22 (bracketed text original).
648. *Id.* at 1412.
649. BECKMAN, *supra* note 86, at 75.
650. *See* Press Release, Amnesty International, U.K., Proposed "Control Orders" Would Violate Human Rights (Feb. 22 2005), *available at* http://www.amnesty.org/en/library/asset/EUR45/004/2005/en/dom EUR450042005en.html.
651. Ip, *supra* note 640, at 801.
652. *Id.*
653. *See* Secretary of State for the Home Department v. JJ and others, [2007] UKHL 45 (31 October 2007).
654. *See U.K. Joint Committee On Human Rights Tenth Report*, Feb. 20, 2008, *available at* http://www.publications.parliament.uk/pa/jt200708/jtselect/jtrights/57/5706.htm#note45.
655. *See Countering International Terrorism: The United Kingdom's Strategy* (July 2006), http://www intelligence.gov.uk/upload/assets/www.intelli gence.gov.uk/countering.pdf, noting,

> There are limits to what we can say about disruption activity. We cannot be publicly explicit about the detail of many of these operations because of the need to preserve operational security and our capability to conduct similar operations in the future. In addition, where individuals are being prosecuted for terrorist offenses, the Government obviously cannot discuss specific cases until the legal processes are complete. Many disruptions of terrorist networks lead to prosecutions for other, non-terrorist offences—sometimes major offences such as crimes of violence, and sometimes lesser offences such as fraud—or to actions for deportation, or to impose control orders.

656. *Id.* at 19.
657. *Id.* at 20.
658. *See Pre-Charge Detention of Terrorist Suspects*, HOME OFFICE (Dec. 2007) [hereinafter Home Office Report], *available at* http://security.homeoffice.gov.uk/news-publications/publication-search/general/pre charge-detention/pre-charge-detention-proposal?view=Binary, noting,

> We are therefore proposing to legislate in the counter terrorism bill to increase the pre-charge detention limit beyond 28 days to 42 days

only for a strictly limited period of time and in response to a specific operational situation. The higher limit could only come into force where there is a specific operation exceptionally requiring the powers, and then remain in force only where there are compelling operational reasons.

659. *See Halt Efforts to Extend Pre-Charge Detention*, HUMAN RIGHTS WATCH, UK (Oct. 22, 2007), *available at* http://hrw.org/english/docs/2007/10/22/uk17137.htm.
660. *See* Nicholas Watt, *Brown Abandons 42-day Detention After Lords Defeat*, THE GUARDIAN, Oct. 13, 2008.
661. *Id. See also* Phillip Webster, *Vote on 42-day Terrorist Detention Bill to Take Place After May Elections*, THE TIMES, Mar. 21, 2008, *available at* http://www.timesonline.co.uk/tol/news/politics/article3593701.ece.
662. *See, e.g.*, Jago Russell, *Terrorism Pre-Charge Detention,* COMP. L. STUD. (Nov. 2007), *available at* http://www.liberty-human-rights.org.uk/issues/pdfs/pre-charge-detention-comparative-law-study.pdf.
663. *Id.*
664. *See* Home Office Report, *supra* note 658.
665. *Id.*
666. *See* William J. Aceves, *Actio Popularis? The Class Action in International Law*, 2003 U CHI. LEGAL F. 353, 361 (citing KIRSTEN A. YOUNG, THE LAW AND PROCESS OF THE U.N. HUMAN RIGHTS COMMITTEE 176 (2002)).
667. SPRACK, *supra* note 433, at 544.
668. Spencer, *supra* note 430, at 143.
669. *Id.*
670. *See* Murray v. United Kingdom, judgment of 28 October 1994, Series A, No. 300-A (1994).
671. OVEY & WHITE, *supra* note 54, at 132.
672. *See* Brogan and others v. United Kingdom, judgment of 26 May 1993, Series A, No. 258-B; (1994) 17 EHRR 539.
673. Fionnuala Ni Aolain, *supra* note 454, at 1366.
674. Fionnuala Ni Aolain, *The Emergence of Diversity: Differences in Human Rights Jurisprudence*, 19 FORDHAM INT'L L.J. 101, 120 (1995).
675. Fionnuala Ni Aolain, *supra* note 454, at 1366.
676. *See* Brannigan & McBride v. United Kingdom, 17 EHRR 539, 63–64 (1994).
677. ALEXANDER & BRENNER, *supra* note 421, at xii (citing CASES AND MATERIALS ON TERRORISM: THREE NATIONS' RESPONSES xvi (Michael F. Noone & Yonah Alexander eds., 1997)).

678. *Id.* at xii.
679. *Id.* at xiii.
680. *See Dunaway*, 442 U.S. at 212.
681. WALKER, *supra* note 425, at 146.
682. *Id.* at 121.
683. JONES, BOWERS & LODGE, *supra* note 486, at 64.
684. WALKER, *supra* note 425, at 138.
685. *Id.*
686. *See* Guillaume Parmentier, *France*, *in* COUNTERTERRORISM STRATEGIES: SUCCESSES AND FAILURES OF SIX NATIONS 48 (Yonah Alexander ed., 2006).
687. *Id.* at 44.
688. *See* MICHÈLE-LAURE RASSAT, MANUEL DE PROCÉDURE PÉNALE 110 (2002).
689. *Id.*
690. *See* Code de Procédure Pénale art. 145-2 (2008).
691. *See* JACQUELINE HODGSON, FRENCH CRIMINAL JUSTICE 26 (2005).
692. *Id.*
693. *Id.* at 27.
694. *Id.* at 30.
695. *See* Code de Procédure Pénale art. 111-1.
696. *See* Jean Larguier, *The Preliminary Investigation and the French Juge D'Instruction*, 19 N. IR. LEGAL Q. 32, 32 (1968).
697. *Id.*
698. *See* Stewart Field & Andrew West, *A Tale of Two Reforms: French Defense Rights and Police Powers in Transition*, 6 CRIM. L.F. 473, 490 (1995).
699. RASSAT, *supra* note 688, at 107.
700. *See* Code de Procédure Pénale art. 75.
701. *See* Richard S. Frase, *Comparative Criminal Justice as a Guide to American Law Reform: How Do the French Do It, How Can We Find Out, and Why Should We Care?*, 78 CAL. L. REV. 542, n.162 (1990).
702. RASSAT, *supra* note 688, at 112.
703. *See* Code de Procédure Pénale art. 53.
704. *Id.* art. 60–62. *See also* Frase, *supra* note 701, at 78.
705. HODGSON, *supra* note 691, at 147.
706. RASSAT, *supra* note 688, at 109.
707. *See* CATHERINE ELLIOTT, FRENCH CRIMINAL LAW 17 (2001) (while Elliott uses the terms *crime prevention police* and *investigation police*, this article uses *administrative police* and *judicial police*, as those terms more closely correspond with the French designations for each).
708. *Id.*

709. *See* Valérie Dervieux, *The French System, in* EUROPEAN CRIMINAL PROCEDURES 224–25 (Mireille Delmas-Marty & J. R. Spencer eds. 2002).
710. Larguier, *supra* note 696, at 32.
711. *See* Reneé Lettow Lerner, *The Intersection of Two Systems: An American on Trial for an American Murder in the French Cour D'Assises*, 2001 U. ILL. L. REV. 791, 801 (2001).
712. *Id.*
713. Valérie Dervieux, *supra* note 709, at 239.
714. *See* Code de Procédure Pénale art. 79.
715. Lerner, *supra* note 711.
716. ELLIOTT, *supra* note 707, at 34.
717. *Id.* at 37.
718. Lerner, *supra* note 711.
719. *Id.*
720. HODGSON, *supra* note 691, at 39.
721. Parmentier, *supra* note 686, at 45.
722. *See* ANNE STEVENS, GOVERNMENT AND POLITICS OF FRANCE 104 (3d ed. 2003).
723. Parmentier, *supra* note 686, at 59.
724. *See* Jeremy Shapiro & Benedicte Suzan, *The French Experience of Counter-terrorism*, SURVIVAL, Spring 2003, at 68.
725. DARTNELL, *supra* note 341, at 77.
726. Shapiro & Suzan, *supra* note 724, at 68.
727. DARTNELL, *supra* note 341, at 77.
728. *Id.*
729. Shapiro & Suzan, *supra* note 724, at 69.
730. *Id.* at 76.
731. Parmentier, *supra* note 686, at 45.
732. *Id.*
733. *Id.*
734. *Id.*
735. *Id.*
736. *Id.*
737. *Id.* at 59–60.
738. *Id.* at 59.
739. Shapiro & Suzan, *supra* note 724, at 77.
740. Parmentier, *supra* note 686, at 59–60.
741. Shapiro & Suzan, *supra* note 724, at 67.
742. *Id.*
743. *Id.* at 73.

744. Parmentier, *supra* note 686, at 47.
745. Shapiro & Suzan, *supra* note 724, at 76.
746. Parmentier, *supra* note 686, at 57.
747. *See* JEAN PRADEL, DROIT PÉNAL COMPARÉ 282 (1995).
748. Shapiro & Suzan, *supra* note 724, at 77.
749. *Id.* at 78.
750. HODGSON, *supra* note 691, at 40.
751. *Id.* at 41.
752. *Id.* at 39.
753. Parmentier, *supra* note 686, at 47.
754. *Id.*
755. *Id.*
756. Shapiro & Suzan, *supra* note 724, at 82.
757. HODGSON, *supra* note 691, at 43.
758. *Id.*
759. *Id.* at 46.
760. *Id.* at 41.
761. *Id.* at 148.
762. *See* Code de Procédure Pénale art. 706–88.
763. Parmentier, *supra* note 686, at 57, noting,

> A law passed on September 9, 1986, which is part of the new penal code, defines an act of terrorism as an infraction that is intentionally 'linked to an individual or collective effort that intends to disturb public order through intimidation or terror.' Such infractions include: murder, degradation of a person's well-being, kidnapping, sequestration, the hijacking of any form of transport, robbery, extortion, destruction, partial destruction, some forms of computer hacking, and finally, the making, storage, and use of explosive devices, and biological and chemical weapons. French legislation also prohibits conspiracy to commit terrorism and ecological terrorism.

764. *See* Code de Procédure Pénale art. 421-1.
765. *Id.* art. 421-1(1).
766. *Id.* art. 421-1(2).
767. *Id.* art. 421-1(4).
768. *Id.* art. 421-1, cmt. 1 (Infractions Terroristes) (citing arts. 441-2 and 441-3).
769. *Id.* art. 421-2-1.
770. Shapiro & Suzan, *supra* note 724, at 85.

771. *Id.* at 86.
772. *Id.* at 78.
773. Parmentier, *supra* note 686, at 57.
774. *Id.*
775. *Id.*
776. Elliott, *supra* note 707, at 20.
777. Shapiro & Suzan, *supra* note 724, at 85.
778. *See* Robert Vouin, *Provisional Release in French Penal Law*, 108 U. Pa. L. Rev. 355 (1960).
779. *See* Code de Procédure Pénale art. 78-1.
780. *Id.* art. 78-2.
781. *Id.* art. 78-3.
782. *Id.*
783. *Id.*
784. *See* Ordonnance du 2 novembre 1945. *See also* Cynthia Vroom, *Constitutional Protection of Individual Liberties in France: The Conseil Constitutionnel Since 1971*, 63 Tul. L. Rev. 265, 297 (1988) (citing Decrees of June 30, 1946, July 2, 1946 J.O. 5920).
785. *See* Loi du 10 Juin 1983, art. 21.
786. *Id.*
787. *See* Code de Procédure Pénale art. 78-2.
788. Frase, *supra* note 701, at 580 (citing Ministere de la Justice Circulaire, September 10, 1986, 1986 Receuil Dalloz-Sirey, legislation [D.S.L.] 487). It is also worth noting that French police do not need to suspect any danger in order to frisk for weapons. *Id.*
789. *Id.*
790. *See* Sophie Bourtez, La Garde à Vue 7 (2005).
791. Elliott, *supra* note 707, at 20.
792. Hodgson, *supra* note 691, at 147.
793. Bourtez, *supra* note 790, at 7.
794. Hodgson, *supra* note 691, at 147.
795. *Id.*
796. *See* Code de Procédure Pénale art. 63.
797. Elliott, *supra* note 707, at 20.
798. Bourtez, *supra* note 790, at 14.
799. *Id.*
800. *Id.*
801. *See* Code de Procédure Pénale art. 63.
802. Elliott, *supra* note 707, at 20.

803. *See* Code de Procédure Pénale art. 63-1.
804. *Id.* art. 63-2.
805. *Id.*
806. *Id.* art. 63-3.
807. *Id.*
808. *Id.* art. 63-3.
809. *Id.*
810. *Id.* art. 63-4.
811. *Id.*
812. ELLIOTT, *supra* note 707, at 22.
813. *See* Code de Procédure Pénale art. 63-4.
814. ELLIOTT, *supra* note 707, at 22.
815. *Id.* at 20.
816. *See* Circulaire CRIM 04-16 E8 du 21 septembre 2004, reprinted in Code de Procédure Pénale 201 noting,

> Cette modification ameliore les droits de la defense en permettant l'avocat, en cas de prolongation, d'etre present des le debut de la deuxieme period de la garde a vue et renforce la coherence du dispositif en institutant un parallelisme entre le debut et le renouvellement de la mesure.

817. HODGSON, *supra* note 691, at 119.
818. Bron McKillop, *Anatomy of a French Murder Case*, 45 AM. J. COMP. L. 527, 577–78 (1997).
819. BOURTEZ, *supra* note 790, at 8.
820. *Id.* at 74.
821. Dervieux, *supra* note 709, at 276 (citing Code de Procédure Pénale art. 73).
822. *Id.* at 276.
823. *Id.* at 281.
824. *Id.*
825. *Id.* at 252.
826. *Id.* at 276 (citing Code de Procédure Pénale art. 70(1)).
827. *Id.* at 281.
828. *Id.* at 281.
829. *Id.*
830. PRADEL, *supra* note 747, at 36–37.
831. *Id.* at 37.
832. Vouin, *supra* note 778, at 355.

833. *Id.* (citing Circular of April 2, 1952 [1952] Semaine Juridique 16903).
834. *Id.* (citing Code de Procédure Pénale (1958) art. 137).
835. *Id.*
836. *Id.* at 360 (citing Code de Procédure Pénale (1958) art. 139).
837. *Id.* at 360.
838. *Id.* at 357.
839. *Id.*
840. *Id.*
841. *Id.* at 358.
842. *See* Code de Procédure Pénale art. 137.
843. Dervieux, *supra* note 709, at 278 (noting, however, that there are circumstances in which the *Chambre de l'instruction* or the *tribunal correctionel* or its president may also order someone into *détention provisoire*).
844. *See* Code de Procédure Pénale art. 143-1.
845. *Id.* art. 144.
846. Dervieux, *supra* note 709, at 278 (citing Code de Procédure Pénale arts. 143-1, 145).
847. *See* Code de Procédure Pénale art. 145-1.
848. *Id.* art. 145-1.
849. *Id.*
850. *Id.* art. 144-1.
851. *See* Circulaire CRIM 00-16 F1 du 20 décembre 2000.
852. *See* Code de Procédure Pénale art. 145-2.
853. *Id.*
854. Elliott, *supra* note 707, at 40–41.
855. *See* Code de Procédure Pénale art. 145-4.
856. *See* Code de Procédure Pénale art. 114.
857. *Id.* art. 78-2.
858. Frase, *supra* note 701, at 580 (citing Ministere de la Justice Circulaire, September 10, 1986, 1986 Receuil Dalloz-Sirey, legislation [D.S.L.] 487). It is also worth noting that French police do not need to suspect any danger in order to frisk for weapons. *Id.*
859. Parmentier, *supra* note 686, at 57.
860. Vroom, *supra* note 784, at 297.
861. *See* Code de Procédure Pénale art. 706-73.
862. *Id.* art. 706-88.
863. *Id.*
864. Bourtez, *supra* note 790, at 41.

865. *See* Circulaire CRIM 04-16 E8 du 21 septembre 2004, reprinted in Code de Procédure Pénale 201, *supra* note 816.
866. BOURTEZ, *supra* note 790, at 45.
867. HODGSON, *supra* note 691, at 54.
868. *Id.* at 148.
869. *Id.* at 57.
870. *See* Circulaire CRIM 00-16 F1 du 20 décembre 2000.
871. *See* Code de Procédure Pénale art. 145-2.
872. *Id.* art. 145-2.
873. *See* W. Jason Fisher, *Militant Islamicist Terrorism in Europe: Are France & The United Kingdom Legally Prepared for the Challenge?*, 6 WASH. U. GLOBAL STUD. L. REV. 255, 266–67 (2007).
874. *Id.*
875. Shapiro & Suzan, *supra* note 724, at 80. *See also* Parmentier, *supra* note 686, at 47.
876. Shapiro & Suzan, *supra* note 724, at 84.
877. *Id.* at 80.
878. *Id.*
879. Parmentier, *supra* note 686, at 66.
880. Shapiro & Suzan, *supra* note 724, at 85.
881. Parmentier, *supra* note 686, at 86–87.
882. *Id.* at 85–86.
883. HODGSON, *supra* note 691, at 33.
884. *Id.* at 118.
885. OVEY & WHITE, *supra* note 54, at 132.
886. *Id.* at 201.
887. HODGSON, *supra* note 691, at 34–35.
888. *See* Omer Ze'ev Bekerman, *Torture—The Absolute Prohibition of a Relative Term: Does Everyone Know What is in Room 101?*, 53 AM. J. COMP. L. 743, 755 (2005).
889. *See* David Heffernan, *America the Cruel and Unusual? An Analysis of the Eighth Amendment Under International Law*, 45 CATH. U. L. REV. 481 (1996).
890. *See* Suzanne Galand-Carval, *The European Court of Human Rights Declares War on Unreasonable Delays*, 1996 ST. LOUIS-WARSAW TRANSATLANTIC L.J. 109, 119 (1996).
891. Tomasi v. France (Series A, No 241-A, Application No 12850/87), 15 EHRR 1, 27 AUGUST 1992.
892. *See* Galand-Carval, *supra* note 890, at 119.

893. Ovey & White, *supra* note 54, at 137.
894. *See* Jacqueline Hodgson, *Suspects, Defendants and Victims in the French Criminal Process: The Context of Recent Reform*, 51 Int'l & Comp. L.Q. 783 (Oct. 2002).
895. *See* Circulaire CRIM 00-16 F1 du 20 décembre 2000.
896. *See* Code de Procédure Pénale art. 145-2.
897. *Id.* art. 145-2.
898. Elliott, *supra* note 707, at 20.
899. *Id.*
900. Ovey & White, *supra* note 54, at 80.
901. Elliott, *supra* note 707, at 21.
902. Hodgson, *supra* note 894, at 783.
903. *Id.* at 813.
904. McKillop, *supra* note 818, at 534–35.
905. *See* Code de Procédure Pénale art. 78-2.
906. *See Civil Liberties: Detention Without Trial, The Stuff of Nightmares*, The Economist, Oct. 4, 2007 [hereinafter *The Stuff of Nightmares*], *available at* http://www.economist.com/world/international/displaystory.cfm?story_id=9909351&CFID=7961235&CFTOKEN=39448028.
907. *Terrorist Investigations and the French Examining Magistrate System*, Home Office, 2007, *available at* http://security.homeoffice.gov.uk/news-publications/publication-search/counter-terrorism-bill-2007/examining-magistrates.pdf?view=Binary.
908. *The Stuff of Nightmares*, *supra* note 906, noting,

> But most legal commentators believe that if the French model were copied in this area, an unbearable blow would be dealt to England's common-law system. And despite the fears of civil libertarians, there are still judges and legislators who think that system worth preserving.

909. Jacoby Declaration, *supra* note 2, at 4.
910. *Id.* at 6.
911. *Id.* at 4–5.
912. *General Comment 8*.
913. *Id.*
914. *Id.*
915. Mukasey, *supra* note 7. *See also* Bruce Ackerman, Before the Next Attack: Preserving Civil Liberties in an Age of Terrorism (2006), at 46–52 (arguing

for an "emergency constitution" in the U.S. which would allow for detention of terrorist suspects for up to 45 days based on reasonable suspicion).

916. *Id.*
917. WALKER, *supra* note 425, at 146.
918. *Id.* at 121.
919. Frase, *supra* note 701, at 580 (citing Ministere de la Justice Circulaire, September 10, 1986, 1986 Receuil Dalloz-Sirey, legislation [D.S.L.] 487).
920. RASSAT, *supra* note 688, at 110.
921. BOURTEZ, *supra* note 790, at 14.
922. JONES, BOWERS & LODGE, *supra* note 486, at 64.
923. *Id.*
924. RASSAT, *supra* note 688, at 110.
925. *See* Code de Procédure Pénale art. 137.
926. *Id.* art. 145-2.
927. WALKER, *supra* note 425, at 138.
928. *See Circulaire CRIM 04-16 E8 du 21 septembre 2004*, *in* CODE DE PROCÉDURE P ÉNALE (2008) 201, *supra* note 816.
929. BOURTEZ, *supra* note 790, at 45.
930. *See Terry*, 392 U.S. at 20–21.
931. *See Royer*, 460 U.S. at 502–03.
932. *See Watson*, 423 U.S. at 417–18.
933. *See Chandler*, 520 U.S. at 309.
934. *See Edmond*, 531 U.S. at 44.
935. Frase, *supra* note 701, at 580.
936. *See* Illinois v. Wardlow, 528 U.S. 119, 123 (2000) (noting, "'reasonable suspicion' is a less demanding standard than 'probable cause' and requires a showing considerably less than preponderance of the evidence").
937. Iraola, *supra* note 254, at 410.
938. MOORE'S FEDERAL PRACTICE, *supra* note 226, at § 605.03(2)(c).
939. *Id.* at 411.
940. JONES, BOWERS & LODGE, *supra* note 486, at 64.
941. *See* Code de Procédure Pénale art. 706-73.
942. *See* 18 U.S.C. § 3501(c) (2009).
943. JONES, BOWERS & LODGE, *supra* note 486, at 64.
944. Hodgson, *supra* note 894, at 147.
945. *See, e.g.*, Ricardo J. Bauscas, *The Unconstitutionality of "Hold Until Cleared": Reexamining Material Witness Detentions in the Wake of the September 11th Dragnet*, 58 VAND. L. REV. 677, 682–95 (2005); *see also* Josh Gerstein, *Under Charge*, THE NEW REPUBLIC, Apr. 22, 2002, at 22

(noting that the material witness statute has been used to hold detainees without charge for over seven months).

946. *Id.*

947. Mukasey, *supra* note 7, noting,

> The material witness statute has its perils. Because the law does not authorize investigative detention, the government had only a limited time in which to let Padilla testify, prosecute him or let him go. As that limited time drew to a close, the government changed course. It withdrew the grand jury subpoena that had triggered his designation as a material witness, designated Padilla instead as an unlawful combatant, and transferred him to military custody.

948. *See Awadallah*, 349 F.3d at 56.

949. WALKER, *supra* note 425, at 138; Code de Procédure Pénale art. 706-73; Parmentier, *supra* note 686, at 86–87.

950. *See Miranda*, 384 U.S. at 459 (citing United States v. Grunewald, 233 F.2d 556, 579, 581–82 (Frank, J., dissenting), *rev'd*, 353 U.S. 391 (1957)).

951. *Id.*

952. *Id.*

953. *Id.*

954. WALKER, *supra* note 425, at 138.

955. ELLIOTT, *supra* note 707, at 22.

956. *See* 8 U.S.C. § 1226(a) (2009).

957. *Zadvydas*, 533 U.S. at 701.

958. *Id.*

959. *Id. See also* Miller, *supra* note 286.

960. *See, e.g.*, *Moya*, 74 F.3d at 1119; *Henry*, 604 F.2d at 914.

961. *See Vasquez-Trujillo*, 151 F. App'x 509 (citing *Trias-Hernandez*, 528 F.2d 366); *Alderete-Deras*, 743 F.2d 645.

962. *See Turkmen*, 2006 U.S. Dist. LEXIS 39170.

963. *See Awadallah*, 349 F.3d at 56.

964. Mukasey, *supra* note 7.

965. *See* 18 U.S.C. §§ 2339A, 2339B.

966. DYCUS, BANKS & RAVEN-HANSEN, *supra* note 339, at 491 (noting, "Congress has not made it a crime to be a member of a [foreign terrorist organization]").

967. *See* United States v. Warsame, 537 F. Supp. 2d 1005, 1014 (D. Minn. 2008).

968. *See* Elfbrandt v. Russell, 384 U.S. 11, 15–16 (1966).

969. *See Scales*, 367 U.S. at 224–25.

970. *Id.*
971. *Id.* at 206 n.1 (quoting 18 U.S.C. § 2385).
972. David Henrik Pedle, *Charity of the Heart and Sword: The Material Support Offense and Personnel Guilt*, 30 SEATTLE U. L. REV. 777, 794–95 (2007).
973. *See Scales*, 367 U.S. at 226–28.
974. *See* WALKER, *supra* note 425, at 146.
975. Frase, *supra* note 701, at 580.
976. *See* Stulin, *supra* note 197, at 1459.
977. *See* Hiibel, 542 U.S. at 187–88.
978. *See* Dickerson v. United States, 530 U.S. 428, 437 (2000).
979. *Id.*
980. *Id.*
981. Darmer, *supra* note 253, at 274–75.
982. *See Quarles*, 467 U.S. at 655–56.
983. *See* United States v. Corley, 500 F.3d. 210, 213 (2007).
984. *Id.* at 216–18.
985. *Id.* at 218.
986. *Zadvydas*, 533 U.S. 678.
987. *Id.* at 701.
988. *Id.*
989. *Id.* at 690.
990. *See* Code de Procédure Pénale art. 145-2.
991. *See Hendricks*, 521 U.S. at 357.
992. *Id.*
993. *Id.*
994. Tung Yin, *supra* note 21, at 211.
995. *Id.* at 197.
996. *Id.* at 211.
997. *Id.*
998. *Salerno*, 481 U.S. at 750.
999. *Id.* at 750.
1000. *Id.* at 747.
1001. Jacoby Declaration, *supra* note 2, at 6.
1002. Mukasey, *supra* note 7.
1003. TURNER & SCHULHOFER, *supra* note 322, at 40.

Appendix

Tables of Proposed Legislative Language

Note. Bold type indicates language that deviates from the existing statute.

Table A-1. Proposed federal anti-terrorist membership statute.

Smith Act	Proposed Terrorist Membership Statute
18 U.S.C. § 2385 Whoever organizes or helps or attempts to organize any society, group, or assembly of persons who teach, advocate, or encourage the overthrow or destruction of any such government by force or violence; or becomes or is a member of, or affiliates with, any such society, group, or assembly of persons, knowing the purposes thereof—	18 U.S.C. § _____ Whoever organizes or helps or attempts to organize any society, group, or assembly of persons who teach, advocate, or encourage **international or domestic terrorist activity**; or becomes or is a member of, or affiliates with, any such society, group, or assembly of persons, knowing the purposes thereof—
Shall be fined not more than $20,000 or imprisoned not more than twenty years, or both, and shall be ineligible for employment by the United States or any department or agency thereof, for the five years next following his conviction.	Shall be fined not more than **$100,000** or imprisoned not more than twenty years, or both, and shall be ineligible for employment by the United States or any department or agency thereof, for the five years next following his conviction.

TABLE A-2. Proposed federal "stop and identify" statute.

Nevada Statute	Proposed U.S. Statute
171.123. Temporary detention by peace officer of person suspected of criminal behavior or of violating conditions of parole or probation: Limitations. 1. Any peace officer may detain any person whom the officer encounters under circumstances which reasonably indicate that the person has committed, is committing or is about to commit a crime. 2. Any peace officer may detain any person the officer encounters under circumstances which reasonably indicate that the person has violated or is violating the conditions of his parole or probation. 3. The officer may detain the person pursuant to this section only to ascertain his identity and the suspicious circumstances surrounding his presence abroad. Any person so detained shall identify himself, but may not be compelled to answer any other inquiry of any peace officer. 4. A person must not be detained longer than is reasonably necessary to effect the purposes of this section, and in no event longer than 60 minutes. The detention must not extend beyond the place or the immediate vicinity of the place where the detention was first effected, unless the person is arrested.	18 U.S.C. § _____. Temporary detention by **federal law enforcement** officer of person suspected of **international or domestic terrorism or terrorism-related activity:** Limitations. 1. Any **federal law enforcement** officer may detain any person whom the officer encounters under circumstances which reasonably indicate that the person **is engaged in, is engaging in, or is about to engage in international or domestic terrorism or terrorism-related activity.** 2. The officer may detain the person pursuant to this section **in order to** ascertain his identity and the suspicious circumstances surrounding **his presence.** Any person so detained shall identify himself, but may not be compelled to answer any other inquiry of any **federal law enforcement** officer. 3. A person must not be detained **under this section** longer than is reasonably necessary to effect the purposes of this section, and in no event longer than 60 minutes. The detention must not extend beyond the place or the immediate vicinity of the place where the detention was first effected, unless the person is arrested. 4. **Nothing in this section shall be interpreted as limiting any other ability by federal law enforcement to lawfully detain a terrorist suspect.**

TABLE A-3. Proposed federal terrorism public safety/confession statute.

Proposed Terrorism "Public Safety/Confession" Statute
18 U.S.C. § _____. **Given that terrorism poses enormous risks to national security and the lives of others, in any criminal prosecution by the United States or by the District of Columbia involving an individual suspected of international or domestic terrorism or terrorism-related activity, a confession or any other statement made or given by a person who is a defendant therein, while such person was under arrest or other detention in the custody of any law-enforcement officer or law-enforcement agency, shall not be inadmissible solely because that individual was not advised of his or her rights when that statement or confession was given during an on-the-scene interrogation, immediately upon the individual's apprehension, and where the interrogation was conducted in order to attain further information regarding past, future, or ongoing terroristic activity.**

TABLE A-4. Proposed federal terrorism detention statute.

Omnibus Crime Control and Safe Streets Act	Proposed Amendments
18 U.S.C. § 3501(c). In any criminal prosecution by the United States or by the District of Columbia, a confession made or given by a person who is a defendant therein, while such person was under arrest or other detention in the custody of any law-enforcement officer or law-enforcement agency, shall not be inadmissible solely because of delay in bringing such person before a magistrate [magistrate judge] or other officer empowered to commit persons charged with offenses against the laws of the United States or of the District of Columbia if such confession is found by the trial judge to have been made voluntarily and if the weight to be given the confession is left to the jury and if such confession was made or given by such person within six hours immediately following his arrest or other detention: Provided, That the time limitation contained in this subsection shall not apply in any case in which the delay in bringing such person before such magistrate or other officer beyond such six-hour period is found by the trial judge to be reasonable considering the means of transportation and the distance to be traveled to the nearest available such magistrate or other officer.	18 U.S.C. § 3501(_). In any criminal prosecution by the United States or by the District of Columbia **involving an individual suspected of international or domestic terrorism or terrorism-related activity,** a confession made or given by a person who is a defendant therein, while such person was under arrest or other detention in the custody of any law-enforcement officer or law-enforcement agency, shall not be inadmissible solely because of delay in bringing such person before a magistrate [magistrate judge] or other officer empowered to commit persons charged with offenses against the laws of the United States or of the District of Columbia if such confession is found by the trial judge to have been made voluntarily and if the weight to be given the confession is left to the jury and if such confession was made or given by such person within **twelve** hours immediately following his arrest or other detention: Provided, that the time limitation contained in this subsection shall not apply in any case in which the delay in bringing such person before such magistrate or other officer beyond such six-hour period is found by the trial judge to be reasonable considering the means of transportation and the distance to be traveled to the nearest available such magistrate or other officer.

TABLE A-5. Proposed alien terrorism detention statute.

Existing Alien Detention Statute	Proposed Statute
8 U.S.C. § 1231(a)(6). Inadmissible or Criminal Aliens. An alien ordered removed who is inadmissible under section 212 [8 U.S.C. § 1227(a)(1)(C), (a)(2), or (a)(4)] or who has been determined by the Attorney General to be a risk to the community or unlikely to comply with the order of removal, may be detained beyond the removal period and, if released, shall be subject to the terms of supervision in paragraph (3).	8 U.S.C. § 1231(a)(_). **Aliens suspected of Terrorist Activity or Associations.** An alien ordered removed who is inadmissible under section 212 [8 U.S.C. § 1227(a)(1)(C), (a)(2), or (a)(4)] or who has been determined by the Attorney General to be **a terrorist suspect or who is suspected of any involvement in international or domestic terroristic activity** may be detained beyond the removal period **until such time as the Attorney General determines that the alien no longer poses a continued danger** and, if released, shall be subject to the terms of supervision in paragraph (3).

Bibliography

8 U.S.C. § 1231(a)(2).

18 U.S.C. § 2332b(g)(5).

18 U.S.C. § 2339A.

18 U.S.C. § 2339B.

18 U.S.C. § 3077(1).

18 U.S.C. § 3142.

18 U.S.C. § 3144.

18 U.S.C. § 3161(b)(1).

18 U.S.C. § 3501(c).

Abdallah Higazy v. Templeton, 505 F.3d 161 (2d Cir. 2007).

Aceves, William J. *Actio Popularis? The Class Action in International Law*. 2003 U. Chi. Legal F. 353 (2003).

Ackerman, Bruce. *Before the Next Attack: Preserving Civil Liberties in an Age of Terrorism*. New Haven, CT: Yale University Press, 2006.

Alexander, Yonah. "United States." In *Counterterrorism Strategies, Successes and Failures of Six Nations*, edited by Yonah Alexander, 9–43. Dulles, VA: Potomac Books, 2006.

Alexander, Yonah, and Edgar H. Brenner. *The United Kingdom's Legal Responses to Terrorism*. Oxon, U.K.: Routledge-Cavendish, 2007.

Al-Marri v. Pucciarelli, 2008 U.S. App. Lexis 14979.

Aolain, Fionnuala Ni. *The Emergence of Diversity: Differences in Human Rights Jurisprudence*. 19 Fordham Int'l L.J. 101 (1995).

———. *Legal Developments: The Fortification of an Emergency Regime*. 59 Alb. L. Rev. 1353 (1996).

Amann, Diane Marie. *International Law Weekend Proceedings: The Rights of the Accused in a Global Enforcement Arena.* 6 I.L.S.A. J. Int'l & Comp. L. 555 (2000).

Atwater v. City of Lago Vista, 532 U.S. 318 (2001).

Baxter, Richard. *A Skeptical Look at the Concept of Terrorism.* 7 Akron L. Rev. 380 (1974).

Bauscas, Ricardo J. *The Unconstitutionality of "Hold Until Cleared": Reexamining Material Witness Detentions in the Wake of the September 11th Dragnet.* 58 Vand. L. Rev. 677 (2005).

Bekerman, Omer Ze'ev. *Torture—The Absolute Prohibition of a Relative Term: Does Everyone Know What Is in Room 101?* 53 Am. J. Comp. L. 743 (2005).

Beckman, James. *Comparative Legal Approaches to Homeland Security and Anti-Terrorism.* Burlington, VT: Ashgate Publishing Company, 2007.

Blakesley, Christopher L. *Terrorism, Drugs, International Law, and the Protection of Human Liberty.* New York: Transnational Publishers, 1992.

Bilder, Richard B. "An Overview of International Human Rights Law." In *Guide to International Human Rights Law Practice*, edited by Hurst Hannum, 4–6. Philadelphia: University of Philadelphia Press, 1999.

Blum, Stephanie Cooper. *The Necessary Evil of Preventive Detention in the War on Terror.* Amherst, NY: Cambria Press, 2008.

Boim v. Quranic Literacy Institute, 291 F.3d 1000 (7th Cir. 2002).

Bourtez, Sophie. *La Garde à Vue.* Paris: Editions L'Harmattan, 2005.

Bradley, Craig M. *Criminal Procedure: A Worldwide Study.* Durham, NC: Carolina University Press, 2007.

Brannigan & McBride v. United Kingdom, 17 Eur. H.R. Rep. 539 (1994).

Brewer v. Williams, 430 U.S. 387 (1977).

Brogan and Others v. United Kingdom, Judgment of 26 May 1993, Series A, No. 258-B; (1994) 17 EHRR 539.

Brown v. Illinois, 422 U.S. 590 (1975).

Campbell, Colm, and Ita Connolly. *A Deadly Complexity: Law, Social Movements and Political Violence*. 16 Minn. J. Int'l L. 265 (2007).

Carlson, Ronald L. *Distorting Due Process for Noble Purposes: The Emasculation of America's Material Witness Laws*. 42 Ga. L. Rev. 941 (2008).

Cassel, Doug. *Pretrial and Preventive Detention of Suspected Terrorists: Options and Constraints Under International Law*. 98 J. Crim. L. & Criminology 811 (2008).

———. International Human Rights Law and Security Detention. Notre Dame Law School Legal Studies Research Paper No. 08-32. *Available at* http://www.ssrn.com/link/notre-dame-legal-studies.html.

Chaliand, Gerard, and Arnaud Blin. *The History of Terrorism: From Antiquity to Al Qaeda*. London: University of California Press, 2007.

Chandler v. Miller, 520 U.S. 305 (1997).

Circulaire CRIM 00-16 F1 du 20 décembre 2000.

Circulaire CRIM 04-16 E8 du 21 septembre 2004.

City of Indianapolis v. Edmond, 531 U.S. 32 (2000).

"Civil Liberties: Detention Without Trial, The Stuff of Nightmares." *The Economist*, Oct. 4, 2007. *Available at* http://www.economist.com/world/international/displaystory.cfm?story_id=9909351&CFID=7961235&CFTOKEN=39448028.

Clarke, Richard A. *Al Qaeda, the Organization: A Five-Year Forecast*. 618 Annals 14 (2008).

Clifford, Mary. "Criminal Justice System in the United States: General Overview." In *Criminal Justice in the United States, Comparative and International Criminal Justice Systems: Policing, Judiciary, and*

Corrections, edited by Obi N. Ignatius Ebbe, 11–28. Woburn, MA: Butterworth-Heinemann, 2000.

Code de Procédure Pénale. Paris: Dalloz, 2008.

Congressional Research Service ("CRS") Report for Congress, Arrest and Detention of Material Witnesses: Federal Law in Brief and Section 12 of the USA PATRIOT and Terrorism Prevention Reauthorization Act (H.R. 319), Sept. 8, 2005. *Available at* https://www.policyarchive.org/bitstream/handle/10207/2557/RL33077_20050908.pdf?sequence=1.

Conte, Alex, Scott Davidson, and Richard Burchill. *Defining Civil and Political Rights: The Jurisprudence of the United Nations Human Rights Committee*. Aldershot, U.K.: Ashgate, 2005.

Countering International Terrorism: The United Kingdom's Strategy, July 2006. *Available at* http://www.intelligence.gov.uk/upload/assets/www.intelligence.gov.uk/countering.pdf.

County of Riverside v. McLaughlin, 500 U.S. 44 (1991).

Darmer, M. K. B. *Lessons from the* Lindh *Case: Public Safety and the Fifth Amendment*. 68 Brooklyn L. Rev. 241 (2002).

———. *Miranda Warnings, Torture, the Right to Counsel and the War on Terror*, 10 Chap. L. Rev. 631 (2007).

Dartell, Michael Y. *Action Directe: Ultra-left Terrorism in France, 1979–1987*. London: Routledge, 1997.

Davies, Malcolm, Hazel Croall, and Jane Tyrer. *Criminal Justice: An Introduction to the Criminal Justice System in England and Wales*. White Plains, NY: Longman Publishing Group, 1995.

Declaration by Vice Admiral Lowell E. Jacoby (USN), Director of the Defense Intelligence Agency, Jan. 9, 2003. *Available at* http://www.pegc.us/archive/Padilla_vs_Rumsfeld/Jacoby_declaration_20030109.pdf.

Declarations Recognizing the Competence of the Human Rights Committee under Article 41, Office of the United Nations High Commission for

Human Rights, last updated Jan. 5, 2009. *Available at* http://www2.ohchr.org/english/bodies/ratification/docs/DeclarationsArt41ICCPR.pdf.

Decree of June 30, 1946, July 2, 1946 J.O. 5920.

Dervieux, Valérie. "The French System." In *European Criminal Procedures*, edited by Mireille Delmas-Marty and J. R. Spencer, 218–291. Cambridge, U.K.: Cambridge University Press, 2002.

Doggett v. United States, 505 U.S. 647 (1992).

Donohue, Laura K. *Counter-Terrorist Law and Emergency Powers in the United Kingdom 1922–2000.* Dublin: Irish Academic Press, 2001.

Doran, Sean, John D. Jackson, and Michael L. Seigel. *Rethinking Adversariness in Nonjury Criminal Trials*. 23 Am. J. Crim. L. 1 (1995).

Dunaway v. New York, 442 U.S. 200 (1979).

Dunoff, Jeffrey L., Steven R. Ratner, and David Wippman. *International Law, Norms, Actors, Process: A Problem-Oriented Approach.* 2nd ed. New York: Aspen Publishers, 2006.

Dycus, Stephen, William C. Banks, and Peter Raven-Hansen. *Counterterrorism Law.* New York: Aspen Publishers, 2007.

Elfbrandt v. Russell, 384 U.S. 11 (1966).

Elliott, Catherine. *French Criminal Law.* Portland, OR: Willan Publishing, 2001.

European Convention on Human Rights, art. 5(1)(c), art. 5(3), art. 15(1).

Failer, Judith Lynn. *Who Qualifies for Rights? Homelessness, Mental Illness, and Civil Commitment.* Ithaca, NY: Cornell University Press, 2002.

Federal Rules of Criminal Procedure, 5(a)(1)(A), 5(c), 15(a)(2), 46.

Field, Stewart, and Andrew West. *A Tale of Two Reforms: French Defense Rights and Police Powers in Transition.* 6 Crim. L.F. 473 (1995).

Fisher, W. Jason. *Military Islamicist Terrorism in Europe: Are France & the United Kingdom Equally Prepared for the Challenge?* Wash. U. Global Stud. L. Rev., 266–267 (2007).

Florida v. Royer, 460 U.S. 491 (1985).

Fox, Campbell and Hartley v. United Kingdom, Series A no. 182 (1990).

Frase, Richard S. *Comparative Criminal Justice as a Guide to American Law Reform: How Do the French Do It, How Can We Find Out, and Why Should We Care?* 78 Calif. L. Rev. 542 (1990).

Galand-Carval, Suzanne. *The European Court of Human Rights Declares War on Unreasonable Delays.* 1996 St. Louis-Warsaw Trans'l 109 (1996).

General Comment No. 08: Right to Liberty and Security of Persons (Art. 9): 30/06/82. CCPR General Comment No. 8 (General Comments). *Available at* http://www.unhchr.ch/tbs/doc.nsf/(Symbol)/f4253f9572cd4700c12563ed00483bec?Opendocument.

Gerstein v. Pugh, 420 U.S. 103 (1975).

Gerstein, Josh. "Under Charge." *The New Republic*, Apr. 22, 2002.

Goodnough, Abby. "Jose Padilla Convicted on All Counts in Terror Trial." *N.Y. Times*, Aug. 16, 2007.

Gramenos v. Jewel Co., 797 F. 2d 432 (7th Cir. 1986).

Griffin, Lissa. *The Correction of Wrongful Convictions: A Comparative Perspective*. 16 Am. U. Int'l L. Rev. 1241 (2001).

"Halt Efforts to Extend Pre-Charge Detention." *Human Rights Watch, U.K.*, Oct. 22, 2007. *Available at* http://hrw.org/english/docs/2007/10/22/uk17137.htm.

Hamdi v. Rumsfeld, 542 U.S. 507 (2004).

Hannum, Hurst. Book review of *Ten Years On in Northern Ireland: The Legal Control of Political Violence*, by Kevin Boyle, Tom Hadden, and Paddy Hillyard. 75 A.J.I.L. 705 (1981).

Harding, Andrew. *Preventive Detention and Security Law: A Comparative Survey.* Dordrecht, the Netherlands: Martinus Nijhoff Publishers, 1993.

Harwin, Michael. *Detaining for Danger under the Bail Reform Act of 1984: Paradoxes of Procedure and Proof.* 35 Ariz. L. Rev. 1091 (1993).

Hayes v. Florida, 470 U.S. 811 (1985).

Heffernan, David. *America the Cruel and Unusual? An Analysis of the Eighth Amendment Under International Law.* 45 Cath. U.L. Rev. 481 (1996).

Hiibel v. Sixth Judicial District Court of Nevada, 542 U.S. 177 (2004).

Hirschel, J. David, and William Wakefield. *Criminal Justice in England and the United States.* Westport, CT: Preager Publishers, 1995.

Hodgson, Jacqueline. *French Criminal Justice.* Oxford, U.K.: Hart Publishing, 2005.

———. *Suspects, Defendants and Victims in the French Criminal Process: The Context of Recent Reform.* 51 I.C.L.Q. 783 (October 2002).

Illinois v. Caballes, 543 U.S. 405 (2005).

Illinois v. Wardlow, 528 U.S. 119 (2000).

International Covenant on Civil and Political Rights New York, December 16, 1966 (List of Signatories). *Available at* http://www2.ohchr.org/english/bodies/ratification/4.htm.

International Covenant on Civil and Political Rights Optional Protocol to the International Covenant on Civil and Political Rights, March 23, 1976. *Available at* http://www.ohchr.org/english/law/pdf/ccpr-one.pdf.

Ip, John. *Comparative Perspectives on the Detention of Terrorist Suspects.* 16 Transnat'l L. & Contemp. Probs. 773 (2007).

Iraola, Roberto. *Terrorism, Grand Juries, and the Federal Material Witness Statute.* 34 St. Mary's L.J. 401 (2003).

Jackson, John D. *Making Juries Accountable.* 50 Am. J. Comp. L. 477 (2002).

Jones, Alun, Rupert Bowers, & Hugo D. Lodge. *Blackstone's Guide to the Terrorism Act 2006.* Oxford, U.K.: Oxford University Press, 2006.

Jorgensen, Nina H. B. *The Right of the Accused to Self-Representation Before International Criminal Tribunals*. 98 A.J.I.L. 711 (2004).

Kansas v. Hendricks, 521 U.S. 346 (1997).

Lafave, Wayne, Jerold H. Israel, and Nancy J. King. *Principles of Criminal Procedure: Investigation*. St. Paul, MN: Thomson/West, 2004.

———. *Principles of Criminal Procedure: Post-Investigation.* St. Paul, MN: Thomson/West, 2004.

Langbein, John H. *The Origins of Adversary Criminal Trial.* New York: Oxford University Press, 2003.

Larguier, Jean. *The Preliminary Investigation and the French Juge D'Instruction*. 19 N. Ir. Legal Q. 32, 32 (1968).

Law & Order (NBC television broadcast, 1990–present).

Lenihan, Brian P. *Unsound Method: Judicial Inquiry and Extradition to Northern Ireland.* 34 B.C. L. Rev. 591 (1993).

Lerner, Reneé Lettow. *The Intersection of Two Systems: An American on Trial for an American Murder in the French Cour D'Assises*. Univ. Ill. L. Rev. 791 (2001).

Lewis, Neil A. "Moussaoui Given Life Term by Jury over Link to 9/11." *N.Y. Times*, May 4, 2006.

Lillich, Richard B. *The Growing Importance of Customary International Human Rights Law*. 25 Ga. J. Int'l & Comp. L. 1 (1995).

Loi du 10 Juin 1983, art. 21.

Maguire, Mike. *Effects of the "P.A.C.E." Provisions on Detention and Questioning: Some Preliminary Findings*. 28 Brit. J. Criminol. (Winter 1988).

Mallory v. United States, 354 U.S. 449 (1957).

Mathews v. Diaz, 426 U.S. 67 (1976).

McIntyre, Tasia E. *Protecting Against Terrorism or Symbolic Politics? Fatal Flaws in Ohio's Terrorism Statute.* 56 Case W. Res. 203 (2005).

Michigan Dept. of State Police v. Sitz, 496 U.S. 444 (1990).

Michigan v. Tucker, 417 U.S. 433 (1974).

Miller, Teresa. *Blurring the Boundaries Between Immigration and Crime Control After September 11th*. 25 B.C. Third World L.J. 81 (2005).

Miranda v. Arizona, 384 U.S. 436 (1966).

Moeckli, Daniel. *The Selective War on Terror: Executive Detention of Foreign Nationals and the Principle of Nondiscrimination*. 31 Brooklyn J. Intl'l L. 495 (2006).

Moore, James W. *Moore's Federal Practice*. 3rd ed. 2007. LexisNexis Matthew Bender.

Mukasey, Michael B. "Jose Padilla Makes Bad Law: Terror Trials Hurt the Nation Even When They Lead to Convictions." *Wall Street Journal, Aug. 22, 2007.*

Murphy, Sean D. *Canadian Deportation to United States of Death-Penalty Convict*. 98 A.J.I.L. 180 (2004).

Murphy, Sean D. *Second Circuit Rejection of Presidential Power to Declare U.S. National "Enemy Combatant."* 98 A.J.I.L. 186 (2004).

Murray v. United Kingdom, Series A no. 300-A (1994).

Nash (Leich), Marian. *Contemporary Practice of the United States Relating to International Law*. 89 A.J.I.L. 96 (1995).

Nesbitt, Katherine. *Preventative Detention of Terrorist Suspects in Australia and the United States: A Comparative Constitutional Analysis*. 17 B.U. Pub. Int. L.J. 39 (2007).

New Jersey v. T. L. O., 469 U.S. 325 (1985).

New York v. Quarles, 467 U.S. 649, 655–656 (1984).

Nevada Revised Statute § 171.123.

Northern Ireland (Emergency Provisions) Act 1973, 11(1), 12.

O'Connor, Michael P., and Celia M. Rumann. *How to Avoid Getting Burned by the Same Mistakes Made Fighting Terrorism in Northern Ireland.* 24 Cardozo L. Rev. 1657 (2003).

Office of the Inspector General, United States Department of Justice. *The September 11 Detainees: A Review of the Treatment of Aliens Held on Immigration Charges in Connection with the Investigation of the September 11 Attacks*, Apr. 2003. *Available at* http://www.usdoj.gov/oig/special/0306/full.pdf.

Optional Protocol to the International Covenant on Civil and Political Rights New York, December 16, 1966 (List of Signatories). *Available at* http://www2.ohchr.org/english/bodies/ratification/5.htm.

Ordonnance du 2 Novembre 1945.

Ovey, Clare, and Robin White. *Jacobs & White, the European Convention on Human Rights*. 4th ed. Oxford: Oxford University Press, 2006.

Parmentier, Guillaume. "France." In *Counterterrorism Strategies: Successes and Failures of Six Nations*, edited by Yonah Alexander, 44–71. Dulles, VA: Potomac Books, 2006.

Police and Criminal Evidence Act ["PACE"].

Police and Criminal Evidence Act ["PACE"], Code A (Stop and Search).

Padilla v. Bush, 233 F. Supp. 2d 564 (S.D.N.Y. 2002).

Padilla v. Hanft, 423 F. 3d 386 (4th Cir. 2005).

Padilla v. Hanft, 432 F. 3d 582 (4th Cir. 2005).

Padilla v. Rumsfeld, 352 F. 3d 695 (2d Cir. 2003).

Payton v. New York, 445 U.S. 573 (1980).

Pendle, David Henrik. *Charity of the Heart and Sword: The Material Support Offense and Personnel Guilt.* 30 Seattle Univ. L. R. 777 (2007).

Pradel, Jean. *Droit Pénal Comparé.* Paris: Dalloz, 1995.

Pre-Charge Detention of Terrorist Suspects. Home Office, Dec. 2007. *Available at* http://security.homeoffice.gov.uk/news-publications/publication-search/general/pre-charge-detention/pre-charge-detention-proposal?view=Binary.

Prevention of Terrorism (Temporary Provisions) Act 1989, § 20(1).

Profile: Jose Padilla (BBC News television broadcast, Aug. 16, 2007). *Available at* http://news.bbc.co.uk/1/hi/world/americas/2037444.stm.

"Proposed 'Control Orders' Would Violate Human Rights." *Amnesty International, U.K.*, Feb. 22, 2005. *Available at* http://www.amnesty.org/en/library/asset/EUR45/004/2005/en/dom-EUR450042005en.html.

Rassat, Michèle-Laure. *Manuel de Procédure Pénale.* Paris: Presses Universitaires de France (PUF), 2002.

Regina v. Dodd, 74 Crim. App. 50 (C.A. 1981).

Regina v. Mackintosh, 76 Crim. App. 177 (C.A. 1982).

Roberts, Adam. *Transformative Military Occupation: Applying the Laws of War and Human Rights.* 100 A.J.I.L. 580 (2006).

Romany, Celina. *Black Women and Gender Equality in the New South Africa: Human Rights Law and the Intersection of Race and Gender.* 21 Brooklyn J. Int'l L. 857 (2006).

Roth, Kenneth. "After Guantanamo: The Case Against Preventive Detention." *Foreign Affairs*, May/Jun. 2008.

Roosevelt, Franklin D. "Fireside Chat of September 11, 1941." In *Dictionary of Military and Naval Quotations*, by Robert Debs Heinl, 247. Annapolis, MD: US Naval Institute Press, 1966.

Rumsfeld v. Padilla, 542 U.S. 426 (2004).

Russell, Jago. *Terrorism Pre-Charge Detention, Comparative Law Study*, Nov. 2007. *Available at* http://www.liberty-human-rights.org.uk/issues/pdfs/pre-charge-detention-comparative-law-study.pdf.

Ryder, Chris. *The RUC: A Force Under Fire.* 2nd ed. London: Mandarin, 1992.

Sampson, Fraser, Glenn Hutton, and David Johnston. *Blackstone's Police Investigators' Manual.* Oxford, U.K.: Oxford University Press, 2007.

Saltzburg, Stephen A., and Daniel J. Capra. *American Criminal Procedure: Cases and Commentary.* 5th ed. St. Paul, MN: Thomson, 1996.

Scales v. United States, 367 U.S. 203 (1961).

Secretary of State for the Home Department v. JJ and Others. 2007 U.K.H.L. 45 (31 October 2007).

Semple, Kirk. "Padilla Sentenced to 17 Years in Prison." *N.Y. Times*, Jan. 22, 2008.

Shapiro, Jeremy. "Detention of Terrorism Suspects in Britain and France." *Brookings Institution*, Jul. 15, 2008.

Shapiro, Jeremy, and Benedicte Suzan. "The French Experience of Counter-Terrorism." *Survival*, Spring 2003.

Slapper, Gary, and David Kelly. *The English Legal System.* New York: Routledge-Cavendish, 2004.

Slobogin, Christopher. *A Jurisprudence of Dangerousness*. 98 Nw. U.L. Rev. 1 (2003).

Sprack, John. *A Practical Approach to Criminal Procedure*. Oxford, U.K.: Oxford University Press, 2006.

Spencer, J. R. "The English System." In *European Criminal Procedures*, edited by Mireille Delmas-Marty and J. R. Spencer, 142–217. Cambridge, U.K.: Cambridge University Press, 2002.

Steiner, Henry J., and Philip Alston. *International Human Rights in Context: Law, Politics, Morals*. 2nd ed. Oxford, U.K.: Oxford University Press, 2000.

Stevens, Anne. *Government and Politics of France.* 3rd ed. New York: Palgrave Macmillan, 2003.

Stoller, Heidee, Tahlia Townsend, Rashad Hussain, and Marcia Yablon. *Developments in Law and Policy: The Costs of Post-9/11 National Security Strategy*. 22 Yale L. & Pol'y Rev. 197 (2004).

Stulin, Jamie L. *Does Hiibel Redefine Terry? The Latest Expansion of the Terry Doctrine and the Silent Impact of Terrorism on the Supreme Court's Decision to Compel Identification*. 54 Am. U. L. Rev. 1449 (2005).

Terrorist Investigations and the French Examining Magistrate System. Home Office, 2007. *Available at* http://security.homeoffice.gov.uk/news-publications/publication-search/counter-terrorism-bill-2007/examining-magistrates.pdf?view=Binary.

Terry v. Ohio, 392 U.S. 1 (1968).

Thornton, Brenda Sue. *The New International Jurisprudence on the Right to Privacy: A Head-On Collision with* Bowers v. Hardwick. 58 Alb. L. Rev. 725 (1995).

Tomasi v. France, Series A, no. 241-A, Application no. 12850/87, 15 EHRR 1, Aug. 27, 1992.

Trias-Hernandez v. INS, 528 F.2d 366 (9th Cir. 1975).

Turkmen v. Ashcroft, 2006 U.S. Dist. LEXIS 39170 (E.D.N.Y. June 14, 2006).

Turner, Serrin, and Stephen J. Schulhofer. *The Secrecy Problems in Terrorism Trials*. New York: Brennan Center for Justice at NYU School of Law, 2005.

U.K. Joint Committee on Human Rights Tenth Report, February 20, 2008. *Available at* http://www.publications.parliament.uk/pa/jt200708/jtselect/jtrights/57/5706.htm#note45.

U.N. Human Rights Committee, General Comment 8: Right to Liberty and Security of Persons (Art. 9): 30/06/82 (June 6, 1982).

United Nations Commission on Human Rights, Working Group on Arbitrary Detention, Fact Sheet No. 26. *Available at* www.ohchr.org/english/about/publications/docs/fs26.htm.

United Nations Office on Drugs and Crime (Terrorism Prevention Branch), Preventing Terrorist Acts: A Criminal Justice Strategy Integrating Rule of Law Standards in Implementation of United Nations Anti-Terrorism Instruments (2006). *Available at* http://www.unodc.org/pdf/terrorism/TATs/en/3IRoLen.pdf

U.S. Const. amend. IV.

U.S. Const. amend. V.

U.S. Const. amend. VI.

U.S. Const. amend. XIV.

United States v. Alderete-Deras, 743 F.2d 645 (9th Cir. 1984).

United States v. Alvarez-Sanchez, 511 U.S. 350 (1994).

United States v. Awadallah, 349 F.3d 42 (2d Cir. 2003).

United States v. Brignoni-Ponce, 422 U.S. 873 (1975).

United States v. Corley, 500 F.3d 210 (2007).

United States v. Cortez, 449 U.S. 411 (1981).

United States v. Duarte-Acero, 208 F.3d 1282 (11th Cir. 2000).

United States v. Henry, 604 F.2d 908 (5th Cir. 1979)

United States v. Loc Tien Nguyen, 313 F. Supp. 2d 579 (E.D. Va. 2004).

United States v. Martinez-Fuerte, 428 U.S. 543 (1976).

United States v. Mitchell, 322 U.S. 65 (1944).

United States v. Moreno, 475 F.2d 44 (5th Cir. 1973).

United States v. Moussaoui, 382 F.3d 453 (4th Cir. 2004).

United States v. Moya, 74 F.3d 1117 (11th Cir. 1996).

United States v. Padilla, 2007 U.S. Dist Lexis 26077 (S.D.Fla. Apr. 9, 2007).

United States v. Perez, 733 F.2d 1026 (2d Cir. 1984).

United States v. Place, 462 U.S. 696 (1983).

United States v. Ramsey, 431 U.S. 606 (1977).

United States v. Salerno, 481 U.S. 739 (1987).

United States v. Sharpe, 470 U.S. 675 (1985).

United States v. Skipwith, 482 F.2d 1272 (5th Cir. 1973).

United States v. Sokolow, 490 U.S. 1 (1989).

United States v. Timothy McVeigh and Terry Lynn Nichols, 940 F. Supp. 1541 (1996).

United States v. Warsame, 537 F. Supp. 2d 1005 (D. Minn. 2008).

United States v. Watson, 423 U.S. 411 (1976).

University of Missouri-Kansas Law School. "The Zacarias Moussaoui (September 11) Trial: A Chronology." *Available at* http://www.law.umkc.edu/faculty/projects/ftrials/moussaoui/zmchronology.html.

Upshaw v. United States, 335 U.S. 410 (1948).

Vachon, Christyne J. *Hong Kong's 1997 Transition: U.N. Enforcement Mechanisms to Guarantee Hong Kong's Human Rights Will Endure After the Transition*. 28 Denv. J. Int'l L. & Pol'y 97 (1999).

Van Kessel, Gordon. *The Suspect as a Source of Testimonial Evidence: A Comparison of the English and American Approaches*. 38 Hastings L.J. 1 (1986).

Vasquez-Trujillo v. Gonzales, 151 Fed. Appx. 509 (9th Cir. 2005).

Vouin, Robert. *Provisional Release in French Penal Law*. Pa. L. Rev. 108 (1960).

Vroom, Cynthia. *Constitutional Protection of Individual Liberties in France: The Conseil Constitutionnel Since 1971*. 63 Tul. L. Rev. 265 (1988).

Walker, Clive. *Blackstone's Guide to the Anti-Terrorism Legislation*. Oxford, U.K.: Oxford University Press, 2002.

———. *Keeping Control of Terrorists Without Losing Control of Constitutionalism*. 59 Stan. L. Rev. 1395 (2007).

Walton v. United States, 334 F.2d 343 (10th Cir. 1964).

Watt, Nicholas. "Brown Abandons 42-Day Detention After Lords Defeat." *The Guardian*, Oct. 13 2008.

Weaver, Matthew, and James Sturcke. "British Army Ends Northern Ireland Operation." *The Guardian*, Jul. 31 2007. *Available at* http://www.guardian.co.uk/uk/2007/jul/31/northernireland.military/print.

Webster, Phillip. "Vote on 42-Day Terrorist Detention Bill to Take Place After May Elections." *The Times*, Mar. 21, 2008. *Available at* http://www.timesonline.co.uk/tol/news/politics/article3593701.ece.

Wittes, Benjamin. *Law and the Long War*. New York: Penguin Press, 2008.

Wong, Kam C. *Legalism and Constitutionalism in the People's Republic of China*. 1 Int'l Journal of Crim. Justice Sciences (July 2006).

Yin, Tung. *Coercion and Terrorism Prosecutions in the Shadow of Military Detention*. 2006 B.Y.U. L. Rev. 1255 (2006).

———. *Ending the War on Terrorism One Terrorist at a Time: A Noncriminal Detention Model for Holding and Releasing Guantanamo Bay Detainees*. 29 Harv. J.L. & Pub. Pol'y 149 (2005).

Young, Kirsten A. *The Law and Process of the U.N. Human Rights Committee*. New York: Transnational Press, 2002.

Zadvydas v. Davis, 533 U.S. 678 (2001).

Zweigert, Konrad, and Hein Kotz. *An Introduction to Comparative Law*. Translated by Tony Weir. 3rd. rev. ed. Oxford, U.K.: Oxford University Press, 1998.

Index